Postcolonial Eyes
Intercontinental Travel in Francophone African Literature

Contemporary French and Francophone Cultures 11

Contemporary French and Francophone Cultures

This series aims to provide a forum for new research on modern and contemporary French and francophone cultures and writing. The books published in *Contemporary French and Francophone Cultures* reflect a wide variety of critical practices and theoretical approaches, in harmony with the intellectual, cultural and social developments which have taken place over the past few decades. All manifestations of contemporary French and francophone culture and expression are considered, including literature, cinema, popular culture, theory. The volumes in the series will participate in the wider debate on key aspects of contemporary culture.

AEDÍN NÍ LOINGSIGH

Postcolonial Eyes
Intercontinental Travel in Francophone African Literature

LIVERPOOL UNIVERSITY PRESS

First published 2009 by
Liverpool University Press
4 Cambridge Street
Liverpool L69 7ZU

British Library Cataloguing-in-Publication data
A British Library CIP record is available

ISBN 978-1–84631-049-2 cased

Typeset in Sabon by Koinonia, Manchester
Printed in Great Britain by the MPG Books Group, Bodmin and King's Lynn

I gcuimhne m'athair 's mo dhearthbáir:
'Anois ba mhaith liom bualadh [leo]
Nuair nach féidir é
Ó dheas a ghabh [siad]
Aneas ní thiocfaidh [said].'

Contents

Acknowledgements

This project was made possible thanks to the Arts and Humanities Research Council who granted me extended research leave. In addition, the British Academy awarded me research funding to conduct vital work on the project and an overseas conference grant to present a paper related to the project in Frankfurt. The support of both bodies is gratefully acknowledged.

I am sincerely appreciative of the support and intellectual companionship of former colleagues and students in Edinburgh. Thanks are also due to the University of Stirling for more recently providing me with an intellectual base. Liverpool University Press, and especially Anthony Cond, deserve special thanks for their understanding and forbearance when life simply got in the way. I am grateful too to both my readers: Dominic Thomas for his astute comments, and Charles Forsdick whose encouragement at different stages of this book's preparation was hugely influential. I also want to extend my thanks to Rachel Douglas, Nicki Hitchcott, Claire Launchbury, Lorna Milne, Andy Stafford and Michael Syrotinski for invaluable suggestions and/ or practical support.

I am especially privileged to thank five people for their ideas and constructive criticisms: David Murphy, as always, provided unwavering support at every stage as well as contributing enormously to shaping the critical approaches informing this study; Maeve McCusker was a masterful critical reader who generously gave of her time to read drafts of several chapters; Estelle Epinoux played an invaluable role in helping me to formulate the ideas for Chapter 6 and providing me with bed and board in Paris; I also greatly appreciated the engagement and sophistication of Claire Boyle's reading of Chapter 4. Finally, Emily Harding engaged with my work from an entirely different perspective in order to design this book's cover image.

Another key person behind this project is Roger Little who has encouraged and believed in me since my postgraduate days. Whatever the failings of this work they in no way reflect the exemplary scholarly standards he sought to instil in his students with patience, wit and extraordinary generosity.

Finally, I would like to thank friends and family in Glasgow and Cork who understood that what I needed most was time, and gave it to me when they could. Roddy Buchanan, Jacqueline Donachie, Emily Harding, Caroline Kirsop, Halena McAnulty, Anna Miele and Dougie Taylor stepped in to do nursery pick-ups, babysitting, sleepovers, or simply organize nights out away from all of it... My thanks and love too to Moira, Eoin, Éanna, and of course Elton, for always reminding me of how fortunate I am to have started from where I did. To my mother, who has remained her generous, inspirational, travelling self throughout, I am more than grateful. Without her support, and the incalculable influence of my late father, I know for certain that I simply couldn't have done this. Lastly, Dave, Ailbhe and Gabriel have shown me that when all is said and done travelling home to them in Glasgow and with them to Cork are the journeys I cherish most.

Abbreviations and Note on Translations

The works examined are abbreviated as below. Where they exist, translations of quotations are provided from existing versions in English with the page numbers included in brackets. Where translations of critical works in French exist, only the English version is quoted. All other translations are my own.

AG	*L'Africain du Grœnland*
CH	*Chalys d'Harlem*
Kocoumbo	*Kocoumbo, l'étudiant noir*
MAM	*Maman a un amant*
MP	*Mirages de Paris*
NP	*Un Nègre à Paris*
PNY	*Patron de New York*
PPB	*Le petit prince de Belleville*

INTRODUCTION

History, Genre and New Ways of Reading Travel

Critical research in travel writing has done much over the past two and a half decades to decolonize the genre and confront its tainted legacy. In particular, greater awareness of the historical, political and cultural factors influencing the textual representations of different cultures and places has revealed travel writing's role in supporting the phantasmic dynamics of Europe's perception of its 'others' and in upholding the asymmetrical power relations of Europe's colonial project. Analysis of the imperial ventriloquism of colonial travel writing has shown how a hierarchical relationship developed between the authoritative European observer and the passive, silent and immobile object of the latter's gaze. In addition, recuperative projects within the field of travel writing have been successful in presenting a more inclusive and complex generic genealogy that takes account of the influence of variables such as gender, social class, and, to a lesser extent, ethnic identity. Studies focusing on literature of the so-called postcolonial era have also contributed greatly to new understandings of the ways in which cultures travel and interact in the modern world. And whilst it is right to criticize the abstractions that can arise from an over-emphasis on metaphorical and epistemological journeys, their recurrence in much critical discourse nonetheless points to a recognition of the central place of travel in today's world.

These critical developments have undoubtedly contributed to the transformation of the Western academic landscape and are certainly welcome. However, in an assessment of future directions in the study of travel writing, Tim Youngs argues that 'the simple picture of a subject that has freed itself from its colonial legacy through greater introspection needs to be redrawn'.[1] Youngs's sentiments find an echo in Patrick Holland and Graham Huggan's highly influential study of contemporary travel writing, *Tourists with Typewriters*: 'the freedom of travel writers should not be equated with freedom in the truest sense of the term: it is the privilege of mobility that allows them to travel, and to write.'[2] Nowhere is such decontextualization of travel more evident, I believe, than in the critical neglect of representations of travel by African writers and the failure to develop a coherent theoretical framework within which to analyse the connections between ethnicity and textualizations of travel. Unlike anthropology, whose '*crise de conscience*', according to James Clifford, has rightly undermined its position as 'the unique purveyor of anthropological knowledge about others', our recognition that we live in a world of generalized travel has not led, I believe, to a sufficiently radical reassessment of twentieth-century developments in the representation of travel.[3] It is true, of course, that, following on from work by Clifford, Paul Gilroy, Mary Louise Pratt, Charles Forsdick and, more recently, Debbie Lisle, there has been clear recognition of the agency of non-Western subjects and the ways in which they participate in, and reconfigure, eurocentric modes of travelling, seeing and narrating. It is also true that critics have begun to pay more attention to the place of travel in the work of diasporic travel writers. However, despite the existence of studies on African American and Caribbean travel writers, not to mention the significant number of studies devoted to colonial travel writing on Africa, and also to the recurrence of colonialist tropes in contemporary travel writing, few critical projects have considered the important contribution of Africans themselves to the development of the genre.[4] With regard to Africa's place within critical and historical studies of travel and its textualization, it is notable that despite an undeniable sophistication in approach, the landscapes, cultures and peoples of this continent continue to be analysed as raw material for the literary aspirations of travel writers (for the most part Western) who journey *to* the continent. In contrast, the journeys of Africans who depart *from* their continent are recognized not for their contribution to the literature of travel and cultural encounter but for their historical value (e.g. slave narratives), contribution to the development of intellectual movements (e.g. Negritude), sociological importance (e.g. immigrant literature) or for their illustration of abstract and ahistorical theories of a cosmopolitan hybridity and interstitiality. It is not my intention in this study to suggest that the conspicuous absence of African writers from recent critical considerations of travel literature is evidence of any bad faith on the part of critics associated with these modes of analysis. Instead, in *Postcolonial Eyes* I hope to elaborate on what might be gained by including African textualizations of travel within important contemporary theoretical configurations, particularly postcolonial theory.

In answer to the question 'what does the study of African literature bring to the field of literary studies?' Christopher L. Miller submits that it 'demands nothing less than a reconsideration of all the terms of literary analysis, starting with the word "literature" itself'.[5] The answer encapsulates, of course, the critical framework by which we read travel writing and reminds us of the dangers inherent in confining critical approaches within one's own culture where, as Miller stresses, 'theory and reading will operate within a closed circuit, smoothly confirming each other and leaving an appearance of universal validity'.[6] In the remainder of this introduction, therefore, I tentatively suggest ways in which we might begin to untie travel writing from its Western moorings and open up a space for African representations of travel. In order to do this, I look briefly at some of the key literary and historical issues characterizing European colonial travel writing on Africa, and discuss also some of the meanings and practices of travel that derive from African contexts. I also look closely at the issue of travel writing's generic identity in order to suggest a way of prising open what I see as its overly restrictive categorizing tendencies. In a related way, I explore the critical tendency to dematerialize travel practices and thereby subtly exclude those whose material concerns force them to reinvent ways of travelling. Throughout, I discuss some of the key critical terms and ideas employed in contemporary theories of travel and suggest the modifications needed once they are applied to African contexts.

Destination Africa

Where intercontinental travel is concerned, recognizing Africans as travellers and producers of travel texts requires an awareness of what it takes to overcome the obstacles to travel, and to write about it. In this regard, identifying an African literature of travel involves at some level acknowledging the influence of Western travel practices and travel writing. This is not to imply that African travel practices and representations of travel derive exclusively from Western models and traditions: as we shall see, there is an entire tradition of representing and understanding journeys that is specific to Africans. However, to reconstruct the key features of Western colonial travel writing on

Africa, as I do briefly below, is a necessary attempt to come to grips with the complex issues governing an understanding of the nature of postcolonial African travel and its representation.

One of the most influential concepts underpinning postcolonial criticism concerns the notion that various European representational practices 'produced' non-European cultures for its own consumption. Fundamental to such practices, as critics such as Martine Astier Loutfi, Edward Said and Mary Louise Pratt have demonstrated, has been the literature of travel in its various forms. Non-fictional travel writing and fictional foreign adventure narratives formed a key ideological apparatus of the inland expansionist initiatives of European colonial powers from the eighteenth century. Coinciding with these ambitions was a specifically European knowledge-building project in which various 'scientific' accounts of other life forms were 'rewoven into European-based patterns of global unity and order'.[7] As the frontiers of expansion grew ever wider, the borders distinguishing the so-called scientific travel accounts of naturalists and botanists became ever more hazy and increasingly infused with the 'sentimental' tones of adventurous narratives. Pratt highlights the descriptions in Mungo Park's 1799 *Travels in the Interior Districts of Africa* as 'exemplif[ying] the eruption of the sentimental mode' into European accounts of travel and exploration.[8] As she explains, several key thematic and rhetorical features of this text would subsequently influence European writers (colonial and postcolonial) of fictional and non-fictional accounts of travel both to Africa and elsewhere. First, Park portrays himself as an intrepid hero whose resourcefulness enables this lone male to survive a series of testing challenges. This, of course, had the effect of suggesting that travel to the African interior was fundamentally a risky undertaking both because of the continent's particular landscape and the predominant characteristics of its inhabitants. Park's adventures, as Pratt illustrates, are also reported in self-dramatizing language where emotions are stressed. Despite this stylistic difference with more staid, scientific travel accounts, the end result is, nonetheless, similar. For it has the effect of making European expansionist ambitions appear 'sanitized' whilst at the same time underlining the 'essential', inherently European and masculine characteristics – resilience, authority, entrepreneurship – that will be used to justify the colonization of an Africa in need of civilizing. In terms of our understanding of travel writing's development, Pratt's analysis of Park's 'sentimental' narrative of travel and exploration also reveals both the ways in which the power relations of that era became encoded within the genre and the pervasive way in which imperial ideology came to dominate perceptions of travel and cultural encounter.

Critics of travel writing have demonstrated how the mid-nineteenth-century penetration of Africa's 'dark' interior by European explorers consolidated authoritative 'knowledge' of Africa. As Pratt describes it, this is the era when 'discovery rhetoric' emerges most clearly with its unmistakable 'relation of *mastery* predicated between the [European] seer and the [colonized] seen'.[9] Referring to texts by explorers such as Richard Burton and John Speke, Pratt demonstrates how the European traveller to Africa arrogated to himself the authority to interpret Africa, to assess its potential value to European culture and to suggest where 'intervention' was needed. Crucially, despite ever more creative and imaginative reworkings of travel and exploration literature, the issue of the Western traveller's supposed authority to describe and interpret Africa remained largely unchallenged. This is true of accounts such as Park's where the recognition of African agency and the potential for critical relativism remain nonetheless 'anchored securely in a sense of European authenticity, power and legitimacy'.[10] Such contradictory positions are also true of colonial women's travel writing. For example, in her analysis of Mary Kingsley's account of travelling through British and French West Africa, Sara Mills identifies a decided undermining of travel writing's generic conventions, including its masculinist and colonialist ethos. Despite these subversive elements, Mills nonetheless concludes that characterizing Kingsley's writing as either 'feminist' and/or 'anti-colonial' is simplistic and fails to take account of the ways in which it 'seems to be caught up in the contradictory clashes of these discourses one with another'.[11] More disturbingly, critics of contemporary Western travel literature have underlined the ways in which characteristics of a blatant colonial ethos can resurface in subtle ways despite the development of more self-conscious and self-reflective writing practices.[12]

I do not wish to suggest here that European travel writing on Africa must invariably be seen as fully aligned with imperial ideology. Nor is it my intention to uphold uncritically the Manichean logic that is frequently said to define such travel discourses. (Postcolonial criticism has increasingly demonstrated the ways in which even apparently clear-cut articulations of 'racist' or exoticizing ideologies

are destabilized by their own inherent ambivalence and hybridity.)
Nonetheless, there is broad critical consensus that whatever the
contradictory features of texts recounting the experiences of travel
in Africa, they are underwritten by a rigid sense of boundaries that
construct Africa as irreducibly 'other'. For Syed Manzul Islam, this
'principle of opposition' informed what he dubs the 'sedentary' travel
practices of many colonial travellers:

> When the European colonialists, in their sedentary voyages,
> ventured into other places, they moved folded in the inside, and
> replicated the same old boundaries in distant places. They created,
> like Robinson Crusoe, their enclosed spaces, so that they need not
> risk the encounter with the other or open themselves to the trace of
> the outside.[13]

Sedentary travel reinforced received 'wisdom' on Africa, and colonial
travel writing's reproduction of this disjunctive space undoubtedly
contributed to a lurid fascination in metropolitan Europe with the
landscape of the continent. The undifferentiated vision of Africa in
both 'factual' and imaginative writing gave rise to complex fantasies
that constructed the continent as savage and primitive, exotic and
mysterious. In a specifically French context, for example, Martine
Astier Loutfi explains how an intensified policy of colonialist expansion in Africa dramatically increased demand for travel-inspired
writing amongst the reading public from the early 1870s.[14] It is true
that the nineteenth century in France is dominated, in travel writing
terms at least, by the 'Voyage en Orient', and narratives of travel to
Sub-Saharan Africa, such as René Caillié's 1830 *Voyage à Tombouctou*,
remained relatively unknown.[15] However, the availability of French
translations of Henry Morton Stanley's sub-Saharan exploration
narratives from the late 1870s changed this situation and explains the
subsequent popularity of Pierre Loti's unashamedly exoticist *Roman
d'un Spahi* (1881), and, following the Berlin Conference, the writings
of explorer Pierre Savorgnan de Brazza. Other publications worth
mentioning in this context are the serialized adventure narratives of
the *Journal des voyages* (1877–1915) with titles such as *Les Aventures périlleuses de Narcisse Nicaise au Congo* and *La Vengeance
d'un noir* deliberately designed to evoke the motifs of 'more serious'
literary accounts of travel in Africa.[16] As with the accounts of Stanley,
Loti and de Brazza, these publications largely upheld the 'travelling
subject' as white, male and Western, and, along with other fora such
as exhibitions, museums, fine art and public lectures, contributed to

the specific idea of a dark, uncivilized Africa. Needless to say, the historical context of this French rise in popularity of accounts of travel in Africa is not irrelevant. For as Emmanuelle Sibeud notes in her magisterial account of the institutionalization of a French 'Africanist' science, the 'construction imaginaire d'une Afrique française' [imaginary construction of a French Africa] lay at its heart and formed a vital part of France's post Franco-Prussian War attempts to restore national pride in the form of its 'mission civilisatrice'.[17] The representation of a savage Africa that such 'knowledge' promoted persisted throughout the early part of the twentieth century, underpinning, as we shall see in the next chapter, the ethos of the 1931 Colonial Exhibition 'spectacle' and emerging in supposedly more enlightened texts such as André Gide's 1927 *Voyage au Congo*, where Pierre-Philippe Fraiture sees the attitude towards Africans as oscillating between 'le dédain, une bienveillance paternaliste et l'admiration' [disdain, paternalistic benevolence and admiration].[18]

Gide's attitude is a reminder of how the ambiguously described landscape of Europe's 'imagined Africa' is echoed in a complex system of stereotypes that characterize the 'natives' as culturally and intellectually arrested yet also exotically different. During the nineteenth century the very colour of African skin emerged as both a 'biologically' and culturally significant factor. Speculative 'scientific' theories such as those submitted by Arthur de Gobineau in his 1854 *Essai sur l'inégalité des races humaines* meant that 'blackness' came to be seen as the fundamental marker of difference which in turn provided proof of the 'natural' inequality between supposedly biologically distinct 'races'. Needless to say, Gobineau's insistence on 'racial' difference becomes fundamental to underlining all that the African 'other' is not – physically, culturally, sexually, emotionally, intellectually – in relation to the colonizer. In this way, all the negative qualities of the white European are displaced onto the African, who becomes at once a source of fascination and contempt, as well as providing confirmation of Europe's cultural superiority and intellectual authority. In his examination of nineteenth-century accounts of colonial exploration in Africa, Johannes Fabian interprets the consistent emphasis on 'difference' in such travel writing as the refusal of European explorers and travellers to recognize the existence of shared cultural practices between themselves and Africans. Fabian expands on the intellectual concept of recognition by reference to German-language nuances for the act of recognizing: '*Erkennen*, as in "I know these persons or objects when I see them" (cognition), *Wiedererkennen*, as in "I know them because I remember them (memory), and *Anerkennen*, as in "I give them the recognition they deserve" (acknowledgement).'[19] Although the anthropologist does unearth some exceptional instances of 'recognition' and *déjà vu* by European observers of African cultural norms and practices, these are frequently partial or quickly retracted. More important for these travellers, as Fabian notes, is receiving recognition. For this reason any appeal to mutual recognition, particularly in the form of *wiedererkennen* and *anerkennen*, would jeopardize their authority and 'be incompatible with the European's mission as the emissary of a superior race'.[20]

Other critics, such as Petrine Archer-Straw, have demonstrated the ways in which late nineteenth-century and early twentieth-century popular images of black people in France 'converted fears of difference into "safe", accessible images where whites were given control'.[21] In the specific context of colonial travel writing on Africa, Laura Franey observes how white Europeans frequently removed themselves from their descriptions of African landscapes and thereby made themselves appear as 'bodiless entities'. However, she stresses that:

> This self-removal represented not a loss of power but a fundamental increasing of it, since travellers thereby claimed absolute power of the sovereign – and the deity – who occupied space invisibly yet powerfully. These travellers participated, then, in what Radhika Mohanram calls 'an embodiment of blackness with a simultaneous disembodiment of whiteness, a disembodiment accompanied by two other tropes at the level of discourse. First, whiteness has the ability to move; second, the ability to move results in the unmarking of the body. In contrast, blackness is signified through a marking and is always static'.[22]

In colonial travel writing it is clear too that skin colour served to mark not just difference, but also to indicate distance. In Africa, the somatic feature of the 'natives' blackness was one of the first indicators that the European traveller was no longer at 'home'. For Africans travelling to Europe, as we shall see in subsequent chapters, the inescapable nature of their blackness is constantly mirrored back to them by a culture and people determined to remind them of the place from where they have come. In the colonial and postcolonial texts examined here, skin colour serves at all times to delineate Africans as 'outsiders' who are often seen as conforming in subtle (and sometimes not so subtle) ways to the distorted representations of European travel writing. Certainly, this study recognizes the complex criteria by which 'ethnic' groups can be defined (both by themselves and others). Nonetheless, 'ethnicity' will be seen here to rest overwhelmingly on somatic features. This is in no way intended to suggest that 'ethnicity' is, therefore, primarily biological. Rather, my use of the term in the present study serves to highlight the complex ways in which 'blackness' continues to function in postcolonial textualizations of international travel by Africans. Indeed, although the texts studied here clearly challenge the association of whiteness with 'movement' and 'blackness' with immobility, their underlining of the persistent and disproportionate attention paid to skin colour serves as a constant reminder of the power relations that continue to structure the encounter between Africans and their 'others' in postcolonial contexts.

Of course, underpinning all the above features of nineteenth- and early twentieth-century travel writing on Africa is the notion of the continent's 'discovery' and the assimilation of the unknowable into the knowable through the essentially European faculty of reasoning. In such an epistemic project, the silence and passivity of the African 'natives', whose only role has been as the object of travellers' observations, is vital. However, as Laura Franey suggests above, the silencing tendencies of colonial travel writing's representations of Africa were further reinforced by immobilizing propensities that led to the normalization of African bodies as motionless bodies (or 'travelees' to use Mary Louise Pratt's term[23]) and Africa as a peripheral space. This refusal to recognize Africans as either travellers or narrators of travel encounters undoubtedly feeds into a vision of them as somehow incapable of contributing authoritatively to transcultural debate. For underlying the notion of European exploration and discovery of Africa is the assumption that if 'primitive natives' could reveal nothing about the 'Dark Continent' that Europeans did not already know or would ultimately 'discover' themselves, then African travellers to Europe (or anywhere else) clearly had nothing of value to say about other cultures.

Travelling Africans

Occasionally Africans are recognized as travellers, and even as travel writers, in different colonial contexts. However, the purpose and nature of their movement is seen to be a consequence of colonization, and, as with much colonial travel writing, their observations function as propaganda for colonialist ideas. For example, in the 1919 colonial school text, *Moussa et Gigla*, the eponymous young characters (one from Soudan and one from Dahomey) are 'fortunate' enough to meet Monsier Richelot, a French businessman who hires them as his 'boys' as he travels along the Niger river.[24] However, the boys' 'travels' are little more than a pretext for highlighting the 'positive' changes brought about by France's colonization of West Africa. The boys' role as domestic helpers and Moussa's subsequent decision to become a soldier in the colonial army also serve to underline the fact that rather than being independent travellers, the young men are mere cogs enabling the colonial wheel to travel to where it wants to go. Roland Lebel's comments on travel writing in francophone African literature bear out this dependence mobility of Africans in a different way. Although he appears to acknowledge a genuine African contribution to the genre of travel writing, he just as quickly and patronizingly suppresses it by emphasizing *French* exploration of Africa as the inspiration for these texts and by highlighting the mixed-race heritage of these authors (there seems little doubt that for Lebel the 'white' aspect of their heritage explains their decision to adopt the genre):

> On comprend assez bien que la littérature de voyage n'offre qu'un très petit nombre de publications écrites par des indigènes. L'exploration du pays n'est pas leur fait et, d'autre part, ils ne pratiquent pas encore le tourisme à notre façon. On ne trouve donc, en principe, ni relation documentaire, ni carnet de route, ni souvenirs et impressions de voyage chez les auteurs indigènes de langue française, du moins à l'origine. Les deux ou trois ouvrages de ce genre qui ont été publiés au moment de notre extension territoriale sont dûs à des mulâtres.[25]

> [Quite understandably travel writing is represented by a very small number of texts written by natives. The exploration of the interior is not their responsibility; moreover, they do not yet travel as tourists in the way that we do. Thus, in principle, one finds no documentary report, no travelogue, no memories or impressions of travel by native, French-speaking authors, at least not at the beginning. The two or three examples of the genre published at the time of our territorial expansion are by persons of mixed-race.]

The persistent 'travelling over' of 'natives' also exposes the widespread ignorance of specifically African conceptualizations and practices of travel. As the authors of one study of British overseas exploration note: 'While from London these places [discovered by explorers] appeared as a periphery reached, studied and known from an imperial metropolis that commanded it, they did not appear so to the peoples who lived there, people who were often considerable voyagers themselves.'[26] The historical fact of African travel and mobility is also evoked by Madeleine Borgomano who speaks of the exclusively utilitarian function of travel and journeying in a pre-colonial Africa that was 'en mouvement perpétuel' [perpetual movement].[27] Borgomano also highlights the colonizers' tendency to portray Africans as immobile whilst simultaneously exploiting the latter's traditional readiness to travel in order to facilitate European exploration of the continent's interior, the construction of transport routes and the extraction of natural resources. Where literary representations of travel are concerned, Mildred Mortimer provides the beginnings of an answer as to how to acknowledge more effectively an African tradition of representing travel by underlining the 'dual origin' of the journey motif in fiction by authors such as Camara Laye, Mongo Beti and Mariama Bâ.[28] For Mortimer, this motif is a result of 'cultural blending' that sees African authors adopt a European genre (the novel) in order to represent physical journeys that are both semi-autobiographical in nature yet also clearly inspired by traditional tales where the journey is used to reinforce symbolically such notions as the quest for self-knowledge, endurance, and rites of initiation. Significantly, in a comment borne out by some of the 'travellers' tales' studied here, Mortimer also explains how, 'in traditional [African] society, which emphasizes communal values, the journey is shown to benefit both the individual and the community'.[29] Ursula Baumgardt also alludes to these symbolic functions of the journey in her useful attempt to identify a generic 'typology of travel' in Peul oral literature.[30] Her conclusions point to the extraordinary wealth of meaning attached to travel in this oral tradition but also underline the diverse motivations that prompt characters to undertake journeys in tales, epics and oral poetry. Needless to say African orature is a rich and complex area of study worthy of separate analysis and will not be the focus of any detailed discussion in the present study's examination of intercontinental journeys. However, the following two examples from African oral traditions usefully sketch out other important symbolic and generic meanings of 'local' travel practices that have particular resonance for the intercontinental travel practices examined in subsequent chapters.

In his discussion of legends of flight in African-American literature, Gay Wilentz examines how an earlier, clearly African myth is seen to replay in the conscious and subconscious minds of slaves and their descendants. He illustrates how legends and contemporary fiction use the idea of flying both as a symbol of transcendence and resistance but also quite literally to designate a marvellous ability of certain African slaves to negotiate their transatlantic journey in reverse.[31] Wilentz's study of this particular myth is an important reminder of the historical and critical urgency of broadening the discussion of African intercontinental travel beyond the abject conditions of the middle passage. In addition, as well as underlining in its own way the embodied nature of travel, the myth also stresses the agency, resilience and resourcefulness of African travellers. Finally, in its focus on Atlantic criss-crossing, the myth of flight also tentatively suggests the geographical breadth of Africa's connections with the wider world and points to a geographical diversity of African experiences of travel that is not always sufficiently recognized.

In addition to travel's symbolic importance, Liz Gunner describes the *jamooje nai*, a poetic genre of oral literature exclusive to the nomadic Fulani of West Africa that describes the journeys of young herdsmen. Although this genre is said to be 'individual and confessional' it also exists 'within the clear parameters of a recognized form [and the young men's] making of the poetry becomes the means by which they map and control, mentally, the harsh terrain through which they travel'.[32] Gunner's point raises two vital issues for the study of African textualizations of travel: first, as with Baumgardt's study mentioned above, it reminds us that representations of journeys have not always been confined to written (even prose) genres originating in the West. Secondly, the mental mapping of these herdsmen underlines culturally specific navigational skills and travel practices that are no doubt as effective as the more technological methods of European explorers and frequently complemented them. For, as Johannes Fabian illustrates, 'solitary travellers never travelled alone' and European colonial expeditionary travel in Africa was an 'operation' that depended heavily on local skills and knowledge for information gathering.[33] Like Fabian's work, Gunner's example reminds us how the history of slavery, colonization and the tradition of European writing on Africa has obscured the practical travel skills of Africans and reinforced a vision of them as either transported commodities or static features of the landscape.

Although the role of orature is vital to any understanding of African authors' understanding of travel, it is unlikely that franco-phone African writing more widely would have developed as it did were it not for Africans' 'voyage à l'envers [inverted travel] to the metropolitan centre since the First World War.[34] Colonized Africans first travelled to Europe in large numbers during the Great War when Marc Michel estimates that 11.7% of the 134,000 who made the journey lost their lives.[35] The experiences of one of these soldiers, who travels from a remote Senegalese village to France via Casablanca, is recorded in Bakary Diallo's *Force-bonté*, a text Mortimer describes as 'the first francophone African novel to introduce the journey motif'.[36] From the 1920s, colonized Africans slowly began to travel to France for education, lured by the promise of enhanced social status upon their return to Africa that they believed would be guaranteed by more prestigious qualifications. Indeed, many of the Francophone African writers who came to prominence in the 1930s, 40s and 50s travelled to France in order to pursue an education begun in French colonial educational establishments.[37] Whether structuring the narrative, as in Cheikh Hamidou Kane's *L'Aventure ambiguë*, or informing an attempt to reverse roles and present the African as the educator of French students, as is arguably the case in Pius Ngandu Nkashama's 1987 text *Vie et Mœurs d'un primitif en Essonne quatre-vingt-onze*, the educational journey along the 'Chemin d'Europe' [road to Europe], to borrow the title of Ferdinand Oyono's novel, has remained an enduring topos of francophone African literary production.[38] Histori-cally speaking, the intellectual, artistic and political paths chosen by such figures as Léopold S. Senghor, Bernard Dadié, Oyono, Ousmane Socé, Camara Laye, Aké Loba and Kane were indelibly marked by the sense of displacement provoked by the encounter with France, and more particularly with its capital. For Dominic Thomas this ulti-mately becomes less a physical journey than a psychological process through which 'greater consciousness was achieved as a mechanism for deconditioning and questioning colonialism'.[39] Of course, the particular gravitational pull of Paris and its significance as the capital of an emerging global Black cultural and intellectual movement from the 1920s has been well documented by critics. Within the context of African writing on intercontinental travel, the central role of Paris is reinforced by the disproportionate number of texts devoted to encoun-ters with the city. Indeed, the very geography of this study seems to suggest an inevitability of the passage through Paris, and it is fair to say that all the Paris-bound journeys examined here do reveal to varying degrees the persistence of the French capital's mythical seductiveness in the eyes of the (post)colonial African traveller. Nonetheless, the different travel experiences of these texts also draw attention to evolving realities and trajectories that move beyond, bypass, or simply question, the central position of the French capital.

The importance of student mobility as a literary trope has been overtaken in recent decades by the travel practices of postcolonial migrants. In one respect, the particular conditions of immigrant travel highlight the disappointment of the post-independence era and could be said to follow on from a particular tendency in 1960s fiction that, in Mildred Mortimer's view, used journeys culminating in death to underline the corruption and repression that was impoverishing the lives of Africans. From the 1990s, authors such as Calixthe Beyala, Jean Roger Essomba, Daniel Beyala and Alain Mabanckou began to represent the consequences of this failed politics by focusing on the harsh experiences of those propelled out of their continent by economic need yet rejected by the societies in which they had hoped to make a better life. However, rather than presenting migrant mobility as hopelessly wretched and marginalizing, these writers also stress a new relationship to travel that, for Jacques Chevrier, qualifies these writers and their characters as 'nomads' for whom the absence of any fixed identity means that travel and instability have become the norm.[40]

It is important to remain wary of simplistic descriptions, and the above synopsis of African examples of intercontinental travel should not be seen as conveniently distinguishing an entire tradition. For the emphasis on collective travel by soldiers, students and immigrants obscures both the diverse experiences within these groups as well as travel practices and textualizations that are unusual or not so easily categorized. For example, non-fictional travel writing and the particular journeys they record, although rare, form, as I will demonstrate, an important subcategory of African literature in French since the late 1950s. Other texts such as Pius Ngandu Nkashama's abovementioned 'memoir' recounting a period spent in Paris as an African cultural advisor, Massaër Diallo's 'reverse ethnological' study of the white clients of Paris-based African marabouts, 'Les marabouts de Paris', or *L'Ombre d'Imana* in which Véronique Tadjo deftly weaves fictional short stories into a factual account of two journeys to Rwanda suggest that, no less than contemporary Western travel writers, African writers are acutely aware that the representation of travel often demands playing with form.[41] Both these writers also remind us of other important issues that must be taken into account in any attempt to establish the extent of Sub-Saharan representations of intercontinental travel. The particular origins of Ngandu, for example, suggest a related tradition of francophone textualizations of travel from the Democratic Republic of the Congo (former Belgian Congo) that could complement this study's focus on writing from the former French colonies.[42] As a rare example of a female-authored text on travel, *L'Ombre d'Imana* also raises the important issue of gender in assessing the history of travel practices and textualizations in francophone African literature. As will be clear from Chapter 7, African women's experiences of intercontinental travel have differed significantly from male travellers, not least because their movement takes place within the complex convergence of colonial/postcolonial distrust of their ethnic identity and patriarchal constraints that shape that identity.

The complex history of African intercontinental travel since the early twentieth century must influence any reading of colonial and postcolonial textualizations of intercontinental journeys by African authors. Above all, it emphasizes ways of travelling that differ markedly from the experiences foregrounded in European colonial travel writing. Taken together with the examples of African travel practices just mentioned, the texts analysed in this study provide us with a crucial fact: it is not that Africans have remained motionless bodies but that the colonial evolution of Western travel writing has obscured their input into the development and understanding of new ways of travelling, and writing about it. But before any conclusions can be drawn about this issue it is necessary to look a little more closely at the question of literary taxonomies and the exclusionary forces contained within the genre of travel writing as it is widely understood. This will allow for a more dynamic understanding of the category so as to make way for the contribution of African authors.

Travel and genre

Accepting the existence of an African literature of travel requires a certain leap of faith on the part of critics conditioned to working within the framework of a long-established generic tradition. If we are to move away from seeing the African continent exclusively in terms of a destination for others' journeys, and their accounts of them, then it is vital that we first begin to tackle the 'double absence' characterizing travel writing by African authors:[43] the paucity of works that appear to fit the generic bill and their neglect by contemporary critics of travel literature. Of the authors studied here, two – Dadié and Kpomassie – have, between them, published four works that along with lesser-known texts by Valentin Y. Mudimbe and Zamenga Batukezanga appear to be the only francophone African texts that might unproblematically be located within the recognized, if sometimes hazy, parameters of the Western travelogue.[44] All of these texts recount non-fictional journeys to destinations outside Africa, and although the circumstances that allow these authors to travel are very different, there is an explicit link in their writing between travel, recreation and pleasure that appears to locate them more easily within commonly held Western notions of the genre. But how are we to classify the substantial number of colonial and postcolonial texts (largely but not exclusively fictional) in which travel out of Africa constitutes the main plot impulse and frequently forms the central organizing principle? Texts that relate the encounters of African soldiers, students, civil servants, writers, immigrant workers, housewives, mothers, and children living within non-African cultures may not always foreground the geographical stages of the journeys that lie at their heart, but then this is hardly a condition for including Western texts within the category of travel writing.

The problem then is clearly one of genre. We have already seen how, historically, European colonial travel writing on Africa bears out John Frow's contention that 'genres actively generate and shape knowledge of the world; and [...] generically shaped knowledges are bound up with the exercise of power, where power is understood as being exercised in discourse, but is never simply external to discourse'.[45] As Frow sees it, this mutually reinforcing relationship between power and genre permits any given category to produce 'effects of truth and authority that are specific to it, and projects a "world" that is generically specific'.[46] As we shall see below, the boundaries of travel writing are far from hard-edged. Nonetheless, the exclusion of African texts would suggest that a subtle but an effective patrolling of its parameters has somehow taken place since the colonial era. This conclusion tallies with the findings of other important theorists of genre such as Alistair Fowler, who see the existence of 'kinds' of literature as necessarily exclusionary.[47] The act of describing, Jacques Derrida demonstrates, can quickly become proscribing, and 'as soon as a genre announces itself, one must respect a norm, one must not cross a line of demarcation, one must not risk impurity, anomaly or monstrosity'.[48] The history of African literature's relationship to travel writing illustrates better than most how the borders of genre operate not only to exclude others but also to prevent these others from seeing themselves as contributing to a literary category even when they most clearly are. The authors discussed in *Postcolonial Eyes* all combine accounts of individual journeys to the West with observations on its culture. As such, their narratives, be they fictional or non-fictional, deserve to be considered within the critical frameworks used for other texts of cultural encounter, including most obviously travel writing. It is, therefore, in order to take account of these texts' contribution to our understanding of literary travel and travel practices more generally that the generic boundaries of travel writing need to be probed and tested.

On first analysis, such an approach to genre is not quite so radical as it might initially appear. In Western critical circles we have become so accustomed to the genre bending and blending tendencies that define postmodern literature in particular that, at times, it hardly seems innovative, or even productive, to point them out any more. Generic innovation has also led to the by now almost standard discussion relating to the blurred forms of different literary categories that struggle to contain the growing number of texts that prefer to straddle different forms. Indeed, although above I refer to Derrida, Fowler and Frow to support the notion of genres as ideologically infused and exclusionary taxonomies, each of these critics is primarily concerned with demonstrating how this concept (whether literary or otherwise) invariably contains within it the conditions that allow its boundaries to be exceeded. For Derrida, in particular, 'the law of genre' may be disabling, senseless and exclusionary but he also exhorts us to consider the 'counter-law' contained within it, a principle of excess and contamination that can be enabling, meaningful and inclusive, and allow for 'participation without membership'.[49] Equally important for the present study are the notions of context and socio-historically generated transformations that explain the range of factors bearing upon the development and reception of travel writing as a genre. For Stephen Heath, context is intrinsic to 'genre politics' as it explains how:

> Different contexts of reading or listening produce new or altered genre identifications, as kinds of writing with little or no formal recognition become accredited as genres in response to changing socio-historical pressures (so African-American slave narratives gain acknowledgement and are read as a specific genre in the light of contemporary awareness of matters of race and identity and the renegotiation of history and the literary canon). Equally they produce new genres and generic transformations, as classes or groups define and redefine the conditions and understanding of their existence [...]. We can grasp the politics of genre here as a politics of representation, with change and innovation implicated in crises as to whom and what is represented and how and to whom.[50]

Needless to say, generic modulations, innovations and evolution all give rise to growing uncertainty about the identity of existing literary categories, a fact which is particularly evident when it comes to representations of travel and the body of work to which the term supposedly refers. Indeed, confusion surrounding the genre's very appellation is the first indication of this uncertainty: is it travel writing, travel literature, writing on travel? Is it exclusively non-fiction, and if not what features do imaginative and real journeys share? For Jan Borm, travel writing 'is not a genre, but a collective term for a variety of texts both predominantly fictional and non-fictional whose main theme is travel'.[51] In her study of French modernist travellers, Kimberley J. Healy proposes travel literature, in its simplest form, as being 'merely a list of destinations and a series of descriptions'.[52] Loredane Polezzi's examination of contemporary Italian travel writing characterizes the genre as 'marked by alterity, by distance, and by multiple allegiances'.[53] Other critics see the colonial past of Western travel writing and travel practices as justification for jettisoning 'travel' as an unsuitable concept for analysing the myriad forms of journeying in the modern world. For Mark Simpson, it is both the 'self evidence' of travel and writing and the growing critical tendency to use 'travel' as a 'signifier for distinct, even irreconcilable, experiences, relations [and] events' that persuades him to opt for the notion of 'mobility' in his examination of patterns of human movement in nineteenth-century American literature.[54] As Simpson sees it, the importance of travel must not be denied but rather than forming an umbrella term for movement it should be seen as a 'key term' within a much broader theoretical discussion of the 'material and ideological determinations of human movement, particularly as these bear on the making and breaking of subjectivities: local, national, and imperial; classed, racialized and engendered'.[55]

Simpson's particular method of analysis provides evidence of the growing influence in literary and cultural studies of what Tim Cresswell has dubbed the 'mobility turn' of certain theoretical paradigms within the social sciences.[56] As Cresswell explains, mobility is a dynamic concept that has come to designate the opposite of movement, the latter being, like Simpson's understanding of 'travel', 'abstracted mobility' or 'mobility abstracted from contexts of power'.[57] Cresswell also identifies 'mobility as a social and cultural resource [that] gets distributed unevenly and in interconnected ways' and plays a crucial role in the 'differentiation of society'.[58] Of course the advantages for the present study of such a cross-disciplinary, historical and material approach to journeys are obvious and compelling. And yet I also believe that where the study of African literature is concerned it would be premature to abandon entirely the notion of travel as a generic organizing principle before its relevance has been tested or the possibilities of its 'decolonization' more fully explored. Indeed, the value of such an approach is underlined by Charles Forsdick in his study of travel in France and the Francophone world where he opts for 'travel literature' over 'travel writing', arguing that the former

> depends more on a sense of dynamic genericity that presents the material to which the label relates in terms of intergeneric uncertainty or transgeneric voguing between different forms. 'Travel literature' accordingly avoids the prescription attached to fixed notions of genre, and exists as an often unpredictable category in which is assembled a variety of texts. What these share [...] is their representation of journeys, actual and/or imagined, through places with which those undertaking them are unfamiliar – or with which they had thought they were familiar, but through travel discover they no longer are.[59]

Used productively, in the way that Forsdick uses it, the term 'travel literature' brings into focus a wide-ranging corpus of works that reveal evolving attitudes to travel and travel practices over time. The term also allows for a recognition of the value of genre as an important organizing and meaning-making principle whilst at the same time positing resistance to any restrictions the term might suggest. 'Travel *literature*' also introduces what John Frow sees as 'an absolute generality, that of literature' or 'literature not as one genre or another but as at once the totality and dissolution of kinds'.[60] From a critical perspective, situating the texts examined here within the category of 'travel literature' allows for an important development of the approach adopted by Mildred Mortimer's groundbreaking study on the journey motif in Francophone African literature. For although Mortimer sees the incorporation of this oral motif as reinvigorating and revolutionizing the novel, her theme-based, structuralist focus prevents her from exploring the extent to which these fictionalized autobiographies (as she identifies them) are also playing with form. Examining textualizations of journeys within the open-ended genre of travel literature, as this study does, opens up new critical perspectives and prompts a reappraisal of the division within the literature of travel between the categories of fiction and non-fiction by high-lighting how each can infiltrate the other. Such cross-fertilization has the potential, I believe, to build a bridge across the gulf dividing the African representations of travel examined here from more formalized Western traditions of writing about travel. Indeed, just as the journeys in these texts urge Western readers to reflect upon their own culture, so their sometimes uncertain categorization supports John Frow's conception of genre as a 'reflexive model' where texts become '*uses of genre*, performances of or allusions to the norms and conventions which form them and which they may, in turn, transform'.[61] Consequently, apart from instances where other terms and categories are deemed more appropriate to specific discussions, this study shall adopt the more inclusive term of 'travel literature' to distinguish the corpus of works examined.

Questioning generic boundaries or highlighting their fluidity has become an important critical approach of many postcolonial studies of non-Western literatures, a fact which might appear to mitigate against any claims for the radical nature of reappraising the generic boundaries of travel literature. The danger too when it comes to highlighting travel literature's generic uncertainty is that the term can quickly become shorthand for everything, and, in Peter Hulme's view, '[make] the definition nugatory'.[62] Nonetheless, within the context of African literary studies, it is clear that the stakes are high and if we are to take Christopher Miller's comments on the reappraisal of literature seriously then a reconceptualization of generic boundaries is a necessary and inclusive process that deepens our understanding of the nature of cultural flows and cultural production. In addition, although by now it might constitute a standard approach, the generic investigation of such works as Simon Gikandi's orderly and original proposal for grouping well-known African works of fiction, Stephanie Newell's study on Ghanaian popular fiction, Charles Forsdick's above-mentioned study of francophone travel literature, and recent explorations of francophone North-African and Antillean autobiography by Debra Kelly and Maeve McCusker all reveal that this approach is far from straightforward and the conclusions frequently thought-provoking and unexpected.[63]

Accepting that Africans have something vital to contribute to travel literature and possess valuable insights into Western culture brings us to the crucial question of readership. To whom are these textualizations of travel addressed? For Patrick Holland and Graham Huggan, readers of Western travel writing tend to be predominantly metropolitan and this has crucial implications for how such texts are read and produced. For example, readers 'back home' tend to process and defuse such accounts of *difference* through 'the comforting reiteration of *familiar* exotic myths'.[64] It is precisely this sense of home that Western travel writers share with their readers and that explains another layer of familiarity underpinning writing that ultimately 'operate[s] within a readily identifiable semantic field'.[65] For his part, Michel de Certeau sees the tripartite structure of travel writing – departure, descriptive narrative of place visited, return – as revealing not just an unbreakable tie with the Western travel writer's 'home' but also a form of mutually empowering framing whereby:

> The two histories (the departure and the return) [have] the status of meta-discourses since the narration speaks of themselves in them. In travel accounts, this historical 'frame' entertains a double relation to the picture it supports. On the one hand, the frame is necessary to assure the strangeness of the picture. On the other, it draws upon the representation for the possibility of transforming itself: the discourse that sets off in search of the other with the impossible task of saying the truth returns from afar with the authority to speak in the name of the other and command belief.[66]

Needless to say, African travellers also hold up their own cultural origins as the implicit referent for interpreting and representing others. However, as we shall see, the relationship based on familiarity and authority mentioned by de Certeau does not quite pertain in African textualizations of travel to the West, particularly those from the colonial era. Quite apart from the fact that material reasons mean a round trip can rarely be taken for granted in most of the texts examined here, the relationship with 'home' is never straightforward. First, the particular linguistic contexts of these francophone texts mean that the readership is not necessarily African and consequently not one that shares the cultural values and attitudes to difference of the authors. This is complicated by the fact that many of these African authors, because of their Western education, understand important aspects of the cultural and moral framework within which their metropolitan readers operate yet are not fully part of it. Publishing contexts must also be taken into account when assessing questions of readership, and the fact that these texts are largely edited, produced and marketed in the West is not, of course, insignificant. Indeed, Jean Malaurie's foreword to *L'Africain du Grœnland*, for all its generosity and insightfulness, is clearly addressed to a French readership, and is largely concerned with highlighting the 'difference' of the interconti-nental African traveller. This signals the dangers involved for Western readers and critics anxious to create a space for African textualiza-tions of travel. Careless readings mean roles will simply be reversed rather than travel models questioned, and instead of the colonial emphasis on the Black 'object' of the traveller's gaze, the Black trav-eller will simply be gazed upon as a new 'object' of ethnographic-style inquiry. It is vital, therefore, that Western readers pay careful atten-tion to what is being said to them and learn to extract themselves from the cosy relationship they have heretofore enjoyed with Western travel writers. How and why is their familiar cultural and physical landscape being reflected back to them? What is being revealed about their expectations of the genre of travel literature, of travellers and of travel practices? How are these expectations subverted, and what might the resulting processes of defamiliarization mean?

Despite the overwhelming evidence supporting a majority metro-politan readership for these texts, it would be wrong, nonetheless, to assume that the African reader is absent from the intentions of these authors. For example, even if the question of readership is far from straightforward, the epistolary form of Bernard Dadié's *Un Nègre à Paris* explicitly addresses an African reader, and calls upon him/her to make sense of what is being described. The in-between cultural posi-tion of these writers can also impact negatively on their relationship to their 'African home'. For many, a sense of belonging to Africa is never self-evident and the adoption of Western narrative forms and modes of address can operate as a distancing process between both the author and his/her African reader.

What emerges from the texts studied here is the presence of a split readership. This becomes an explicit textual issue in both *Chalys d'Harlem* and *L'Africain du Grœnland* and is worth focusing on briefly. In both texts, the notion of split readership emerges in the subtle highlighting of a distinction between conventional Western-style travelogues and the form required to convey travel's significance to a non-literate and/or non-French-speaking African audience. For example, when the eponymous protagonist of *Chalys d'Harlem* is asked by Omar Fall, the narrator of the text, if he would be willing to have his travel experiences recorded in written form, Chalys agrees. In a manner that evokes the significance of travel in traditional myth mentioned earlier, Chalys is convinced that the insights he has gained on his travels could be of positive, practical and *communal* benefit to his fellow Africans. However, because he is illiterate, Chalys expressly asks that his words be conveyed in the following manner: 'Si tu me promets de relater mes dires devant mes concitoyens, à la manière des conteurs de notre enfance je suis prêt à accéder à ton désir. Quelle école de la vie que celle de nos conteurs. [...] Notre voyage commençait dans le monde du merveilleux.' [If you promise to relate my words to our compatriots like the storytellers of our childhood then I am happy to satisfy your request. What a school of life those story-tellers provided. [...] Our journey began in the realm of the marvellous] (*CH*, p. 62).

Chalys goes on to describe the power of being transported to imaginary worlds and seems to suggest that the challenge for Omar Fall is to relate the account of his particular intercontinental journey so that so-called factual accounts and fiction feed into each other for the benefit of African audiences. In Kpomassie's text, the written narrative ends when the author decides it is time to return to Africa. Once here, he implies, the challenge will be not just to recount what he has seen but to apply what he has learned in a practical context that will benefit those who remained at home. Together, these examples reveal the way in which the challenge for African authors is to (re)shape a genre for an African audience familiar with the specific representation and symbolic significance of travel in oral myth but unused to the types of intercontinental travel practices that shape much Western travel literature. In order to reach both audiences, it would seem that it is not enough to dwell on the individual experience of travel but that its heuristic benefit must be both textually demonstrated and, where possible, practically conveyed and applied.

To conclude this section on generic considerations, I stress that discussion of written African literature, whether we like it or not, cannot simply deny the significance of conceptual models associated with the West. For this reason it will be necessary at times to incorporate the African texts discussed here into an overarching system of explanation that is rooted in Western critical practices. However, as the above discussion makes clear, African textualizations of travel are also given shape by specific cultural and historical realities and must, therefore, not simply be made to fit a generic tradition that is essentially Western. To be sure, not all the texts examined here are knowingly subversive, and some, as we shall see, could even be described as formally conservative. Nonetheless, the sorts of rhetorical devices, thematic reworkings and genre blending that will be highlighted in subsequent chapters can all be said to blur any boundaries that travel literature may imply. For this reason it is important to stress again that a reappraisal of Western travel writing's boundaries is vital for developing ways of identifying an African literature of travel and learning to read it against and alongside its Western equivalent.

Travel and Leisure

As I mentioned above, there exists a very limited corpus of francophone African texts that appear to slot unproblematically into the category of non-fictional travelogue as it is more generally understood. What distinguishes these particular texts from other accounts of travel out of Africa is the apparent representation of travel for travel's sake and the clear implication that most of the authors appear to retain a quite clear traveller/tourist identity. In my brief listing of the other types of Africans who travel out of their continent, it is clear that another identity, in most cases 'professional' (and here I include mothers and housewives), tends to overshadow, or even obliterate their status as travelling subjects. The difficulty of establishing their identity as travellers is compounded by the fact that they themselves, the societies from which they come and in which they arrive, do not always recognize their traveller status. There is no doubt that as well as the historical and literary explanations discussed above, part of the problem is linked to a dominant Western idea of travel that links it to purposes of rest and recreation. Other largely positive associations influence perceptions of travel as being linked to a capacity to provide instruction and fulfilment, and notions of the traveller as being courageous and intrepid, but also suspended (whether permanently or temporarily) from professional obligation.

What the above observations suggest is that when thinking about African representations of travel it is vital to destabilize the term 'travel' itself, to question the logic of what it has come to mean. Despite claims that the 'art' of travel is dying, or has died, substantial numbers of people around the globe travel each day and provide evidence enough of the continued significance of travel as an important culturally shaping phenomenon. Certainly, some of the developments in critical theory already mentioned have been influential in establishing new ways of analysing the social, cultural and physical ramifications of contemporary travel practices. However, this theoretical movement has not always been accompanied by progress in our understanding of literary representations of travel, and we remain stuck in an earlier era of travel for pleasure where its meaning is closely linked to that of the holiday, i.e. a temporary surcease of work for the types of self-satisfying purposes mentioned above.

In an article examining the evolution of the Western tourist, and which is relevant to a broader discussion of travel, Jószef Böröcz examines how this largely positive perception of travel derives from the Grand Tour of the eighteenth century. He argues persuasively that this focus on an elitist and aristocratic way of travelling has meant that other historical precursors for travel are ignored such as the working-class movement of craftsmen, the purpose of which was also educational and which, he suggests, covered a broader geographical area than its elite counterpart. Böröcz concludes that 'the one-to-one association of the aristocracy with early tourism – and its corollary, the assumption of a simple, unilinear descending cultural pattern of leisure travel – is empirically untenable'.[67] The model he provides is important for establishing the ways in which Western perceptions of travel have for far too long elided any relationship to labour. (Indeed, criticism and the travel literature industry have also been complicit in this by underplaying or erasing the travel writer's professional identity, and by failing to highlight the utilitarian and professional dimension of travelling to write as well as the undeniable market value of travel writing.) However, Böröcz's travel-work model becomes even more enabling when it comes to recognizing the development of an African literature of travel and for including African travellers whose journeys are not necessarily or exclusively motivated by leisure purposes.

Similarly, in her study of antebellum black and white American women travellers, Cheryl J. Fish explains how travel for Nancy Price, Mary Seacole and Margeret Fuller was not undertaken solely for the sake of adventure and education as in the Grand Tour but because it enabled these women to find what Fish refers to as a '"field of usefulness" through which to explore the wider world'.[68] Although Fish's notion of usefulness largely refers to the professional vocation these women discover on their respective journeys, it also refers to the way in which the individual traveller's insights are subsequently applied in practical ways for the benefit of others. In other words, Fish's identification of travel as a field of usefulness ties in with the communal benefits of travel and journeys stressed in African orature.

Taken together in an African context, both Fish's concept of travel as a 'field of usefulness' and Böröcz's link between travel and labour are crucial for establishing not just the motivation for travel, but also African ways of travelling. For the soldier who leaves Africa to fight for the metropolitan 'mother country' in a major war, for the student who journeys to France to further his education before returning with a view to bettering the lives of his family and fellow countrymen, for the immigrant workers and their families whose destination is employment and better material conditions, travel is essentially a means, or journey, to an end, a way of enabling them to play a useful role. These models are also relevant to texts that appear to privilege recreational travel. For example, in *L'Africain du Grœnland*, as we shall see, Kpomassie is inspired by the travel practices of a semi-nomadic Nigerian tribe who provide him with a practical 'work' model to reach his destination. In *Un Nègre à Paris* it is important to remember that Dadié's trip is paid for by an unnamed friend and it is likely that his particularly critical manner of observing is part of a wider intellectual and political project that he hopes will be of benefit to the imminently independent Ivory Coast. Indeed, although he never explains it, the American trip recounted in *Patron de New York* is undertaken when he has become a government minister and the manner in which he delivers his conclusions on American society suggests they will be used to influence subsequent political and cultural decisions at home. (The nature of this trip also means, of course, that it is almost certainly not self-financed.)

The connection between travel and labour in the context of African literature is important because it also raises the issue of travel's material contexts, and reminds us that, as well as being a product of literary and cultural forces, travel writing is also socially and economically rooted. For Patrick Holland and Graham Huggan, the economic power of Western travellers 'enables them to mobilize resources' that allow them to contemplate and execute return journeys.[69] Similarly, John Urry reminds us that if Westerners travel for leisure and pleasure it is simply because they have the means to buy time.[70] Put bluntly, this is not an option available to many Africans. For if money makes the world go around, we also need money to go around the world.[71] And as with labour, the significance of money – or lack thereof – is crucial to understanding certain representations and practices of travel in African literature.

Michael Cronin, in his thought-provoking study of travel and translation, suggests that literary travel involves 'constant shifts between the macroscopic scale of [...] horizontal travel and the microscopic scale of [...] vertical travel. For Cronin:

> Horizontal travel is the more conventional understanding of travel as a linear progression from place to place. Vertical travel is temporary dwelling in a location for a period of time where the traveller begins to travel down into the particulars of place either in space (botany, studies of micro-climate, exhaustive exploration of local landscape) or in time (local history, archaeology, folklore).[72]

Although's Cronin's assessment of this structural pattern is an accurate description of much Western travel writing, his theory, as with so many others, needs to be modified when applied to African representations of travel. The representation of the linear progression from interesting place to interesting place described by Cronin suggests a certain 'romantic' wandering or 'aimlessness' that is frequently present (though by all means not a constant feature) in Western travel literature, particularly non-fiction. Moreover, the nature of horizontal travel implies a certain level of financial security that enables stopovers in the succession of places visited. Although, as we shall see, there are African texts that describe the stages of an international journey, most representations of travel by Africans gloss over, or minimize the importance of horizontal travel. Instead, whether it is the representation of educational or bureaucratic structures, observations on architecture, local environment and cultural mores, or the description of the cultural encounters of restrictive domestic spaces the majority of African textualizations of travel focus overwhelmingly on 'travelling down'. This is not, however, to be equated with the type of sedentary travel mentioned earlier where cultural encounter is eschewed. On the contrary, many of the texts studied here suggest that vertical travel is an intense and more self-reflective encounter with difference yet also one that reaffirms the unending possibilities of travel and (re)discovery.

Studying African textualizations of travel reminds us, therefore, of the need to pay closer attention to the practices of those who travel without money or for whom the financing of travel is never straightforward. Needless to say, this is of particular importance in the context of immigrant literature where the reality of travel's material conditions is most obvious, and where the type of mobility involved appears most irreconcilable with the travel practices of tourists and recreational travellers. However, extending the borders of travel literature to include this figure is an urgent task that has the potential to emphasize the human dimension of immigrant travel without losing sight of differences between more privileged forms of journeying.

* * *

The present study does not present itself as an archaeological unearthing of 'lost' travel texts or as an exhaustive history of a francophone African literature of travel. The texts studied here are chosen as case studies that together underline the diversity of African textualizations of travel in formal and geographical terms, but also in relation to the travelling subjects represented and their motivation for and ways of travelling. The presentation of these texts in largely chronological order is not meant to suggest a single, smooth line of development but is instead intended to highlight the ways in which particular socio-historical contexts shape attitudes to intercontinental travel in an African context.

I have chosen to begin this study by examining Ousman Socé's *Mirages de Paris* because I believe it illustrates the distinctiveness of colonial African intercontinental travel experiences in important ways, and underlines the invaluable contribution such writing makes to the broader genre of travel literature. In the first instance, *Mirages de Paris* illustrates the symbiotic relationship between the earliest colonized travellers and the French capital, a relationship that, in travel terms, appears to reinforce the notion of Western destinations as the centre and Africa as the periphery, a geographical configuration that endures well beyond the colonial era. The second reason for beginning this study with Socé's text is that it highlights an important exilic dimension of colonized Africans' journeys to Europe that is linked to a particular politics of visualizing Africans in inter-war Europe. Nonetheless, despite the manner in which the text's protagonist appears forever fixed in the gaze of the European, *Mirages de Paris* also reveals the way in which the colonial 'centre' is uncovered/discovered by the African travelling gaze in unexpected ways that tentatively destabilize its claims to cultural and political authority.

Chapter 3 focuses on Aké Loba's *Kocoumbo, l'étudiant noir*. As the text's title suggests this is an account of student travel that further explores the centripetal pull of Paris in the context of colonial education. The particular alienation and exile of the young travelling protagonist links him in important ways to the travel experiences described in *Mirages de Paris*. However, in this instance courage and resilience enable the student to complete his journey, return home and transform the benefits of travel into the type of cultural capital needed for individual social advancement within colonized African society. This chapter will also launch a discussion of transport and travel technologies, an issue that re-emerges in Chapter 5. Invariably, travel presupposes a body, and the intercontinental journeys structuring all the texts studied in *Postcolonial Eyes* raise the important issue of modes of transport. If not quite a study of trains, planes and automobiles, Loba's text nonetheless underscores the symbolic importance of transport technologies for Africans keen to embark on the route to 'progress' and 'modernization'. Like many Western travel writers, African authors are, in their way, attuned to the growing mechanization of travel and its effects on the traveller's ways of seeing. References to increased speed and technology are also rooted in the dual perspective of these authors for whom such features can be as much a symbol of Africa's 'underdevelopment' as of the West's 'modernization'.

Chapter 4 considers another text that chooses Paris as its destination. However, *Un Nègre à Paris* represents an important break with preceding portrayals of Paris in its questioning of the French capital's status as the centre of the colonial universe. By boldly adopting the recognizable forms of the travelogue, and subjecting his travel narrative of the City of Light to his own particular form of interpretative framework, Bernard Dadié succeeds in approaching some of the key issues of travel writing from a genuinely innovative angle. At the same time, the account of his 'holiday' reminds the reader that

Dadié's African identity is not incompatible with that of the tourist or with the elaboration of a critical postcolonial gaze.

Dadié's positive experience of travel, and the preliminary steps he takes to 'decentring' African intercontinental travel, also link him in important ways to the texts examined in Chapters 5 and 6. It is perhaps no coincidence that the historical context of *Un Nègre à Paris*, *L'Africain du Grœnland*, *Chalys d'Harlem* and *Patron du New York* is the period leading to, or immediately succeeding African independence. As the chapters devoted to these texts underline, the period from the late 1950s to the mid-1960s emerges as significant for the elaboration of more geographically diverse and conceptually sophisticated textualizations of intercontinental travel by a small but important group of African authors. Disenchantment with postcolonial regimes has not yet set in, Africa sees itself as beginning to play a part on the world stage, and these writers, buoyed no doubt by the international connections of the anti-colonial movement, clearly see themselves as citizens of the world. In the same way as other contemporary African writers imagined 'their works and words had an innate and functional capacity to intervene in everyday life and to transform the tenor and vehicle of political discourse', it is highly plausible that both Dadié and Tété-Michel Kpomassie in particular detected in the particular formal conventions of non-fictional travel writing a means to contribute to the mood of hope and optimism.[73] For them, as well as the fictional characters of Diakhaté's text, international travel is seen both as a confident, individual reaction to the times the authors (or fictional characters in the case of *Chalys d'Harlem*) live in and a means of instilling their own self-confidence in the wider African community. In all of these texts, travel's 'field of usefulness' is evidenced most clearly in an inherent process of comparison, and at times *widererkennen*, that derives from the encounter with another culture. In the same way as other African writers of this era stressed the connection between art and politics Dadié, Kpomassie and the characters of Diakhaté's text stress a similar link between travel and politics. For all three authors, intercontinental travel encourages a self-reflexive assessment of the traveller's own culture which in turn leads to a renewed commitment to that culture. Together, their texts stress that part of Africa's movement away from colonization requires it to be released from a blinkered fascination with its past and awakened to its potential role within a postcolonial, globalizing world.

In Chapter 7 I will explore the travelling reality that replaces the optimism of the previous chapters. Together, Calixthe Beyala's *Le petit prince de Belleville* and *Maman a un amant* allow us to begin to assess the impact that economic migration has had on the development of African travel literature. At first glance, the role of Paris as the centre of its former African colonial world appears to have been reinstated. In addition, the living conditions and social marginalization of Beyala's African characters appear to support the association of immigrant travel with a less optimistic and abject form of mobility. However, in their way these texts provide a very clear, constructive engagement with ideas of travel that open up new directions for African writing. In particular, the privileging in *Le petit prince de Belleville* and *Maman a un amant* of the female experience of intercontinental travel allows Beyala to trace the possibilities available for women who take to the road. As an African account of postcolonial France, these immigrant texts also reveal a society whose culture and society is equally on the move and undergoing radical transformation, not least in terms of leisure travel patterns and tourism.

Reading together the corpus of works examined in *Postcolonial Eyes* it is possible to establish how their deployment of various attitudes to, and practices of, travel produce very different, yet in other ways familiar, possibilities for cultural encounter. Consequently, if we are to grasp their potential contribution to the literature of travel they need to be understood in relation to that particular generic tradition. This is not to say that we must ignore the places from where the authors have come. Instead, being aware of the ways in which African writers repeat, rework, and subvert the conventions of the genre will better reveal where travel literature might be going as it comes to terms with ever increasing global mobility. For Western readers, it is also vital that we acknowledge the particular 'field of usefulness' these texts represent for us, and recognize the value of being the object of the other's gaze. To do so means beginning a dialogue that would genuinely enable us to fulfil Dennis Porter's aspiration to 'read ourselves as the others of our others and replace the notions of a place of truth with that of a knowledge which is always relative and provisional'.[74]

CHAPTER ONE

Mirages de Paris: Staged Encounters of the Exotic Kind

Ousmane Socé Diop's novel, *Mirages de Paris*, is not the first franco-phone African text to base its structure on intercontinental travel. That honour most likely belongs to *Force-bonté*, Bakary Diallo's autobiographical-inspired account of a Senegalese *tirailleur* published in 1926.[1] However, whereas *Force-bonté* is largely acknowledged to be a panegyric to the French colonization of West Africa, Socé's text is crucial to establishing the fundamental link between travel and exile that informs the psychological drama of so many subsequent African accounts of journeys (to France, in particular, but also to other Western destinations). What is also especially unusual about *Mirages de Paris* is the identity of its travelling protagonist, Fara. As was already mentioned, where African journeys to the West are concerned, it is professional and domestic identities that tend to be highlighted and any affinity to the figure of the traveller is either ignored or underplayed. Fara, on the other hand, is not a soldier, civil servant, spouse, student or labourer. Instead, his journey to Paris takes place against the background of the 1931 Exposition Colo-niale, an event one commentator has described as the apotheosis of French colonial history.[2] The Exposition, to which Socé devotes only a brief chapter, is key to the novel's plot as it provides the setting for Fara's meeting with Jacqueline Bourciez, the young French woman who will eventually become his lover and the mother of his child.[3] However, rather than focus on the broader issue of miscegenation and cultural *métissage* raised by their relationship, this chapter will use the Exposition as a starting point for a detailed examination of its symbolic significance in the context of African intercontinental travel and cultural encounter in the colonial era.[4] This approach will serve to clarify first how the event stages, in an artificial context, the reality of what happens when representatives of a colonized culture travel to a colonizing culture. Analysis of the Exposition also provides an invaluable insight into the mechanisms of representing what Christopher Miller terms a 'form of state-sponsored hallucination'.[5] Examining this more closely reveals the complex interdependency between negative, hierarchical perceptions of the colonized Other and the Exposition's politics of visualizing 'other' culture. Finally, the focus of this chapter's concluding section diverges somewhat from other recent studies of *Mirages de Paris* by examining the ways in which the Exposition's travelling themes shed light on an external reality, 'the West', that ultimately reveals itself to be as artificial a construct as the fabricated world within the perimeter walls.[6]

Travel sickness? Home sickness?

The complex significance of the Exposition may seem ill-served at first by the apparently unsophisticated structure and limpid style of *Mirages de Paris*. Like other novels of intercontinental travel to be examined here, Socé's text begins with a seemingly idyllic description of the point of departure, Fara's native village, Niane, where, we are told, this 'petit noir poussait comme les tamariniers de la brousse, libre dans l'espace' [little black boy grew, untamed, like the tamarind trees of the bush] (*MP*, p. 9). However, as we shall see in other apparent juxtapositions of idyllic African points of departure and alienating Western destinations, such simplistic binaries fail to take account of the cultural encounter of colonization and its importance as an impetus for travel. For example, in *Mirages de Paris*, a careful reading of the geography and layout of Niane reveals that not only has colonization transformed the local landscape and culture, it has also introduced the technological conditions – in the form of mechanized transport – that facilitate travel out of the village, and ultimately out of Africa:

> Le village de Niane se campait sur la plaine de Cayor, terre de prédilection de l'arachide. Un jour des blancs y firent leur apparition, ils construisirent un chemin de fer qui transporta des outils. Ils tracèrent de larges rues droites, y plantèrent une double rangée de fromagers qui, maintenant, se donnaient l'accolade au-dessus des boulevards pour arrêter les rayons du soleil. (*MP*, p. 7)

> [The village of Niane was situated on the plain of Cayor, where the groundnut flourished. One day, white men appeared; they built a railway line that transported tools. They laid out straight, wide streets and planted two rows of kapok trees that now stood proudly over the avenues, blocking the sun's rays.]

Despite the rigid lines of European town planning highlighted by this short extract, the co-existence, and indeed permeability, of two very different cultures is also implied. Nonetheless, until the age of nine, Fara seems sheltered from the cultural and political realities of the French colonial presence and grows up in a community described in terms that evoke the cultural stability associated with Negritude literature. However, as Bernard Mouralis notes, the corollary of this essentialist portrait of a stable, pure and traditional Africa is an unspoken notion of pathological soundness:

> Tranquillité de l'esprit, harmonie des rapports qu'il entretient avec le cosmos comme avec les autres hommes, égalité de l'humeur: voilà quelques-uns des traits qui semblent définir l'état psychique du Nègre et font ainsi de lui un être particulièrement équilibré, doté d'une constitution spécifique qui le préserverait en somme de toute dérive névrotique ou psychotique.[7]

> [Peace of mind, harmonious relationship with both the cosmos and other individuals, stable mood: these are some of the characteristics that appear to define the black man's psyche, thereby making him a particularly balanced individual with a specific constitution that would, in short, protect him from any neurotic or psychotic deterioration.]

For Mouralis, this positive portrayal is nonetheless destabilized by the undeniable tones of sadness and depression that underwrite much Negritude literature, and which can be explained, in part, by the shadow cast over African lives by European colonization.

The question of mental stability, and instability, figures strongly in Socé's account of Fara's intercultural experiences both at home and abroad and is worth examining before turning in more detail to issues relevant to the Exposition. It is first raised when the young Fara is taken to the 'école des blancs' [white school] (*MP*, p. 12) by his father. Significantly, this early encounter with Western culture is not explicitly presented as evidence of a psychological trauma. Indeed, the presence on the classroom wall of familiar scenes of African life appears to suggest that Fara and his fellow African pupils may move effortlessly between two very different cultural realities. However, the portrait of the French teacher in her strange attire and the confusion engendered by the French language undermine any notion of these cultures co-existing harmoniously. If anything, it is the *seeming normality* of the classroom scenes, and in particular the introduction to the French language, that should alert us to the cultural alienation that is taking place. As philosopher Paulin Hountondji remarks: '*Il n'est pas normal* en effet que des individus apprennent d'emblée à lire et à écrire dans une langue qu'ils ne comprennent pas. *Il n'est pas normal* d'être obligé de traverser, pour accéder au savoir le plus élémentaire, le dur apprentissage d'une langue étrangère.' [Effectively, *it is unnatural* that individuals should first learn to read and write in a language they do not understand. *It is unnatural* that in order to acquire the most basic knowledge one should first have to undergo the difficult process of learning a foreign language.][8]

The issue of language and its role in colonial and postcolonial politics and writing has, of course, been a central feature of post-colonial criticism.[9] However, in order to understand better how the question of language might be seen in relation to this study's focus on intercontinental travel it is helpful to look at Mary Besemeres's notion of 'language travel'.[10] For Besemeres, narratives of language-immersion – or language travel – in contemporary literature in English constitute a sub-genre of travel writing which she argues

> represent[s] an attempt to communicate with people of another culture on those others' own terms. [...] Through their focus on the experience of learning another language as a foreigner and cultural outsider – and translating the self in the process – memoirs of language immersion arguably extend the possibilities of the larger travel genre, possibilities foreclosed in the canonical, often mono-lingual writers whose narratives typically observe and comment on, rather than engage with, cultural others.[11]

Mirages de Paris, and the other narratives of travel and cultural encounter studied here, all explore, implicitly or explicitly, the ques-tion of language travel. However, unlike the corpus of works exam-ined by Besemeres – where the authors relate their encounter with the space of the other language through the medium of their own native language – African narratives of travel in French reveal a very different relationship between language, culture, place and identity. Essentially, this is due to a spatio-linguistic reality that has been shaped by colonization and which, as *Mirages de Paris* repeatedly emphasizes, appears to transform the French language into a sort of boarding pass for the colonized African traveller. Four times in the course of the novel our attention is drawn to the scholarly perfection of Fara's spoken French, as if this linguistic competence will smooth his journey to France and render his quest for acceptance by the host culture easier.[12] This appears to be borne out when some insidiously friendly white fellow-passengers agree to show Fara around Bordeaux only when they discover him to be intelligent and well-spoken.[13] However, as with so much in this text, appearances are deceptive, and the African's mastery of French does not mean integration is a given, nor does it quell the sense that beneath this grammatical perfection is a non-verbalized and devastating inferiority complex. For Paulin Hountondji, this curious obsession of the colonized with grammatical perfection is a further element of the particular psychological make-up of the educated colonized elite and provides an interesting insight into how 'language travels' might operate in African textualizations of journeys to the West:

> Ce désir d'une perfection toujours plus grande atteint [...] un degré proprement pathologique. L'intellectuel colonisé est un obsédé de la grammaire – et de la correction en générale. [...] Le langage ordinaire ne sépare pas, il unit. [...] Il ne faut pas s'y arrêter, mais se laisser porter vers lui, vers l'Autre, qui est seul véritablement visé. [...] L'intellectuel vit une communication tronquée, avortée. L'Autre, pour lui, ce n'est pas l'interlocuteur, c'est le langage. [...] Disons le mot: le comportement linquistique de l'Africain, quand il s'exprime en français, a tous les caractères d'une névrose.[14]

> [This desire for an ever greater perfection reaches [...] a genuinely pathological level. The colonized intellectual is obsessed with grammar – and with what is correct in general. [...] Ordinary language does not separate, it unites. [...] One must not become stuck on it but must allow oneself to be carried towards it, towards the Other, who is its only real target. [...] The intellectual communicates in a truncated, aborted way. For him/her, the Other is not the interlocutor, it is language. [...] Let us be clear: the linguistic behaviour of the African, when s/he speaks in French, has all the characteristics of a neurosis.]

It is through the main character's relationship with literary texts, however, that Socé alerts us most explicitly to a troubling relationship with elsewhere. Tales of French adventurers give rise, we are told, to a 'dangereux amour de l'exotisme' [a dangerous love of exoticism] (*MP*, p. 15) on the part of Fara and an obsession with seeing Paris for himself. Certainly, literature's role as an invitation to, and impetus for, travel, has long been acknowledged, particularly in African accounts of colonial education. What is notable here, however, is the opening up of a new axis of travel through the explicit reversal of the term 'exotic' to denote not the colonial periphery, but the colonial centre. Yet in Fara's case, as in the case of many other colonized African travellers to France, the desire to travel does not appear to be informed by a longing for the unfamiliar but by the yearning to close a distance that he believes separates him from where he will truly feel at 'home'. Indeed, although Fara is said to have 'le pied marin' [a sailor's constitution] (*MP*, p. 19) and to be immune from travel sickness, he appears to experience a particular form of 'home' sickness characterized by a constant longing for an idealized but unattainable Parisian 'home'. Being in Paris does not heal this homesickness because his encounter with the French capital does not correspond to his pre-conceived image of it.[15] In sum, the elusiveness of a Parisian 'home', the sense that it is a destination that the colonized African traveller will never reach, is seen to a be a major contributory factor to the text's pathological tone.

Clearly, then, whilst the reversal of exoticism's usual referent is a welcome development, the price to be paid by the African traveller is a heavy one. For if Paris becomes the exotic destination *par excellence*, the yearning for its supposed familiarity instigates a relationship with reality that is destabilizing in an entirely different way. For Christopher Miller, novels such as *Mirages de Paris*, which relate the experiences of Africans in France during the colonial era, present 'a strong current of altered consciousness. [...] These texts seem to address questions of political and cultural identity from within a hall of mirrors. They stage the encounter between Africans and French as a matter of *hallucination, mirage, anesthesia,* or *phantasm*.'[16] Whilst Miller, here, is using the notions of hallucination and mirage to describe an essentially literary phenomenon, he also stresses the relevance of a more psychopathological meaning for Fara's obsession with France. Undoubtedly, the idea of Fara's 'pathological francocentrism', as Miller terms it, is lent greater support by the text's all-pervasive melancholic tone.[17] This is evident in the importance of minor details such as the foggy landscape that first greets Fara upon his arrival in France and the more obvious focus on the distressing split between 'reality' and *mirages* that recurs throughout the text. More importantly, this blurred line between illusion and 'reality' ties in with the novel's emphasis on the main character's psychological well-being as he swings from almost euphoric excitement to moments of deep despair and anguish. At such moments, it is tempting to view Fara's growing sense of despair and his eventual suicide as evidence of an endogenous psychiatric disorder. However, one must be wary here of making clinical 'diagnoses' of strictly textual personae, particularly when closer analysis suggests that Socé is more concerned with using the psychological portrait of his main protagonist to examine broader issues relating to the effects of colonization on the psyche. Accordingly, my use of the term 'pathology' in relation to Socé's novel reflects the open meaning attributed to it by George Revill and Richard Wrigley, who conclude that as well as 'implying a causality that can be clinically determined, [the term] is also diffuse, carrying with it a marked social and moral charge'.[18]

Needless to say, the link between travel and pathology is not new. Indeed, as Revill and Wrigley remind us, travel has long been seen as a cause of ailments and malaise (personal and social), as well as their cure.[19] Where Sub-Saharan Africa and international travel is concerned, the threat of tropical diseases, including mental illness, has always been of particular concern to Western travellers to the continent.[20] Interestingly, *Mirages de Paris* presents us with the reverse scenario when a minor character, in a comment worthy of contemporary rightwing Western opposition to mass Third World immigration, warns Jacqueline of the risk of being contaminated by African illnesses because of her close relationship with Fara. Jonathan Andrews also notes important associations between travel practices and psychopathologies. Many of these are culturally contingent, but others, such as the link between travel and 'mental healing', transcend specific contexts and attain a more universal value:

> Whether as a symptomatic response to mental unrest and trauma [...]; or a means of working out trauma and of pursuing, or accidentally arriving at, self-knowledge, wandering and journeying have long had an association with mental unrest. Culturally, travel has meant and still means radically different things to different societies, be it the dreamtime walkabouts of aboriginals, the many-faceted routes taken in American road movies, or the mental journeys pursued during certain forms of meditation. Yet many of these modes of travel have had aspects of mental healing at their very centres.[21]

It is clear that in the texts I am concerned with in this study, travel is often motivated by the promise of healing and the possibility of finding answers to traumatic questions of identity and belonging. However, the key deviation from 'mental healing' in francophone African narratives of travel to the West – and in particular to the centre of colonial power – hinges on the degree to which travel itself further prises open these questions and heightens, rather than heals, feelings of trauma and loss. In this way, an emphasis on pathology and travel in Socé's text allows us to see the ways in which Fara's despair connects not only with Fanonian ideas of a specific internalized inferiority complex on the part of the colonized, but also with a particular psychology of travel. Indeed, *Mirages de Paris* sets in place a rhetoric of alienation and exile that will be replicated to various degrees by all the texts examined here and which will emerge as a crucial factor in characterizing African textualizations of intercontinental travel and cultural encounter.

Starting out: being seen

It is certainly possible to see in Fara's desire to travel to Paris a need for a kind of 'healing', or at the very least a form of identity reconciliation. However, although the physical act of travelling away from Africa and towards France clearly marks the beginning of a journey of self-awareness, his experiences in Paris cannot be said to provide any kind of 'cure'. It is during his journey across the sea, in this uncertain space between France and Senegal, that Fara first fears he may never again see the familiar sights of his birthplace. This may be interpreted as a logical consequence of travelling large distances in an era when intercontinental travel was still a rare undertaking for black Africans. However, it is also an indication that Fara is beginning to understand that the distance between himself and his culture of origin is more than physical, and that his in-between position on the sea is the clearest indication of where he really comes from. In the next chapter the question of travel conditions on board steamships will be looked at more closely. Where Fara's particular journey across the sea is concerned, suffice it to say, however, that it is as he moves out of Dakar, past the old slave port of Gorée, that we first detect in him evidence of a nascent awareness of his inalterable 'blackness' and all that this will signify in France.

Two key incidents on the steamship contribute to the African traveller's growing sense of self as seen by others. First, in the dining quarters, Fara notices that the arrangement of tables and the differential quality of service accorded to the diners is explained entirely by 'race'. Secondly, sitting within earshot of a 'white' table, Fara overhears a conversation concerning the intellectual abilities of black Africans. On the one hand, a French colonial teacher, Monsieur Dupont, argues

that experience has shown him how Africans are capable of assimi-
lating Western culture and engaging in genuinely original and critical
thought. Dupont's claims are strongly refuted by his interlocutor, a
businessman, who claims that Africans are little more than parrots.
However, in an almost exemplary illustration of the ambivalence of
colonial discourse, he then proceeds to argue against over-schooling
Africans and exposing them to too much Western culture because
of the risk of transforming them into 'des "elements dangereux" et
le jour où ils verront très clair, ils nous f... à la porte' [dangerous
elements and *the day when they see things clearly* they will kick us
out] (*MP*, p. 22, my emphasis).

These incidents are the first clear indication of the type of objectification and demonization of blackness that, cumulatively, will
have such a destabilizing effect on Fara's sense of self whilst abroad.
What is noteworthy here is the way in which the physical journey
out of Africa coincides with the beginning of a more inward looking
psychological journey. Until now, even if the reader has suspected
that Fara's physical identity is out of joint with his cultural aspirations, he himself has seemed blissfully unaware of this split. If seeing
(and in this case also hearing) is believing, then it is travel that has
allowed Fara to really 'open his eyes' – a development the travelling
French businessman has warned against – and to begin to see that his
image of France and his place in it may be just that: an impression.
Curiously, however, the perspective afforded by travel, both of the
self and of the other, does not develop seamlessly and transform the
text into a more recognizable Western-style travel account. Instead,
Fara becomes tragically trapped in the crossfire of two competing
gazes: his own complex view of France on the one hand, and, on the
other, the iconic Duboisian double perspective of 'always looking at
oneself through the eyes of others'.[22] Nowhere is this intricate play of
looks more forcefully illustrated than by the passage devoted to the
Exposition coloniale.

The 'Exposition coloniale internationale et des pays d'outre-mer'
– to give it its official title – was organized by no less a figure than
the French imperial hero Maréchal Lyautey, and opened by Paul
Reynaud, minister for the colonies, in Paris in May 1931. By the time
the 110-hectacre Exposition closed its doors the following November
it had been visited by millions and was widely accepted to have been a
resounding popular and financial success.[23] In the abundant literature
accompanying the Exposition, and in the numerous critical works

devoted to it, it is evident that the event was a feast for French eyes on a grand scale.[24] From the sumptuous recreation of the Khmer temple of Angkor Wat, to the numerous other exhibits representing France's overseas colonies, and the equally 'exotic' displays by other European colonial powers, it was clear too that France was reminding its citizens of its colonial achievements and its place amongst, indeed above, the other European colonial powers.[25] However, the aim of the Exposition was much more than a simple celebration of French colonialism in this the centenary year of French Algeria. As Herman Lebovics explains, one of the organizers' primary objectives was linked to a notion of 'improvement' whereby 'aesthetic appreciation [was to be transformed into] political ontology: the show became a token of the worth of the colonial effort and of a new grander vision of what it was to be French'.[26] Crucially, what the Exposition aimed to disseminate was a notion of an *enlightened* Frenchness linked to a sense of duty to educate the other, less fortunate cultures that formed part of *la plus grande France*. For Christopher Miller, it was precisely this notion of a French *mission civilisatrice* that provided the 'overarching structure' protecting the Exposition's 'authentic' display of difference.[27] The moral mission to civilize was in turn given its unquestionable political dimension by what Charles Forsdick refers to as the Exposition's 'processes of exoticization [...] employed to create a popular justification of ownership of elsewhere inherent in imperialist expansion: the aim was to demonstrate who was civilized and who required civilization'.[28] Needless to say, a crucial prop for this ambition was the use of 'live exhibits' who became human signifiers of all the Exposition organizers wanted to convey. Although it is never made clear whether Fara has come to the Exposition specifically to perform as a live exhibit, mention is made in the text of fellow Africans who do and who are clearly meant to provide irrefutable evidence of cultural 'authenticity'.[29]

In yet another example of its participation in the broader ideological objectives of colonization, travel was also used by the Exposition's organizers to communicate a particular aspect of 'Frenchness'. Not only were advancements in French technology to be appreciated by viewing achievements in the automobile and aeronautical industries, but the Exposition itself was clearly designed to be an experience of simulated travel, an 'exotic' prolonging of the humble journey begun on the specially extended metro line. Clearly, the 'Frenchness' conveyed was a type defined by the 'adventurous', curious traveller

who has the material means and technological know-how to get where
s/he wants to. In reality, however, this was a safe cultural encounter
of a type akin to Syed Manzurul Islam's 'sedentary traveller' noted
in the introduction. As French visitors interacted with the 'exotic'
spectacles on display, their feet never left French soil, another way of
emphasizing the particular interpretative framework through which
'difference' was to be viewed and understood. In such a set-up, the
politics of the gaze meant that displays of 'otherness' were relegated
to backwardness, and French visitors, and their culture, aligned with
progress.[30] Every object, every action gazed upon, became a 'racial' or
cultural sign, their meaning partially, if not fully, determined by the
lens of France's civilizing mission. Travel, as it was reconfigured by
the ethos of the Exposition, became an essentially hermeneutic exercise that depended on a cleverly manipulated and manipulating gaze
that was backed by the economic and discursive power of the colonial centre. And in *Mirages de Paris*, this becomes a travel practice
and way of seeing that clearly extends outwith the boundaries of the
110-hectacre site: after the Exposition, Fara attends a talk given by
a French cinematographer returning from the fictitious 'Zoulouville'
and is dismayed to hear a series of stereotypes of African barbarity
being presented as fact because they have been witnessed, and interpreted as such, by this highly selective Western traveller. 'Il fallait
beacoup d'audace pour parler de l'Afrique *quand on en avait vu si
peu*' [It took a lot of nerve to speak about Africa *when one had seen
so little*] (*MP*, p. 67, my emphasis) comments Fara, failing to realize
that what matters is not how the traveller travels, how little is seen or
not seen but *how* it is seen: in other words how it is interpreted and
what it confirms.

One of the more curious aspects of the Exposition's politics of
visualizing as explored by *Mirages de Paris* is Fara's tendency to view
and interpret the spectacle as the Exposition would have French visitors see and interpret him, what Mary Louise Pratt might term an
'autoethnographic' gaze.[31] Hence the curious impression we get as
the reader visits the Exposition in his company, but also at other
moments thoughout *Mirages de Paris*, that we are not really being
given an 'African' view of Europe, contrary to what one critic has
claimed.[32] Instead, Fara appears to have internalized a French way of
looking at the world, and particularly the African world from where
he originates. Even when he affords a Malian woman 'on display'
some degree of subjectivity by wondering 'à quoi pensait-elle?' [what

was she thinking about] (*MP*, p. 35), he answers for her, imagining a highly romanticized scenario of life on the banks of the Niger that fits entirely with the 'exotic' view of Africa demanded by the Exposition. In this respect, Fara, the cultural insider, becomes even more of a voyeuristic victim of propaganda than French visitors, concluding at the end of his Exposition-world-tour that if France 'interprétait [le monde] à sa façon' [interpreted [the world] in its own way] (*MP*, p. 40), then history – the French version of it – had accorded it that right:

> En Europe, une longue suite de générations, par un effort tenace, avait accumulé un patrimoine de travail et de savoir gigantesque; et combien le patrimoine de sa pauvre Afrique lui parut faible! Il comprit pourquoi le blanc, héritier et dépositaire de cette richesse, le regardait hautain. (*MP*, p. 41)

> [Thanks to its tenacity over many generations, Europe had bequeathed a culture of hard work and enormous learning; and how meagre his own poor Africa's inheritance looked in comparison! He understood why the European, as both inheritor and depository of this wealth, looked at him in disdain.]

One other intriguing incident in the short passage devoted to the Exposition deserves attention as it illustrates clearly the difficulties for the African traveller to France of escaping objectification and developing a way of seeing that might transform intercontinental travel into an experience of positive exchange rather than exile. It concerns the character of Ambrousse, a rug merchant and former well-travelled sailor in the merchant navy, whom Fara assists on an unofficial basis. Ambrousse's 'marketing' cry provides the first troubling suggestion that both the live colonized 'exhibits' and visitors to the French Exposition are fully cognizant of the artifice governing this authorized version of 'authentic' colonized cultures:

> —Approchez, Messieurs et Dames, criait-il, approchez! Achetez mes tapis! *de vrais*! […] Je suis du pays; j'ai été capturé il y a deux mois seulement!' […]
> Le flot des passants s'arrêtait, amusé par la dialectique *invraisembable* de l'homme de la Forêt. […].
> L'on achetait par convenance. Voir de près un nègre *authentique* de la Forêt valait bien cela. (*MP*, p.36. My emphasis.)

> ["Roll up ladies and gentleman", he cried, "roll up. Buy my rugs, *genuine* rugs […] I'm a native, I was captured only two months ago!"

The passing throng stopped, amused by the *unlikely* argument of
the man from the Forest.
People purchased out of politeness. It was worth it to see at close
hand an *authentic* black from the Forest.]

What is striking here is not so much Ambrousse's understandable
commercial insistence on the '*vrai*' [genuine] but his more complex
recognition of, and seemingly willing participation in the Exposition's meaning-making. What the reader appears at once to read
and witness in this 'mimicry' or dramatization of the captured 'black
man' is a complex illustration of what Homi K. Bhabha describes as
'the process of ambivalence' that underlies the construction of stereotypes in colonial discourse.[33] On the one hand, Ambrousse's 'performance', his ambiguous 'active consent' in Bhabha's terms, suggests
he is cleverly enacting the Exposition's credo of 'authentic' difference
for his own ends: financial gain in the immediate term.[34] Yet, whereas
Bhabha sees in the colonizer's mimicry of difference the potential
for subverting colonial authority, the visitors' reaction to Ambrousse
appears instead to suggest its limits. For they too appear to be aware
that they are witnessing a performance and adopt the role of spectators as readily as Ambrousse agrees to act what they have come to see.
Here, Dean MacCannell's theories of the tourist emerge as complementary critical tools for examining the particular audience reaction
to this scene's 'mimicry'.[35] Mobilizing Erving Goffman's dramatur-
gical-inspired theories of social interaction, MacCannell analyses
the importance of the 'authentic' and the 'inauthentic' worlds that
structure tourist experience. For MacCannell, tourists, like the audience to whom Ambrousse performs, can be seen as semiologists who
are frequently aware of the 'staged authenticity' of certain 'pseudo-
events' such as tours of cultural, institutions or staged 'primitive'
ceremonies.[36] Significantly, however, the tourist is forgiving of, and
even satisfied by, the 'strained truthfulness' of such performances.[37]
This ties in with the Exposition's French visitors who recognize the
various staged markers of 'primitive', 'uncivilized' life as they have
been told to imagine it and appear, therefore, reassured by 'the proba-
bilistic truth', to use Bhabha's terms, of the performance.[38]
    At this point, however, the usefulness of MacCannell's theories
in relation to Ambrousse's performance and its reception outruns
itself. For, ultimately, the sociologist of tourism is concerned with
rehabilitating the tourist by underlining this figure's genuine intellectual
interest in the lives and cultures of those performing. Paradoxically,

if the tourist is satisfied with the performance of authenticity it is because it is felt the contrived nature of the experience conceals some kind of 'authenticity'. In this way, MacCannell seems to imply, a sense of respectful *'mystification'* is sustained regarding the supposedly 'authentic' reality that exists behind the scene being watched.[39] However, in the case of the scene under discussion here, the *unlikely* nature of what is being witnessed does not become evidence of *mystification*. Instead, it reinforces *exoticization* and, therefore, does not alter the implications of the Exposition's broader politics of visualizing. Any idea that Ambrousse's performance can undermine stereotypical images defining how he is seen is negated by the equally active consent of those watching him and interpreting him according to the intentions of the Exposition organizers. What Ambrousse sees, how he sees it, and how he *genuinely* lives is of little concern to those for whom his identity is theatricalized in order to confirm what they have come to see. Once again, this practice will be seen to have implications for Fara's relationships with French people outwith the Exposition: it will be apparent in the daily scenes that, as Bhabha reminds us, 'emphasize *the visible – the seen*': 'le mépris dans le regard d'un passant [...] l'index innocemment levé vers lui d'un tout petit' [the contempt in the eyes of a passer-by [...] the finger of a small child innocently pointing at him] (*MP*, p. 107).[40] And it will be evident too in Fara's dealings with Jacqueline's father, the intransigent M. Bourciez, who will reveal himself incapable of seeing Fara in any way other than that constructed by the images, taxonomies and stories of the exhibitionary order.

Journey's end: seeing

Despite the seeming impossibility of deflecting the objectifying gaze Fara encounters on a daily basis, it would be inaccurate to suggest that *Mirages de Paris* fails to provide us with a subjective, outsider and traveller's view of Paris and of French culture. Focusing once more on the Exposition, it becomes clear how Fara's willingness to intercept, and at times direct, the visitor's gaze points to this character's agency, and tentatively suggests that his experiences as a traveller are not as easily labelled as are inert and voiceless exhibits. If the novel is a hall of mirrors, as Christopher Miller suggests, then as well as revealing the image of Fara and his African origins, it is also, perhaps despite itself, a complex portrait of France itself and the realities that shape its misleading view of Africa and Africans.

At various intervals throughout the novel Fara shows he is not an innocent abroad but is aware of the way Africa, Africans and African culture become distorted in the European lens. At best, he reacts with a quiet sense of injustice and determination to retain his self-respect; at worst, he falls victim to his depressive outlook or simply chooses to concur with the racist, eurocentric perception of Africa. However, at the Exposition, in his self-appointed role as guide to Jacqueline and her friends, he dares to indicate his shock at their way of seeing Africa and actively attempts to influence their perception of it. As Jacqueline and he develop a more intimate relationship, the young French woman is simultaneously given access to African culture from a perspective that seems entirely at odds with that displayed at the Exposition. In Fara's company, she is exposed to aspects of Africa's ethnic and religious diversity, its oral culture, its intellectual and social divisions and its prejudices. Most significantly, like the respected travellers of contemporary criticism, their contact with some of the cultural *milieux* of black Paris also yields unexpected insights into the places they themselves have come from: through Jacqueline's eyes, this experience reveals the cultural complexity elided by the fixed, stereotypical displays of the Exposition but also highlights the ways in which the cultural realms of France and its colonies overlap at the very heart of empire. For Fara, close and positive contact with the socially and culturally diverse members of Paris's black diaspora throws into relief divisions within African society that would have meant he and his new friends 'auraient vécu dans des sphères sociales différentes et se seraient hiérarchisés' [would have lived in different social spheres and would have identified themselves according to class] (*MP*, p. 116).

But to what extent may these 'observations' be said to derive from the consciously critical and objective perspective we tend to attribute to travellers and travel literature? And do these observations really provide any substantive travelling African perspective on French life and culture? Despite the interpretation of black Paris in the above paragraph, Dominic Thomas is right when he illustrates the way in which Socé's depiction of the Cabane Cubaine nightclub in Montmartre appears to repeat the artifice and representational order of the Exposition by displaying 'specimens' of 'blackness'. Thomas's suggestion that Fara's observations of French life and culture lack 'lucidity'

is also confirmed when they are compared to the conclusions drawn
by African protagonists who no longer accept the myth of French
cultural superiority by the time they travel to the metropolitan centre.
Despite these reservations, however, Thomas does agree that *Mirages
de Paris* provides an excellent example of the way in which the 'myth
of French cultural superiority [...] can be unpacked and demysti-
fied by an attentive observer'.[41] I would argue that one of the most
effective ways this is achieved is through the novel's subtle exploration of the way in which Fara comes to see – without necessarily
commenting lucidly upon – precisely how notions of artifice and
performance appear to permeate beyond the Exposition's perimeter
walls in order to influence, and even define, the 'reality' of life in the
French capital.

I have already examined the way in which the Exposition's representation of Africa and Africans both reflects and feeds into interpretations of that continent's culture and peoples to the extent that they
appear to be seen and interpreted as exhibits even when they are not
consciously 'on display'. Indeed, Fara himself is shown to dismiss
Africa and Africans according to the stereotypes of colonial discourse
that dismiss the continent as backward and characterize Africans as
lacking resolve, willpower and decisiveness. But just as significant
as the complex ricocheting of Africanist discourse in the novel is the
manner in which the reader, through Fara's eyes, is shown the Exposition reflected in what Timothy Mitchell describes as 'the external
reality' created by the exhibitionary order.[42]

Mitchell's analysis offers an extremely useful theoretical articulation of artifice as it relates to Fara's particular perception of Paris. In
his reading of nineteenth-century Arabic accounts of visits to world
fairs, Mitchell notes how the Europe beyond the exhibitions' gates
'seemed to be set up before one as though it were the model or the
picture of something. Everything was arranged before an observing
subject into a system of signification, declaring itself to be a mere
object, a mere "signifier" of something further.'[43] In sum, the notions
of artifice and model here function as concepts that allow us to
consider the 'external reality' as an extension of the Exposition and
a fundamental part of what Mitchell terms the 'world-as exhibition'.
Central to pursuing this vision of Paris in *Mirages de Paris* are the
explicit references to artifice and illusion that are woven into the
text's fabric from its very title. For example, after an evening in a club
with Jacqueline, Fara reflects upon what he has seen, or imagines he

has seen, in the background of the dance floor. He concludes that the *illusion* of reality created by the model of a seascape extends beyond the small space to reveal the fact that objects, behaviour, appearances, and Europe more widely, are not what they seem:

> La mer qu'il avait vue était trop verte pour être véritable [...]; les falaises étaient un simulacre de cartons. [...]
> Le garçon du vestiaire n'était pas aussi aimable qu'il en faisait montre. Les broches fixées aux cravates des hommes, les pierreries qui étincelaient aux bracelets des femmes étaient de l'imitation. Il eut de l'Europe l'impression de quelque chose d'artificiel. Il ne fallait pas gratter la façade des choses sinon, comme le visage des femmes, on en faisait tomber le fard. (*MP*, p. 47)

> [The sea he had seen was too green to be real [...]; the cliffs were fashioned out of cardboard. [...]
> The cloakroom attendant was not as friendly has he pretended to be. The men's tiepins and the sparkling precious stones on the women's bracelets were fake. His impression of Europe was of something artificial. Scratch the surface of things and, just like a woman's face, the make-up would fall away.]

In this way Christopher Miller's description of *Mirages de Paris* as a hall of mirrors can be expanded upon to describe how Paris emerges in the novel as a city of glass where the ideas conveyed in the Exposition, as well as the views and behaviours of the French visitors, are reflected constantly and intersect at different angles.

Other significant examples of the exhibitionary order mirrored in the novel's portrayal of 'external reality' are evident in behaviour that is clearly influenced by what Timothy Mitchell defines as 'the machinery of commerce'. According to Mitchell, aspects of nineteenth-century commercial machinery inspired exhibition organizers before being imitated in turn in the architecture and organization of newly established department stores, these 'commercial worlds-in-minature' and 'a further means of engineering the real'.[44] We have already seen how Ambrousse and Fara participate in the Exposition's reconstructed African craft market and sell their produce to French visitors playing at being tourists in this simulated foreign destination. (In this regard it is also possible to argue that their 'native' identity is in some way turned to profit by the commercial aims of an Exposition designed to attract the maximum number of paying spectators.) The purchasing of mementos and souvenirs is described again at a later date, but this time it refers to Senegalese acquaintances of Fara who are returning home after the Exposition, their trunks crammed with 'chaussures "André", chemises achetées à la devanture d'un magasin quelconque' ['André' shoes, their shirts purchased from the outside stall of some shop] (*MP*, p. 69). The most curious example of this type of reflected commercial behaviour, however, is not Fara's post-Exposition decision to sell African crafts in order to survive, but the style in which he and Jacqueline decorate their home. Whilst initially it may be tempting to suggest that the North African tables, the curtains from a well-known Parisian department store, the Malian textiles, Senegalese crafts and various African paintings combine to reflect, in classic realist mode, the successful cultural and racial *métissage* the couple hope to represent, the objects appear in quite a different light when seen as a reflection of the Exposition's commercial machinery. Certainly, it is true that Fara's African identity is an important factor determining the choice of object decorating the room. However, in another respect, the very presence of these objects/ souvenirs in the French capital project forward to the imminent rise of globalized travel and the tourist obsession with 'cosmopolitiza-tion' and the accumulation of 'exotic' objects, a practice which itself harks back to an earlier Western travel practice of collect and display – a principle enshrined, of course, in the Exposition. Finally, the very clear impression created in the description of Fara and Jacqueline's home of objects on display also evokes certain practices of the Exposition, repeated in turn by certain Parisian department stores where large window panes endowed goods on display with a 'distance that [was] the source [...] of their objectness'.[45]

Using Timothy Mitchell's analysis of the exhibitionary order once again it becomes clear that the inability to arbitrate between the 'real' and the simulated – in essence Fara's tragedy – derives from the notions of representation, commodification and artificiality underpin-ning the Exposition. In this artificial world order, 'the West', Mitchell argues, appears as 'a place organized as a system of commodities, values, meanings, and representations, forming signs that reflect one another in a labyrinth without exits'.[46] The labyrinth may well be a hackneyed metaphor but I believe it is an apposite, even arche-typal, image for the place in which Fara and other African travellers to the colonial centre find themselves: they are travellers who are incapable of finding home, condemned as a result to travelling in a state of exile. In Fara's case, the loss of touch with reality is further compounded by the fact that the place to which he wanted to travel,

Paris, only ever existed in the imagination. As such, it is telling that his eventual suicide is again prompted by an illusion: Jacqueline's hand may well beckon him out of this false reality, but his decision to seek out the place and person – his African village and the dead Jacqueline – reflected in the murky waters of the Seine suggests that there is no way out of the labyrinth.

Despite the tragic dénouement of *Mirages de Paris*, its exposé of artifice and simulation provides one final insight into Paris that has wider critical and theoretical implications for identifying what might be termed a view of 'the West' through (post)colonial African eyes. For what the portrayal of the pristine 'West' external to the exhibition reveals is that this 'place' is as artificial as the world recreated and interpreted within. The crucial significance of this notion of the 'West' as artificial construct, or as 'an ideological category *masquerading* as a geographic one', is outlined by Timothy Mitchell:[47]

> This external reality, it can be noted, bears a peculiar relationship to the Orientalist portrayal of the Orient. Like the Orient, it appears that it simply 'is'. It is a place of mere being. Where essences are untouched by history, by intervention, by difference. Such an essentialized world lacks, by definition, what the exhibition supplies – the dimension of meaning. It lacks the plan or program that supplies reality with its historical and cultural order. The techniques of the world exhibition build into an exterior world this supposed lack, this original meaninglessness and disorder, just as colonialism introduces it to the Orient.[48]

In this light, it is obvious why the identification of an African literature of travel to 'the West' is such a vital enterprise. I am not suggesting by this that African textualizations of travel be called upon to counter the 'orientalizing' processes of so much Western travel writing, either by engaging in a meaning-making process of their own, or by searching for a 'true' and 'authentic' West – which is arguably what Fara attempts to do. Instead, what Fara's tragic journey highlights is the potential critical value to be gained when attentive, observing and reflective travellers explore meanings of the 'West' and reveal aspects of the historical and cultural order determining its reality.

An examination of the significance of the Exposition in *Mirages de Paris*, and in particular its revelation of an 'the external order', is key to identifying an emerging critical and complex way of perceiving and understanding Paris – and by extension, 'the West' – in a novel that can otherwise appear to be largely concerned with an inward perspective. What is clear is that this perception is based on a process of comparison between a 'here' and 'there', even if the terms of comparison are hazy, and occasionally illusory. However, this observation does not render straightforward Fara's categorization as a traveller. Part of the problem lies in Fara's inability to capitalize on the new perspective and insights offered to him by travel. It is as if 'seeing' reality from a critical and objective vantage point is too painful, and he cannot move beyond the realization that expectations of his destination have been largely disappointed. Consequently, Fara becomes trapped in a downward spiral: he clings to the hope of finally reaching this romanticized and hallucinatory Paris made familiar in his reading only for this hope to be shattered time and again by the nature of his encounters with 'reality'. Certainly, this is an important reminder of travel's crucial function in correcting preconceived ideas. However, it also explains why *Mirages de Paris* can appear to be more a study in the disappointment of travel rather than a celebration of its possibilities for discovery. What is troubling in Fara's case, however, is that rather than triggering a genuine reflection on why Paris disappoints, his realization that the French capital is not the 'El Dorado' he had imagined reinstates his own sense of inferiority and traps him in a labyrinth of pain and exile from which the only escape appears to be the illusion of happiness offered by death.

In the final analysis, however, the overridingly negative tone of *Mirages de Paris* does begin to tell us something fundamental about African intercontinental travel practices and their textualization. In many respects, Fara represents an anti-traveller, a figure who will re-emerge time and again in African narratives of travel and who reminds us that exile is the other side of travel's much-lauded benefits. To begin to read a text such as Socé's as a travel account is to recognize, therefore, that a black African traveller is constituted by objectification to a significant degree. For, as Fara's experiences in France clearly demonstrate, the African who journeys to the heart of the empire is in danger first of being divested of any effort at self-representation, and from there implied to be incapable of representing others and other places. Above all else, the portrayal of the 1931 Exposition in *Mirages de Paris* reveals that it is this fundamental crisis of representation that lies at the heart of colonial but also, we shall see, postcolonial African narratives of travel to the West.

CHAPTER TWO

Kocoumbo, l'étudiant noir:
Foreign Studies

This chapter underscores the link between education and travel in a colonial context. In the West, travel has long been associated with educational benefit and, more recently, has become virtually enshrined as a fundamental element of the student experience. Indeed, quite apart from the various organizations and institutions that promote and support student mobility, international travel itself, for whatever purpose, has become so inextricably associated with the acquisition of cultural capital that to remain at home has come to be seen by many as an intellectually and professionally limiting choice. Needless to say, the link made between travel and intellectual benefit is a feature found in many cultures and is not simply confined to the West. Once again, however, the particular material and historical circumstances of Western students – and indeed those from other materially advantaged points of origin – mean that although the symbolic value of their travels may have a universal significance, the manner in which they travel differs profoundly from their materially less advantaged counterparts.

Since the emergence of a specifically francophone African literary tradition, the African student in France has remained one of the most well-known and emblematic figures of the intercontinental African travelling experience. As was noted earlier, this is due in part to the significant role played by Paris-based African students such as Ousmane Socé, Léopold S. Senghor and Bernard Dadié in the emergence of early twentieth-century anti-colonialist discourse, and in the affirmation and development of Africa's own literary and cultural tradition. However, the symbolic significance of the student is perhaps also explained by the important place occupied more generally by schools and schooling in francophone colonial literature. Indeed, quite apart from its significance as a figurative means of reflecting upon the more brutal excesses of the colonizing project itself, the colonial school is frequently an important stage for the initial encounter of the colonized student with the foreignness of the colonizing culture. Certainly, for many, this encounter is a traumatic and alienating experience from which they will never recover. For others, however, this encounter plays the same seductive role as certain literary texts and produces a desire to travel out of Africa and 'back' to the centre of empire. Once again, because such travel is dependent on financial means, prolonged participation in education – and in particular through progression to further and higher education – becomes one of the surest means of making this journey a reality.

Before entering into a specific examination of Aké Loba's novel, *Kocoumbo, l'étudiant noir*, it is interesting briefly to examine the issues raised by a text many would argue to be *the* classic account of the educational trajectory of a colonized African student, Cheikh Hamidou Kane's *L'Aventure ambiguë*.[1] Described by Pius Adesanmi as the 'most famous African engagement of the psychic and psychological split' of the colonized subject, Kane's text also 'overlaps with the real life odysseys of most of the francophone African novelists of the first half of the twentieth century' by structuring the narrative around the geographical – and educational – journey from Africa (Senegal) to Paris and back of the novel's protagonist, Samba Diallo.[2] The condensed account of the often conflicting value systems of traditional/Islamic versus colonial education allows a striking crystallization of the specifically ideological journey/confusion that underwrites most African accounts of travel to the West, but which tends to form a more central preoccupation of accounts of schooling and education. For all the text's spareness, *L'Aventure ambiguë* also successfully eschews simplistic cultural assumptions that would cast Africa as a site of traditional and spiritual values and the West as its modern, materialist and rational opposite. No doubt, this cultural and ideological complexity explains the depth of Samba Diallo's confusion and alienation when he is faced with the reality of a hybridity provoked by the transition to the new realities of Western education and society. According to Adesanmi:

> For the African subject in Black Paris – as opposed to Americans and Caribbeans in the same context – the inevitability of *métissage* as a resolution of the latent identity crisis comes at a greater risk: the African American and the Caribbean have an incipient, always present Western-ness as part of their being that the African lacks. Consequently, contact with Paris is fraught with the danger of the psychic split lacking any originary Western-ness to sustain it and this eventuates in an alienation that operates at a deeper level.[3]

It would be erroneous to claim that Aké Loba's *Kocoumbo, l'étudiant noir* possesses the same literary sophistication as Kane's masterpiece. The overly detailed account of Kocoumbo's trajectory does not possess the suggestive powers of Kane's writing, the main protagonist's naivety lacks credibility at times and the text's ending, however unusual, is somewhat abrupt and dissatisfying. However, *Kocoumbo* is not without its importance, particularly within the context of a critical discussion of African literature of travel. Whilst the novel does underscore the almost inevitable nature of the 'psychological split' mentioned above, Kocoumbo's educational achievements ultimately cancel out the series of failures that mark much of his stay in France, and introduce a strong note of optimism that offers an important perspective on the educational benefits of travel, as well as distancing the novel from the essential tragedy of *L'Aventure ambiguë*. Like Kane, however, Loba is keen to avoid falling into simplistic descriptions of African and Western cultures and value systems. Again, the figure of the student is used not just to explore the cultural encounter that forms the meat and bones of all travel writing, but to focus explicitly on the notion of travelling theories and one individual's journey into different ideological systems: capitalism, traditionalism, colonialism, Marxist socialism, trade-unionism, rationalism, etc. Loba's text also offers an unusual contribution to the debate on African accounts of travel because as well as the identity quest that we recognize as central to *L'Aventure ambiguë*, *Kocoumbo, l'étudiant noir* also devotes a certain amount of space to the student's physical journey to France.

Getting there: technologies of travel

In certain respects, the novel's opening portrait of Kocoumbo's native village of Kouamo seems interchangeable with the opening sections of *Mirages de Paris* and, as we shall see, *L'Africain du Grœnland*. Kouama is seen as representative of countless other African villages that appear rooted in tradition and ignorant of their place within Western models of history and geography. However, as with the other texts mentioned, this portrait of a timeless, unchanging Africa is revealed to be misleading. Colonization and contact with the West has introduced new perspectives and challenges largely in the form of educational establishments and the ideologies they represent and impart. From the outset, however, it is clear that colonial education is seen as the first stage of a journey that distances the village's youth from tradition and, in the case of young men, inevitably leads either to the corrupting influences of African urban spaces or to France. Thus, whilst we learn in the opening chapter that the teenage Kocoumbo has progressed as far as the *certificat d'études* – and consequently has already begun the process of alienation from his own cultural origins – we are also informed that Kocoumbo's father, 'le vieil Oudjo', is initially reluctant to allow his son progress any further along this route. Slowly, however, three factors force the latter to review his thinking and to consider sending his son to France to pursue his studies.

First, through listening to his son translate an unnamed French text (which we later learn is most likely a novel by Victor Hugo), Oudjo begins to be persuaded that, unlike the tribeless urban environment within Africa, France is in fact very similar to his own village environment where designated patriarchs are respected for their role in transmitting cultural knowledge from generation to generation. Secondly, this dawning realization that France has something to offer his son is further strengthened by the decision of another less senior but independent-minded villager to send his son, Nadan, for a metropolitan education.[4] Most interesting from the perspective of travel, however, is the influence of air transport on Oudjo's decision. Whilst he discusses with a villager the advantages and perils of submitting his son to the teachings of French schools, Kokoumbo's father notices an aeroplane flying overhead. Earlier in the chapter, the changing mentalities of the village's youth have been explained by their contact with another world represented by the colonial schools but also by the coming and going of trains, planes and ferries. These technologies are symbols, of course, of the encroachment of Western culture upon Africa in the form of scientific progress and speed of mobility. What is interesting about the appearance of the aeroplane at this crucial juncture, however, is that it points to a perception of travel that is clearly rooted in the post-war period leading to decolonization.[5]

At this time, aeroplanes are not the primary mode of international travel for Africans. Indeed, with regard to the question of speed and modes of transport, Charles Forsdick argues that it is 'those with the greatest prestige, wealth and power [who] also have access to the highest velocities'.[6] In the scene where Kocoumbo's future is being discussed, however, the aeroplane is clearly seen as culturally coded, and is also seen as a means to an end, a way of getting young Africans, and Africa, on the road to what the speakers see as 'progress'. The passage of the aeroplane overhead forces Oudjo to recognize that if his son is ever to attain the heights represented by this particular mode of transport, and if air transport is ever to become, in Marian Aguiar's terms, 'a technology of agency', then he will have to agree to send Kocoumbo to France to further his education.[7] Here, Oudjo hopes his son will learn to make, and not just travel in, an aeroplane, thereby using technological knowledge as a catalyst for change in Africa rather than as proof of the continued superiority of the West. In the terms of the other villager, it is this type of 'sacrifice' that will produce not just the rains needed in the short term for crops, but that will also pay dividends when this French-educated youth eventually returns home with new skills. Once again, these new skills and knowledge are evoked through reference to modern Western technology and, in particular, mechanized modes of transport:

> Demain ces jeunes-là reviendront en maîtres pour leur apprendre ce qu'ils n'ont eux-mêmes jamais su. Ces hommes de demain leur diront comment une pesante locomotive réussit à glisser sur deux minces rails, comment un plus lourd que l'air arrive à planer dans l'espace. (*Kocoumbo*, p. 36)

> [Tomorrow these young people would return as masters to teach them what they had never known. These men of the future would explain to them how a heavy engine manages to move along two narrow tracks and how an even heavier one can float in the air.]

The significance of these modern mechanized modes of transport is underlined in two other important episodes in the book. The first example concerns the lengthy Chapter 2 which describes the journey by steamship to France in far greater detail than Ousmane Socé does in *Mirages de Paris*. In keeping with the novel's generally vague African geography, we do not learn precisely from what port Kocoumbo sails. What is more important is the symbolic significance of this mode of transport which, despite the student's initial fears, dominates the sea, literally putting the humble African fishing boats caught in its wash into a spin. Just as these small boats appear to gaze in profound respect at this vessel, the young African students on board learn to their amazement that within the ship there exist luxurious surroundings that symbolize a way of travelling they come to identify as entirely Western:

D'abord [...] il y a des bars exactement comme en ville, des salons pour fumer ou se reposer. Quant aux chambres à coucher, elles ont chacune leur lavabo, leur glace. Elles s'appellent des cabines.

—C'est exagéré! cria quelqu'un.

—Pas du tout! Tu dis ça parce que tu n'en profites pas. Mon vieux, les Européens savent voyager. (*Kocoumbo*, pp. 61–62)

[First of all [...] there are bars just like those in the city, and rooms for smoking or relaxing. As for the bedrooms, they all have their own wash basin and mirror. They're called cabins.

"You're exaggerating!" somebody cried out.

"Not at all. You only say that because you can't enjoy it yourself. Dear fellow, Europeans know how to travel!"]

This particular travelling environment – which we learn is in fact third class – underlines the spatial arrangement of the ship itself, with its clearly demarcated zones designating the travel practices of different types or classes of traveller. Certainly, most Africans appear excluded from the comfortable conditions described above. However, the ship clearly reinforces class difference as much as, if not more than, ethnic difference. Kocoumbo, like the majority of black African travellers, spends the journey in the hold.[8] Here conditions are far from luxurious: there is no privacy, meals are basic and the only concession to comfort is a hammock. However, whilst this appears to be the 'black' section of the ship, the travelling conditions of other African passengers point to social distinctions within the African travelling group itself. For example, François Gogodi (who later comes to be known as Douk) is a stowaway whose status puts the relative privilege of those in the hold into perspective. This character has stolen from his employer in order to get to France, and has been forced to travel hidden amongst the freight containers and the baggage of his more 'advantaged' fellow Africans. Unlike Kocoumbo and the other students, Douk is rootless and has lived a life of poverty and deprivation in Africa. Consequently, his only hope of realizing his ambition to travel to France has been to do it illicitly, grasping at any opportunity that presents itself. (At the same time he points to a way of travelling that will survive into the postcolonial era, and a time of mass migration for impoverished Africans.) At the other end of the spectrum, Nadan and the pretentious Durandeau, a major character in the novel, travel in the superior conditions of third class. In particular, Durandeau's whole-hearted embracing of this travel environment, and his rejection of his 'primitive' African name, Koukoto, points to a desire to disassociate himself completely from the passengers in the hold and the 'primitive' culture they represent.

For Durandeau, buying into the more refined travel culture represented by the ship's class structure is essential proof of what he believes to be his successful assimilation of a European identity. Interestingly, once in France, and on firm ground, this character again clings to the symbolic significance of another form of privileged mechanized transport – the automobile – in order to distance himself from his cultural origins. Amongst Durandeau's many dubious and deceitful methods for social advancement is his treatment of women. Slowly we learn that he selects, and subsequently seduces, women who will be of most use to him in terms of prestige and material comfort. One of his unfortunate victims is Lucienne, the owner of a car to which she has given her lover generous access.

The motor car, argues Brenda Chalfin, can be considered the most enduring commodity of modernity, with its manufacture 'representing modernist ideals of technical efficiency [...], the rise of scientific-management, automation, and the sort of "deskilling" that makes workers as interchangeable as machine-made parts'.[9] In a specifically African context, the motor car, since its introduction on the continent at the beginning of the twentieth century,[10] has also served to differentiate between self and other in terms of class, personal taste, political leanings and geo-political locations. In more recent times, Chalfin notes how the motor car is 'foremost among the many commodities that force the confrontation of the industrial/non-industrial divide' but she also explains that it has a long history on the continent as 'a marker of status and cosmopolitan consciousness'.[11] As with the third-class conditions on the steamship, this is precisely how Durandeau uses the motor car. Indeed his apparent acquisition of this motorized vehicle is intended not just to underline the extent to which he has travelled away from Africa and his fellow Africans, but also from the black *and white* 'horde misérable' [miserable hordes] (*Kocoumbo*, p. 184) in Paris, haughtily dismissed because their journeys are made on foot or in the crowded underground.[12] Indeed, Durandeau's return journey to Africa in Lucienne's car is no way a journey 'back' but a vainglorious attempt to remind his family and village of just how far from them he has managed to travel:

> Il l'avait emmenée [la voiture] avec lui en Afrique, et les enfants avaient fait cercle autour d'elle, tandis que les cris inquiets des parents partaient des seuils pour rappeler la marmaille au respect;

le silence et l'attention du village entier exprimaient les égards du lieu qui l'avait vu naître. Son père avait pris aussitôt une importance primordiale. Un Blanc même avait reconnu qu'il ne fallait pas être n'importe qui pour posséder une machine de cette marque. (*Kocoumbo*, p. 185)

[He had taken [the car] to Africa. The children had formed a circle around it but, from the doorways, the worried cries of their parents had reminded the horde to be respectful. The silence and attention of his homeplace expressed the respect afforded to him by all its inhabitants. His father had immediately become a figure of major importance. One white man had even recognised that you couldn't be just anybody to own a car of that type.]

Whilst it may be tempting to view Durandeau's African journey by car as proof of the true extent of the post-war European democratization of travel and motoring, further analysis shows this not to be the case. This journey is undertaken neither in a spirit of adventure nor as a challenge to the Western travelling gaze in Africa. In fact, rather than use the car to point to what Africans can achieve, and how far they can travel, Durandeau instead mobilizes it as an individual status symbol to reinforce the age-old stereotypes separating the cultural realities of Africa and the West. Despite his ethnic identity, Durandeau's automobile journey to Africa shares vital characteristics of the 1950s 2CV journeys to Africa analysed by Charles Forsdick. For, as Forsdick reminds us, 'the car operates as a vehicle of Frenchness. It is a marker of mechanical modernity presented in a process of inverse exoticism as still foreign to the cultures crossed, but at the same time a fetishized object to which the indigenous populations aspire.'[13]

Durandeau's arrogant and uncritical adoption of Western ways of travelling and seeing Africa is also underlined by his ignorance of what Forsdick refers to as the 'preceding journeys' upon which Western motoring depended. By this, Forsdick is referring to:

the journeys of thousands of immigrants (many from North and West Africa) drawn to what was then perceived as mainland France by the car manufacturers' need for cheap and abundant labour at a time of demographic deficit and rapid economic growth. Affordable motoring depended above all on both an affordable workforce and an accelerated shift to the working practices associated with Fordism.[14]

Of course, later in the novel, Loba draws attention to this contrapuntal view of French automobile travel by choosing to have Kocoumbo find menial employment as a cleaner in a factory that produces metal sheeting for cars. This development is also an ironic reminder of the misplaced hopes of his father, who had hoped that Kocoumbo would learn to build aeroplanes in France rather than become an illustration of the heights from which the travelling scholar can fall. The reality illustrated by Kocoumbo's lowly position is not just that Africans face differential access to the fastest and most technologically advanced forms of transport, but that highly specialized knowledge about their production is also largely controlled by Western industry.

Just as interesting as the significance of Kocoumbo's professional trajectory is the idea that Durandeau, for all his arrogance and emulation of Western ways of thinking and travelling, has not quite reached the destination he has set himself. First, concerning his elevated status within the ranks of the ship's passengers it is notable that whilst Durandeau clearly travels in more style than the majority of other African passengers, his status is still far from being that of a first-class traveller. In fact, so inaccessible is first-class travel that it is never mentioned by him, presumably for fear of betraying to the others that he has not risen quite so far as he would have them believe, but also because the existence of first-class travel will serve as a reminder of the constant obstacle of ethnic identity. For clearly Durandeau, as an African, however privileged, can travel only so far in Western society before being faced with the reality that he will never be, to paraphrase Homi Bhabha's well-known formulation, 'quite white', and whatever social standing he attains will primarily serve to differentiate him from other Africans.[15] Durandeau's ability to deceive others is only matched by his own capacity for self-delusion, and his naive belief that it is possible for him not just to live the privileged life of any Westerner, but that of a specific Western social class symbolized by car ownership.[16] Indeed, the true nature of the descent precipitated by the loss of the car can only be fully understood when one realizes that his decline is seen not just in terms of his ethnic identity but also in terms of his perceived social status. For Durandeau, his efforts to cultivate more delicate tastes than those of his 'primitive' compatriots – and indeed of the French lower classes – ought to have spared him from the ignominy of having to use public transport, and worse, from having to rely on a corporeal, primitive form of mobility, walking:

> Lui qui croyait, à son depart d'Afrique [...] que chaque Blanc en
> France avait sa voiture – à cause de l'énorme standard de vie du

plus modeste colon comparé à celui de l'indigène – lui qui pensait
alors devoir, de ce fait, en posséder nécessairement une, lui qui, une
fois débarqué, avait appris que ce moyen de locomotion n'était que
le privilège d'une certaine classe vers laquelle toute son enérgie et
toute sa volonté tendirent aussitôt, lui qui, une fois la Chose en sa
possession, s'était vu enfin dans la classe des Heureux, lorgné par le
piéton blanc comme par le piéton noir […], il retombait aujourd'hui
parmi la horde misérable de ceux qui vont à pied et s'entassent dans
le métro. (*Kocoumbo*, p. 184)

[He who he believed, when he left Africa […], that every white man
in France had a car – because of the significantly higher standard
of life of even the most modest colonizer compared to Africans – ,
he who consequently felt he had to own one, he who learned upon
his arrival that this form of mobility was only the privilege of a
certain class to which he immediately began to devote all his will
and energy, he who, as soon as he had the Thing in his possession,
was finally seen to be part of the Contented class, envied by both
White and Black pedestrians […], today found himself once again
amongst the miserable hordes who travel on foot and pile into the
underground.]

Car ownership, and the elite social and travelling status it bestows,
may be attainable to the African, but Durandeau's case seems to
suggest that this involves deceitful methods which will ultimately
fail and return him unceremoniously to the travel practices of the
masses.

Educational travel

Edward Said's truism regarding the transmission of theories and
ideas bears repeating: 'Like people and schools of criticism, ideas
and theories travel – from person to person, from situation to situation, from one period to another.'[17] Loba's novel, with its emphasis
on intellectual exchange within a colonial context, is clearly rooted
within Said's model of the circulation of ideas. However, as the novel
illustrates, and as Said underlines, whatever the general features that
can be identified in the transmission of ideas, 'such movement is
never unimpeded. It necessarily involves processes of representation
and institutionalization different from those at the point of origin.'[18]
Whilst Said's primary concern in this essay is to examine trends in
the travels and transmission of twentieth-century critical theory, it is,

I believe, helpful to use his paradigm to examine the ways in which ideas about education and different political ideologies are given and received in Loba's text. To do so, however, means to attend, where appropriate, to the ways in which the novel's context shapes the transmission, dissemination and (re)interpretation of these ideas.

Foremost of the theories represented in *Kocoumbo* is the question of education. In the context of empire, education has, of course, always played a key role, and schooling constitutes one of the most enduring topoi of African colonial literature. In the French colonial context, education, the *conquête morale* [moral conquest], was an essential complement to military conquest, and inevitably came to be pressed into the service of the overall 'mission civilisatrice' in a most significant and effective manner. Of course, a fundamental aspect of this civilizing mission was the belief that it was France's duty to bring the Republican values of liberty, equality and fraternity to the 'less civilized' parts of the world, and education, in particular, was seen as a fundamental means of reducing inequalities. It is important to note, however, that despite the belief of French policy makers in education's democratic credentials, the colonial education system was characterized by a distinctive elitism.[19] In other words, the colonial context calls attention to a certain disjuncture between the places of theory's formulation and the places of its practice. This is evident in the simple fact that Republican theories of education, which in France appeared imperative and liberating, lose aspects of their agency and radical nature when transposed to the African colonies. In Said's description of the effects of travel on Lukács's 'revolutionary' theory of reification, the loss of its original 'power and rebelliousness' is largely to be explained by its travelling from the historical circumstances that provoked it to a 'situation [that] has quieted down and changed'.[20] In the case of the transportation of Republican educational theories to the colonies, one aspect of this new context is fundamental for understanding how education came to be viewed. This concerns the central ambiguity or contradiction of the 'civilizing mission' as historians of culture and education in particular have highlighted it. As these studies have amply shown, French colonial educational policy was at best a philanthropic guise with some coincidental positive outcomes, at worst a means to discredit, and arguably wipe out, indigenous cultural institutions.[21] Quite apart from the inherent physical violence of colonization and occupation, the implication (or at times explicitly expressed thesis) that European culture was the only culture worth imparting to colonized students was clearly premised on an entirely destructive intent: namely, the negation of indigenous values and institutions.

For Jean Suret-Canale, the contradiction of colonial education explains the thinking that ultimately shaped the nature and content of the curricula to which African students were exposed:

> For the colonial system, the education of the masses presented a dual danger. In raising the qualifications of its sources of manpower, it also made them costly to employ. Further, it led the masses of people to become aware of the exploitation and oppression to which they were subjected. On the other hand, the economic apparatus of exploitation, and administrative and political oppression, could not function without a minimum of indigenous lower grade personnel to act as executive agents between the European officials and the masses.[22]

This potential danger of exposing Africans to critical thinking and encouraging awareness of their own condition explains the subsequent promotion, through education and its particular manner of disseminating French culture, of the loyalty and deference of colonial subjects who would be encouraged not to lead but to follow. As Tony Chafer reiterates, the aim of French colonial educational policy directors was not to transport educational theories intact from the metropolitan centre in order to create free, equal citizens, but to focus instead on 'adapting education to what was perceived as the lower level of intellectual development of the African'.[23] This meant that education in the colonies largely took on a strictly utilitarian purpose, serving the needs of the imperial project, and maintaining, rather than effacing, inequality. What is clear, then, is that whilst ideas about education did 'travel' between the metropolis and its colonies, this movement, and the ways in which new ideas were implanted and subsequently received, were strictly controlled by the colonizers. In this way the colonized merely became passive recipients rather than being actively involved in the process of adapting such ideas to an African context.

In Loba's novel, Kocoumbo's own educational trajectory provides a clear indication of the ways in which ideas and theories on education are denied free, unimpeded 'travel' between the colonial centre and its 'peripheral' territories. As critics explain, the African's 'certificat d'études' has no equivalent in the metropolitan educational system. Its essential worthlessness is illustrated by the fact that, once in France, the 21-year-old Kocoumbo finds himself placed within a classroom of 12- to 14-year-olds where he struggles initially to meet the standard required.[24] Here, his 'expertise' about his own cultural origins amounts to nothing because he must adapt to French standards, and also, as he explains, because the French students' ideas about Africa were 'absurd': 'loin de s'informer, ils étalaient, sur un ton péremptoire, une documentation des pays dits primitifs qui n'admettait pas la contradiction' [far from informing themselves on the subject, they presented, in a commanding tone, irrefutable documentation on the so-called primitive countries] (*Kocoumbo*, p. 101).

Kocoumbo's all too brief stay within the formal confines of the Anonon-les Bains lycée [upper secondary school] is the story of his struggle with his own perceived intellectual failings, a perception reinforced by his African origins and schooling, the curriculum of the French school itself, the lycée environment and the comments of certain teachers and pupils. From the moment he arrives in the office of the school director, the effects of his colonial education are evident. He is unable (or unwilling) to assess his own ability, lacks confidence in the classroom, and is continuously drawn to highlight his own perceived intellectual and cultural inferiority. Despite the trauma of this initial period of adjustment, Kocoumbo, does, however, slowly begin to show real strength of character. In addition, the outsider status of this 'foreign student' inevitably provokes critical awareness of his own place within a foreign environment. With the help and encouragement of a sympathetic, rational-thinking classmate, Jacques Bourre, Koukoumbo begins to believe he can succeed. (Bourre, a student of modest rural origins also serves to highlight the differential nature of the opportunities provided by French education. As an intellectually gifted white male his promotion to the higher echelons of French society needs to be compared to the pinnacle of achievement available to successful African '*évolués*'.) Jacques's ability to relativize Koucoumbo's situation is, in this respect, crucial. It is he who formulates what Kocoumbo already suspects: failure to integrate is a cultural problem, not an intellectual one. By reminding Koucoumbo that, as an African, he cannot compare himself to his French classmates – he has spent less time in formal education and has not only to master the French language, but also a French way of reasoning – Jacques inadvertently points to the failure of the colonial education system to understand how theories and ideas need to travel. To succeed, Kocoumbo needs to reason *à la française*. His colonial education, however, has taught him that culturally he is incapable of this, or indeed that he cannot combine the less rational aspects of his own cultural with the demands of a 'French' analytical approach. Unfortunately, as Abdou – a communist and successful medical student – will later remark, awareness of this obstacle is no solution to the situation faced by the African student.

Ultimately, the brief period spent within the lycée is less important for what it tells us about Koucombo's *education* than for what it reveals about his *learning*. I use this distinction to highlight what I see on the one hand as the transmission of ideas (education) by teachers and students who believe Kocoumbo must adapt – if he is capable – to a specific way of thinking and problem solving they see as essentially 'French'. On the other hand, 'learning' can be used to describe Kocoumbo's development of a more independent, critical approach to information and the question of cultural difference. As we shall see, this learning can best be understood as a result of the coincidences and human encounters of travelling rather than as a by-product of the African student's encounter with formal education and curricula. It is also important to stress that this learning, if indeed it takes place at all, is not a smooth trajectory from 'ignorance' to 'knowledge' or certainty. As with Cheikh Hamidou Kane's emblematic protagonist Samba Diop Diallo, Koucombo's 'travelling' status in France means he remains within the unsteady and liminal location of the outside observer. This certainly provides the colonized student with useful insights but also leads to the unhappy realization that Western education lies at the heart of the 'psychic split' mentioned earlier in this chapter. So, for instance, whilst Kocoumbo learns, unprompted, to identify a similar genius at work in the plays of Pierre Corneille and the epics of African oral literature, he is traumatized by what he sees as the irreconcilability of his African superstitions and traditions and the rationality of Western ways of thinking:

> Le jeune homme se tournait et se retournait. Il se sentait rejeté de tous, délaissé. [...]
>
> Les croyances africaines, quelle misère! Tout venait des dieux; l'homme ne cherchait, n'avait même pas le droit de chercher à comprendre.
>
> Le sommeil venant, la crédulité ancestrale de Kocoumbo reprenait le dessus: non ses ancêtres étaient toujours ici-bas; il en était sûr.
> (*Kocoumbo*, p. 141)

[The young man tossed and turned. He felt rejected by everything, abandoned. [...]

What a wretched thing were African beliefs! Everything depended on the gods; people didn't try, didn't even have the right to try to understand.

As sleep approached, Kocoumbo's ancestral belief took over once again: no, his ancestors were still on this earth: of this he was certain.]

Despite the emphasis in *Kocoumbo, l'étudiant noir* on one individual's sufferings and achievements, it is important not to overlook the different perspectives engendered by the physical journey that lies at the heart of this text. As part of the substantial body of work representing black Paris, Loba's novel raises important questions about how travelling Africans come to think not just about themselves, but also about their (former) colonial masters. In this respect, Kocoumbo's observations as a traveller play an important role in reminding us of the agency of colonized subjects, and in reversing what Pius Adesanmi terms the 'historical process of the master's gaze, always trained on non-Western peoples'.[25] Consequently, if Loba successfully highlights the very real psychological consequences of Africans' encounters with French theories of education, the 'agential gaze' of Kocoumbo the traveller also subtly points to some of the effects of this one-way theoretical travel for French students.[26] In other words, although the novel's primary focus is on the cultural and intellectual adaptation required of the African student, it also suggests ways in which this education system may be blind to the ways in which its inability to 'travel' also fails French students. We have already seen how student attitudes to Africa reveal an arrogance and ignorance that is also evidence of an absence of critical self-awareness. In addition, Kocoumba's observations on his fellow students suggest that although the latter can satisfy the demands of their teachers, they have acquired no real intellectual curiosity and 'ne [s'intéressent] pas du tout à la lecture en dehors de celle qu'on leur imposait pour les cours' [and are not in the least interested in reading any unprescribed material] (*Kocoumbo*, p. 101). Most damning of all, however, is the failure of some of the educators, most notably the monitor whose racism leads to Kocoumbo's decision to abandon his studies, to understand and accept cultural difference.

Travelling to learn, learning to travel

Kocoumbo's real 'learning' in the novel seems inextricably tied to travel. Indeed, the young student has barely left Africa and the once-solid ground of home when he realizes not only that he is to enter a world of strangers but that he is in fact encountering himself for the first time and has, effectively, become a stranger to himself. Readers of travel literature will identify this as a fundamental lesson of travel whereby distance from the familiar provokes, as David Scott summarizes, 'a reabsorption of the other back into the self'.[27] In Kocoumbo's case, the traveller's sense of self-awareness is accompanied by a foresight of the defamiliarization of home that will await him on his return to Africa – 'il serait un jour un étranger sur sa propre terre' [one day he would be a stranger in his own land] (*Kocoumbo*, p. 52) – suggesting a nascent, but ultimately sophisticated, understanding of the risks as well as the benefits of travel.

As we have seen, formal education, and the need to conform to an established way of thinking, temporarily interrupt, or at least interfere with, the independent process of reflection and deduction prompted by the new experiences and encounters of travel. In certain respects, the period spent in the lycée, described as resembling a fortress or jail, can be seen as an interlude in the real 'education' of this African student. Indeed, it is telling that, despite the novel's title, relatively little space is devoted to descriptions of formal education. Instead, as soon as Kocoumbo decides (or is forced) to leave Anonon-les-Bains, the real process of learning, often slow and painful, recommences. Thrust into a reality without the safety net of school and rote learning, Kocoumbo must learn to rely on his own judgment (which itself has to be developed) to motivate himself and to survive away from the sphere of the privileged cosmopolitan intellectual that he had thought would be his destination.

If, at this point, the novel appears to be taking a *Bildungsroman* turn, it nonetheless retains some of the fundamental features of travel literature, not least the notion of a quest – in this instance for self-knowledge. From the time he leaves the lycée, Kocoumbo's knowledge of Paris, and indeed of himself, is acquired as he encounters others in an unfamiliar environment and in new situations. In order to accentuate the fact that Kocoumbo is a student of travel – and not just a travelling student – and that his journey to France is as much an intellectual as a cultural journey, Loba presents the reader with the assumptions, values, and, in some cases, political preoccupations of various individuals whom the young African meets in different contexts. These African and French characters can be said broadly to represent certain ideologies or moral positions. It is important to stress, however, that although some of these characters would willingly lay claim to such labels, others would strongly refute them. In addition, although Loba captures a certain complexity in some of these characters, others are only very sketchily drawn. In Paris, Kocoumbo's loose-knit group of friends and acquaintances includes the self-centred assimilationist Durandeau; the unscrupulous survivor and cynic Douk (the clandestine passenger from the boat); Nadan, the failed student; Abdou, successful medical student and communist; Mou, the disillusioned and pessimistic seminarian; Tougon, the sanctimonious and authoritarian leader in the 'Cité des étudiants' [halls of residence] whose ideology adapts according to what he feels is personally advantageous, a characteristic, it is implied, of the politician he aspires to become. In addition to these African characters, the influence of certain French individuals is also important: these include Monsieur Gabe, a French friend in Africa; the Brigaud family, relatives of Monsieur Gabe who welcome Kocoumbo to Paris and whose generosity causes them to fall victim to Durandeau's machinations; Jacques Bourre, who befriends Kocoumbo in the lycée and who was discussed above; and most significantly, perhaps, Denise, the Marxist trade unionist Kocoumbo meets in the factory and who becomes his lover.

Encounters and conversations with all of these individuals seem intended to suggest an imminent form of political and moral awakening. In other words, there is a strong sense of a '[shift] in consciousness' that Brent Hayes Edwards sees as characteristic of the Afro-American, African and Caribbean inter-war generation in Paris, and which was 'rooted above all in their experience of migration to Europe, in their exposure to the centers of imperial dominance'.[28] We have already seen how French pupils and teachers force Kocoumbo to undergo an identity crisis and to confront the distorted vision France has of the 'inferior' race he 'represents'. Away from the school, Lucienne, Durandeau's duped French lover, also reminds him of the impossibility of escaping this collective and, crucially, racialized African identity. When she angrily exclaims 'vous êtes tous les mêmes! [you're all the same!]' (*Kocoumbo*, p. 182), the African's response immediately calls the iconic Duboisian notion of 'double consciousness' mentioned in Chapter 2: 'Je suis Africain, tout mon comportement met en cause l'Afrique entière' [I'm an African, all Africa is implicated by my behaviour] (*Kocoumbo*, p. 182). If such 'mirroring' implicitly reflects back upon French attitudes towards African identity, Kocoumbo's reactions to a French Revolution memorial seem to raise more explicit questions about the cultural space of France, and to suggest that reflection on the significance of his individual racial identity may lead to a crucial 'shift' in his general political consciousness. In other words, instead of being merely an object of others' gazes (being seen), Kocoumbo, the traveller, seems ready to learn to see, and, crucially, to develop a critical, indeed anti-colonial, dimension to his observations. Standing in the Parisian 'centre' that spread the 'universal' Republican ideals of equality, liberty and fraternity, the young African reflects upon these Revolutionary ideals but is more explicit in his conclusions than Fara when he notes that this ethos 'avait disparu; où était sa trace, maintenant' [had disappeared; what trace of it was left now?] (*Kocoumbo*, p. 152).

The novel's emphasis on the key issue of class also seems to suggest that, whilst the novel may not be explicitly Marxist in tone, there is a certain awareness of the complex ways in which ethnicity, class and ideology meet in the context of travel and displacement. This in turn implies that Kocoumbo's journey will culminate in a genuinely critical position on questions of social injustice, and perhaps even in political engagement. As we saw earlier, the question of social class initially makes its presence felt on the boat transporting Kocoumbo and his fellow Africans to France. Whilst it is notable that these differences pertain almost exclusively to the travelling black population, Kocoumbo is not, at this point, unduly struck by their significance other than to feel pity for Douk's misfortune and admiration for Durandeau's elegance and achievements. It is in Paris, and in relation to the French population, that Kocoumbo first becomes more critically aware of class. On a walk through the capital with Raymond, the son of the Brigaud family, he notes the differences between the affluent and poor areas of the city and, although he is unable to grasp Raymond's use of the term 'class' – he believes it refers purely to an educational context – it is clear that he is beginning to realize that France's cultural identity is not socially homogenous. It would seem at this point that the positive influence of individuals with the correct intellectual and moral authority is all that is needed to complete Kocoumbo's political education.

Despite its privileging of socialist, Marxist thought – namely through recurrent references to issues of class – one must pause over the idea that *Kocoumbo, l'étudiant noir* could be seen as a representative radical Marxist text, denigrating capitalism and elevating the worker. Part of the problem lies in the portrayal of the two main characters intended to represent radical politics. Abdou, the successful gynaecologist who is said to espouse passionately 'les idéologies extrémistes qui sacrifient l'individu pour le bien de la communauté' [extremist ideologies where individuality is sacrificed for the well-being of the community] (*Kocoumbo*, p. 172), seems initially to be a positive role model. His choice of profession has not been motivated by self-interest or the promise of social standing but by a genuine desire to improve the reproductive health of African women following the death of his own sister in childbirth. In other respects, however, Abdou is less convincing as a political mentor: although we are not given an in-depth insight into this character, his thinking can appear doctrinaire, and whilst he remains convinced that 'le communisme sauvera l'Afrique' [communism will save Africa] (*Kocoumbo*, p. 172), he has no insight to offer on the place of race within communism. Indeed, in their final meeting, Abdou's advice to Kocoumbo suggests that whilst the former is aware of the unequal treatment of Africans within the French education system, the only solution to this is 'plus de travail, plus d'effort [...]. Et puis, il faut assimiler complètement la langue et les idées françaises' [more work, more effort [...]. And after that, you must completely assimilate the French language and French ideas] (*Kocoumbo*, p. 225). In other words, Abdou's version of communism, like French theories of education, is not meant to travel and adapt to other contexts and peoples. Africans must adapt to it, and in the process, he would seem to imply, abandon their own cultural origins.

Like Abdou, Denise is a passionate believer in Marxist ideology as a solution to social injustice and class inequalities. A committed trade union activist, this young white French woman is entrusted with the task of converting Kocoumbo to this ideology – by persuading him to become a member of the Communist Party – so that he will integrate better into life in the metal sheeting factory. For her, Kocoumbo's main problem is his 'bourgeois' intellectual attitude, and his inability to see how capitalism pervades every aspect of society, even the relationship between parents and their children. If Kocoumbo does agree to become a member of the trade union (and the Communist

Party), we get the distinct impression that this is not because of any ideological conversion but simply because it will make life easier for him on the factory floor. For him, Denise's ideological beliefs are no more than empty slogans that prevent her from expressing either her emotions or what he believes to be her feminine side. Ultimately, however, although Denise's political, and later her emotional, sincerity are not to be doubted, her greatest ideological failing, and by implication the failing of the Marxist position she represents, is her inability to even contemplate that Kocoumbo's colonized African identity might not fit neatly into her framework. Nor can she offer an answer to the complex reactions he provokes amongst some of his fellow workers.[29] Despite his lowly position as a cleaner, Kocoumbo is frequently subject to what can best be described as bullying. For his fellow workers, such treatment appears to be provoked by his aforementioned 'bourgeois' attitude and behaviour. In a working atmosphere dominated by inflexible thinking and rigid categorization, his dedication to educational achievement and detachment from political action is seen by many as a betrayal of proletarian values. For the manager, Kocoumbo's ability to answer correctly a mathematical problem is not seen as a betrayal but as a form of arrogance that is quickly dealt with by an order to return to sweeping the floor. Rather than being praised by his fellow workers for upstaging the manager, Kocoumbo is subject to even further bullying.

Although the questions of ethnic identity and 'race' are rarely raised explicitly in the course of these encounters, their relevance cannot be denied. For behind the dismissal of Kocoumbo as a bourgeois, or the treatment of him as an insolent upstart who needs to be put in his place, is a colonialist, indeed racist thinking that unites the capitalist manager and the proletarian workers. Clearly, for them, Kocoumbo's problem is not that he has betrayed his fellow workers or risen above his status as cleaner (in both cases the argument is a class issue), but that he has failed to acknowledge his inferior 'racial' and colonized status. On the only occasion where this thinking is explicitly expressed on the factory floor it is in fact framed in a comparison with Indochina that leaves the reader in no doubt regarding the sentiment governing attitudes to the African: 'Ces gens-là, on leur a apporté la civilisation, ils viennent chez nous pour s'instruire; après, ils nous cassent la gueule!' [Those people, we civilize them, they come here [to France] to be educated and then they kick our heads in!] (*Kocoumbo*, p. 235). Clearly, then, the anticapitalist doctrine espoused by these workers does not translate to an anti-colonial view, and they are unable to see any link between their own class-based oppression and that of France's colonized peoples.

Quite apart from the failure of secondary characters to provide a convincing radical political voice, it is the figure of Kocoumbo himself who does most to undermine any sense of genuine critical intellectual exchange, and who lends the text its tone of essential conservatism. Despite the intellectual failings of these characters' thinking, and the untimely death of Denise, the ultimate problem is that Kocoumbo's own thinking does not seem to be affected in any profound way by these encounters. By the end, it is clear that he has failed to exploit the collision of ideas for any genuine intellectual or political transformative potential. Indeed, in the overall context of the novel it is also arguable that Loba himself fails to use this fundamental consequence of travel for any real dramatic effect. True, Kocoumbo does experience the 'psychological split' of the displaced African and gains some insight into the processes that determine how his African identity is seen and constructed by French society. At times, he also reveals a contemplative consciousness of the ideo- logical failings mentioned above, notably the elision of questions of 'race' from Marxist discourse. However, his response to these issues never becomes genuinely critical or active. Rather he reacts with passive silence inspired, he admits, by 'ennui' [boredom] more than a spirit of 'révolte' (*Kocoumbo*, p. 249). Despite his different travel experiences, his personal aspirations remain middle class. Where he does communicate a broader political vision for Africa, it is clear he envisages its future as lying in the hands of an assimilated, French- educated middle class who, if they do not quite believe in the status quo, subscribe to a form of intellectual and technological progress that remains resolutely French.

Clearly, what these 'évolués' are meant to represent is not a polit- ical viewpoint that will provoke change, but an almost individual moral position based on honesty and a will to rise professionally and socially through hard work and the acquisition of cultural capital – Koucoumbo's dishonest decision to use his repatriation grant to complete his studies in France is justified on this basis. By the time Kocoumbo finally graduates as a magistrate (a profession that has earlier been unequivocally associated by the African students with prestige and social standing), it is clear that the encounters that have proved most influential for him are not those that might have led him to a broader political understanding of his past, present and future, but those that have taken him to what might be called the moral high ground of the stable, rational professional. If Kocoumbo's other African acquaintances have failed in France, it is implied that personal circumstances and cultural and financial obstacles, although significant, ultimately cannot be used as an excuse. Nadan, Mou, Douk and Duranderau all fail because they do not possess the single-mindedness of Koucoumbo and Abdou to devote themselves to study and personal, professional advancement. In other words, they fail to transform their travels into cultural capital that can be cashed in for personal benefit upon their return to Africa. Instead, they are presented as possessing significant moral failings that will ultimately cause their downfall: Nadan's criminal activities (which are never fully explained) lead to his imprisonment; Mou abandons the seminary and develops an alcohol problem; Douk fails to progress beyond a life of dependency and petty crime; and Durandeau, who for much of the novel is the model Kocoumbo seeks to emulate, is finally exposed as a fraud and a liar.

More significantly, this small group of Africans, despite their closeness, highlights a singular lack of unity that belies any sense of the political idealism of the pre-independence era or the earlier decades of black Paris. Certainly, Loba cannot be criticized for presenting the reader with a portrait of a disparate and arguably selfish group of individuals. It would also be wrong, in this period leading to independence, to assume a vision of solidarity amongst Africa's educated elite. (Of course, the particular 'usefulness' attributed to travel in the text also underscores the propensity of African writing on travel to undermine any attempt at neat definitions.) However, it is difficult to ascertain the precise significance of this group's lack of solidarity, or the novel's denial of the geo-political and cultural possibilities of earlier texts dealing with Africans, African-Americans and Caribbeans in Paris. (Jazz, for example, so frequently used as a symbol of the vibrancy and internationalism of black Paris, is associated in Loba's text with a distinctly seedy and morally dubious establishment.) Ultimately, the novel appears to have very little of substance to say about political issues, apart from highlighting what it seems to believe to be the essentially corrupt nature and self-interest of Africa's future politicians – once Durandeau fails to make it into the legal or medical profession he decides to focus on a political career. Koucoumbo's final act, where he knocks the unrepentant Durandeau to the ground, emerges then as final proof that what motivates this 'student' is essentially self-interest and the protection of his 'moral' reputation as an honest and diligent professional. In the final pages, Douk's declaration that 'Koucoumbo n'aime pas la politique' [Kocoumbo doesn't like politics] (*Kocoumbo*, p. 261), suggests that the elite class – whose ranks this student has joined – will not be interested in providing genuine political resistance to the political future represented by Durandeau and the dictator-like Tougon.

If the journey at the heart of *Kocoumbo, l'étudiant noir* is an example of physical travel, it is not, however, quite a journey towards seeing and comparing in the manner of other contemporary travellers such as the narrator of Bernard Dadié's *Un Nègre à Paris* or Tété-Michel Kpomassie in *L'Africain du Grœnland*. True, Kocoumbo does gain invaluable insights into the type of alienation and injustice suffered by Fara in *Mirages de Paris*. However, despite the political context of his journey and the impending nature of decolonization, travel for him does not become the trigger for significant reflection on the future of his country of origin. Essentially, intercontinental travel, as it is portrayed in *Kocoumbo, l'étudiant noir*, appears set to remain the most effective means to achieve personal upward mobility and fulfil the lure of social advancement in the postcolonial order.

CHAPTER THREE

Un Nègre à Paris: Tourist Tales

The period immediately prior to and following African independence has been identified as key to the development of African textualizations of travel. From the 1930s, increasing numbers of francophone sub-Saharan Africans began to travel to the metropolitan centre, and this journey would form a central structural device and thematic preoccupation in several major texts from the 1950s and 1960s. However, *Un Nègre à Paris*, Bernard Dadié's account of his July 1956 trip to Paris, and also later accounts of trips to New York and Rome differ considerably from other key texts of the intercontinental travel experience of this period.[1] In general, novels such as Cheikh Hamidou Kane's *L'Aventure ambiguë*, Ousmane Sembene's *Le Docker noir* and, as we have seen, Aké Loba's *Kocoumbo, l'étudiant noir* seem to retain a fundamental connection with the earlier *Mirages de Paris* by positing as central to the African encounter with Europe experiences of racism, loneliness and alienating cultural encounters. Certainly, Dadié does not deny the significance of ethnicity to his travel experience and is not immune to the racism encountered by other African travellers. However, the Ivorian author's narratives are dominated by an unmistakable light-heartedness and genuine sense of wonder at the traveller's discovery of a 'new' culture.

If the period mentioned above is crucial to understanding a particular development in African accounts of intercontinental travel, this can also be explained, of course, by the socio-political context of impending or recently achieved independence. For underwriting both the descriptions of foreign journeys and the unmistakably instructive tone of Dadié's travel texts is the implication that Africa and Africans themselves are about to begin their own journey of discovery where comparisons with other cultures will prove invaluable for determining future political, economic and cultural directions.

A Parisian holiday

Apart from its distinctive tone, *Un Nègre à Paris* differs in another important respect from the texts mentioned above. In these texts, travel – or more accurately perhaps the psychological reality of *dépaysement* – is a context against which is set the arguably more important professional identity of the main protagonists (students in the case of *L'Aventure ambiguë* and *Kocoumbo* and a manual labourer/novelist in the case of *Le Docker noir*). Of course, this is not to say that the intercontinental journey between Africa and Europe does not form and inform the plot and psychological drama of these texts in significant ways. However, in the case of Dadié's text, travel permeates all aspects of the text from themes, form, ideological debates and even the identity of the narrator, Tanhoe Bertin, who is to all intents and purposes an African tourist on a 'city break' in the French capital.[2]

As we shall see, the appropriation and subsequent subversion of the Western travelogue is fundamental to understanding the form of Dadié's text. However, it is Tanhoe Bertin's identity as tourist that emerges as the most immediately distinctive feature of *Un Nègre à Paris*. Bertin is almost certainly the first Francophone African tourist in literature and, despite the phenomenal global growth in this industry since, remains still today a rare example of an African literary character who goes on holiday in the Western sense of the term, i.e. purely for recreational reasons. In so doing, however, he at once joins the ranks of a group of individuals who, from a Western perspective at least, remain amongst the most maligned of travelling types. In his influential study of the tourist and tourism, for example, French sociologist Jean-Didier Urbain examines the ways in which tourism has come to be seen as the symbol of a world divided between rich and poor, and the tourist as a superficial consumer of other cultures. Most damningly, as Urbain illustrates, the term 'tourist' evokes numerous negative presuppositions that 'dépouill[ent] dans l'instant le voyageur de sa qualité principale: *voyager*' [immediately strip the traveller of his principal characteristic: *travel*].[3]

Significantly, however, if an elitist discourse of travel has categorized the tourist as the 'idiot of travel', there is ample critical support for this travelling figure's rehabilitation as a uniquely perceptive traveller. For Urbain, the tourist is a shrewd observer who is sensitive to cultural difference and not incapable of innovation in terms of travel practices.[4] Such observational skills and careful attention to cultural difference, and similarity, are, of course, immediately obvious in the case of Tanhoe Bertin's description of Paris and Parisians, and will be dealt with in greater detail below. However, it is important to re-emphasize here Bertin's hyphenated identity as a black African tourist. Urbain is surely right to question a vision of the world that is divided between, on the one hand, countries that provide tourists and, on the other, those countries that serve primarily as tourist destinations. However, when he explains that the United States and Europe are not just places from where tourists originate but together represent the preferred destination of 80 per cent of the world's tourist population, he fails to provide statistics for the number of Africans within this population who travel for various reasons either to the preferred destinations of global tourism or to holiday destinations on their own continent.[5] Tourism may well represent an exchange, as Urbain states, but the uneven nature of this exchange, the domination of First World interests and the under-representation of black Africans (and other Third World identities) amongst the holidaying tourist masses – as opposed to tourism's employees – is not always sufficiently recognized.

Tanhoe Bertin does, however, defy trends, by seeming to belong to the disparaged 'hordes' of tourists who, by 1956, had already become established as legitimate targets of the elite group of so-called 'authentic' travellers. For Elisabeth Mudimbe-Boyi, it is primarily the tendency to '[saunter] about and [stop] whenever he pleases, unhindered by external constraints and schedules' that qualifies Bertin as a tourist.[6] However, if, like the other tourists in Paris, he buys a map, follows the crowds and visits the must-see cultural sites and monuments of the French capital, he also appears, despite himself, to succeed in retaining what most self-conscious Western tourists constantly claim for themselves: an individual identity. Skin colour clearly plays a crucial role in distinguishing Bertin as a particular tourist amongst the masses. From the moment he takes his seat on the plane bound for Paris, he is 'le seul Nègre parmi tant de voyageurs blancs' (NP, p. 21) ['the only black amongst all those white passengers', p. 13].[7] As soon as he arrives in Paris, his skin colour threatens not just to mark him out for the particular focus of others' gazes but also threatens to deny him his identity as a tourist. For, if his stated intention at the outset of his visit is to observe and report back, he discovers that he is as much observed as observer, and his 'blackness' is invariably scrutinized as a type of exotic curiosity or attraction in its own right: 'D'aucuns, en me voyant se demandent s'ils ne viennent pas de rencontrer le diable en personne. On n'a pas idée d'être si Noir tout de même. […] Tout est dans le regard. J'étonne' (*NP*, pp. 64–65) ['Some people when they see me think they've encountered the devil himself. Funny, I had no idea I was that black! […] The only thing that matters is what they see. I catch them by surprise', p. 43].

Despite the humour, other reactions to his skin colour deny Bertin his identity as tourist at an even more fundamental level. For example, in a typically understated anecdote, he describes a maid's response to attempts by him and a student friend to book hotel accommodation:

> Cette bonne, après nous avoir déshabillé du regard, refusait même de nous faire visiter les deux pièces que sa patronne nous proposait à des prix différents.
>   —Mais, Mademoiselle…
>   —C'est à prendre ou à laisser. Nous n'allons pas faire visiter nos chambres à tous les clients qui se présentent.
>   —Quelles sont ces manières?
>   —C'est comme ça, ici.
>   —Et ceux qui reviennent de les visiter?
>   —C'est touristes, c'est pas pareil. (*NP*, p.201)

> [After having undressed us with her eyes, this maid refused to let us see the two rooms the proprietor suggested were in our price range.
>   'But Madame…'
>   'Take it or leave it. We don't let just anyone who walks in the door see the rooms…'
>   'Is this the way to do business?'
>   'That's the way we do it here.
>   'What about those people who just left?'
>   'Tourists… it's different with them.' (p. 142)]

Despite the satirical, and uncharacteristically petulant, remarks regarding the maid's physical unattractiveness following this exchange, the scene is important for understanding the complex process involved as Dadié's tourist gaze intersects, and clashes, with that of a member of the host culture. On the one hand, this hotel scene could be interpreted as an example of the fleeting, arbitrary encounters that tell us so much about James Clifford's notion of travelling cultures. In this instance, a white French 'maid', whose role, as one of tourism's employees, is to 'serve', confronts a black African on holiday. However, given the historical context of the novel, and the particular stage in the development of these characters' respective 'travelling cultures', neither is willing to move towards a place where they might begin to recognize each other's individuality and make a connection. In Dadié's case, despite the admirable and genuine sentiments of tolerance that govern most of his reactions to those whom he meets, the 'maid' is never seen as anything more than representative of 'ugly', bad-tempered women. As for the maid, she is unable to accept that a black African could be a tourist deserving of the respect, consideration and service afforded a 'normal' representative of this travelling type.

If others, such as the maid, refuse to acknowledge Tanhoe Bertin's tourist identity, he himself also appears keen to distinguish himself from the tourists he frequently mentions in his letters home. However, this is not, I believe, evidence of the tourist's self-loathing, as Malcom Crick has identified it, nor is it an attempt to align himself with an elite group of travellers who are constantly at pains to differentiate their travel practices from those they see as belonging to the crude and vulgar masses.[8] Certainly, Dadié's narrator is aware of the relative privilege his ability to travel by plane to Paris bestows, and recognizes that, amongst Africans, he is part of the 'chosen few'. But it is worth remembering that this privilege has not been paid for by himself. Dadié's narrator has not bought time in the manner of a Western tourist; he has been given his ticket by an unnamed benefactor. Ultimately, even if Tanhoe Bertin is aware that he is privileged to be travelling as he is, he shows no interest in the value-laden tourist–traveller distinction of Western travel discourse simply because it is of no relevance either to his own travel practice or his 'sight-seeing' plans: 'On ne verra pas pour moi on ne pensera pas pour moi. [...] Je regarderai pour moi, pour toi, pour tous les nôtres' (*NP*, pp. 9–10) ['No one else's eyes will see for me, and no one else will think for me. [...] I'll be seeing for myself, for you, for all our people', pp. 4–5)]. In the same way as Bertin will not allow his travelling gaze to be directed, attempts to categorize his travelling practices by referring uniquely, or uncritically, to culturally specific theoretical concepts will fail to illuminate the precise nature of his project. If the narrator of *Un Nègre à Paris* is keen to set himself apart from tourists it is not because of any qualitative judgement on this particular type of traveller but because he is keen to maintain an outsider, 'objective' position in the face of temptations to assimilate him to any reductive, homogeneous identity, be it 'tourist', black', 'African' or even

'Parisian'. This last category also explains perhaps the absence in the text of any sustained verbal engagement with Parisians, his repeated concern that he is beginning to integrate into Parisian lifestyle, and his related fear of becoming too distanced from his own country and traditions. At the same time, this distance allows Bertin to speak simultaneously to two audiences: his French hosts and his fellow countrymen. As we shall see, this concern with maintaining distance is key to extracting travel's 'field of usefulness' for this particular 'leisure' traveller.

Generic navigations

Bernard Dadié's prolific literary output is characterized by a distinct generic diversity. From folk tale, to prison diary, to poetry and the semi-autobiographical novel, Dadié has consistently shown himself willing to experiment formally in order to convey a particular message:

> Pour moi, tout est moyen. Si j'estime que certaines idées seront plus accessibles au lecteur sous forme de conte plutôt que sous forme de poème, eh bien! j'écris un conte; chaque moyen d'expression a une fonction bien précise, doit remplir une mission différente.[9]

> [For me, everything is a means. If I feel that certain ideas are more accessible to the reader in the form of a folk tale rather than a poem, well then, I write a folk tale; each means of expression has a very precise function and must fulfil a different purpose.]

If this is the case then what ideas, what audience, what purpose lie at the heart of Dadié's decision to choose the travelogue, one of the most under-represented genres in the African literary tradition? True, it is possible to argue, as Fernando Lambert does, that Dadié's fictionalized accounts of journeys to Paris, Rome and New York are not travelogues in the strictest sense of the term but constitute more accurately composite forms that weld together features of the epistolary genre (the entire text is, in fact, a letter addressed to an African friend), the diary and the travelogue.[10] However, as we saw in the introduction, this argument about the generic uncertainty of travel literature could be applied to all manner of different accounts of journeys. What is incontestable where *Un Nègre à Paris*, *La Ville où nul ne meurt* and *Patron de New York* are concerned, however, is that

they reveal Dadié to be one of the exclusive coterie of francophone
African writers whose textualizations of travel are dominated by the
clearly recognizable conventions of the Western travelogue.

Before addressing the possible significance of Dadié's choice of
genre, it is worth pausing to discuss briefly the question of literary
precursors. In her study of Dadié's work, Nicole Vincileoni cites
the influence on Dadié of Pierre Daninos's 1954 fictional account
of the observations of a retired English army major in France, *Les
Carnets du Major Thompson*.[11] For Vincileoni, it is Daninos's style,
as opposed to the form of this text, which provides the major source
of inspiration. Certainly, it is possible to identify similarities between
Daninos and Dadié in the focus of some of their observations and
in the gently ironic tones of their comments on French manners and
customs. However, there are also fundamental differences. Daninos
seems as eager to poke fun, albeit moderately, at the cultural origins of
his English narrator as he is to explore French culture from an (imagined) outsider perspective. Even if Dadié's narrator also comments
from time to time on certain peculiarities of his native African
culture, he is clearly not interested in mocking, or even examining
in-depth, these cultural origins. There is no evidence either to suggest
that Dadié's portrait of the African Bertin is modelled on Daninos's
caricatured 'Englishman'.[12] In addition, although both Daninos's
text and *Un Nègre à Paris* devote a significant amount of space to
questions of language, they do so in very different ways. Daninos
is primarily interested in showing the relationship between travel,
cultural interpretation and interlingual translation:[13] his narrator
employs the services of a translator (Daninos himself), who litters the
text with notes indicating where he has retained the structures and
particularities of the major's English through literal translation. As
such, *Les Carnets du Major Thompson* manages to achieve humour
through its interlingual play with idiomatic expressions whilst simultaneously highlighting Daninos's familiarity with the peculiarities of
the English language. *Un Nègre à Paris* also uses the strangeness of
language as a means to create humour and to underline the realities of
cultural encounter. However, even if Dadié/Bertin is at least bilingual,
it is an almost monolingual mastery of French, and in particular a
fascination with the literal meanings of idiomatic expressions, which
creates humour, and indicates an understanding of certain aspects
of French culture and history.[14] This journey to linguistic competence has clearly begun long before the physical journey to France

and means that the explicit question of translation between French and indigenous African languages is entirely absent from the text.[15] Indeed, any obstacles the travelling Bertin does face in understanding the French are cultural and never purely linguistic.

The question of language points to another issue that indicates a crucial difference not just between Dadié's travelogue and Daninos's text but also between *Un Nègre à Paris* and its most likely literary inspiration, Montesquieu's famous 1721 text, *Les Lettres persanes*.[16] In the case of the two French-authored texts, the strategy adopted is a fictionalized travel account and an 'imagined' outsider perspective on French culture. Dadié, too, fictionalizes his traveller and uses the epistolary format favoured by the eighteenth-century classic in order to send his observations 'home'. With regard to Montesquieu's tone and style, Dadié is also clearly influenced by the 'rhetorical performance' (to use Dustin Griffin's term[17]) of the Enlightenment thinker's satirical mode. The moral purpose of Dadié's text will be discussed later, but what is unquestionable is that in the manner of the best satirical works, including *Les Lettres persanes*, Dadié's use of irony highlights his linguistic brio, and seems in certain respects designed not to provoke but rather 'to win the admiration and applause of a reading audience not for the ardour or acuteness of its moral concern but for the brilliant wit and force of the satirist rhetorician'.[18] The distinctive use of irony in *Un Nègre à Paris* also appears at times to highlight what Linda Hutcheon describes as the 'reinforcing' function of irony which for 'certain discursive communities seem[s] to play a role in proving communicative competence'.[19] However, whilst Dadié the author shares with Montesquieu and Daninos the learned wit and linguistic competence of a 'native' French speaker, he does not have to imagine the perspective of their texts because he also shares with Tanhoe Bertin the *genuine* 'outsider' status of a colonized subject in metropolitan France. In other words, *Un Nègre à Paris* is neither the work of an ethnic imposter in the manner of Daninos's text nor a literary hoax in the manner of *Les Lettres persanes*. In addition, although Bertin (and Dadié) is clearly 'at home' in the French language, the text re-emphasizes the point already underlined in *Mirages de Paris* and *Kocoumbo*: even if linguistic fluency facilitates Africans' travels in France it is not a guarantee of cultural integration. We have seen that this is partly explained by Bertin's reluctance to relinquish his own cultural specificity, thereby protecting his privileged outsider status.

But it is also clear that for many of those he encounters in Paris, and to whom he speaks, fluency in French will never erase the essential difference of his 'blackness'.

Significantly, Dadié never consciously draws attention to language's role within the apparatus of colonialism. Nonetheless, it is possible to argue that his 'rhetorical performance' and his obvious pride at 'inheriting' (*NP*, p. 191 [p. 134]) French culture though fluency in the French language is evidence of what the Martinican intellectual Edouard Glissant identifies as the 'verbal dimension' of the colonized's mimetic drive.[20] Unlike Fara in *Mirages de Paris*, however, whose relationship to the language and culture of the French colonizer more clearly illustrates the negative, 'splitting' effects of colonization on the colonized's psyche, Dadié, through his character Bertin, reveals a genuine intellectual curiosity with regard to the workings of language *per se*. Part of this interest is also motivated by a desire to communicate his beliefs with force and persuasion to a French readership (as we shall see, the moral and political aspects of his beliefs appear to be primarily, though not exclusively, addressed to the French). For this reason it would be inaccurate to suggest that his attitude to language is that of the colonized Martinican *évolués* whom Glissant suggests are more interested in eloquence than the substance of what is being said. Indeed, Dadié's linguistic curiosity is later borne out in his American travel account where American English, with its own particular idiomatic and metaphorical features, provides a similar, if less extensive, source of fascination and entertainment to that of the French language in *Un Nègre à Paris*. Where Dadié's relationship to French is concerned, the only other thing that can be said with any degree of certainty is that his mastery of this language serves to reinscribe, on a textual level, both the fundamental alienation that exists between the travelling observer and the observed travellee as well as the distance that separates the African intellectual from his own people.

Whilst it is impossible to establish the exact extent to which Dadié uses *Les Lettres persanes* and *Les Carnets du Major Thompson* as models for *Un Nègre à Paris*, the question remains as to why Dadié deviates, however slightly, from strict verismilitude by fictionalizing his narrator. One possible explanation is that Dadié is attempting to create a double bluff for readers expecting the type of 'ethnic imposture' of a Montesquieu or Daninos. By aligning himself with such literary strategists, Dadié could then effect a sort of pre-emptive strike against any racist-inspired thinking that might argue that the sophisticated linguistic register and cultural references of *Un Nègre à Paris*'s African narrator are evidence of a literary prank.

Whilst the influence of possible literary precursors provides a starting point for questions of taxonomy, I believe that a more plausible explanation for Dadié's formal choice in *Un Nègre à Paris* can be gleaned if we reverse slightly his justification for using the folk tale to make his first foray into the literary world:

> Pourquoi j'ai débuté par des contes? Je voulais montrer que les contes de chez nous, bien écrits, bien présentés, pouvaient égaler les contes occidentaux. Je suis frappé des analogies qui existent entre les contes, qu'ils appartiennent à l'U.R.S.S., au Japon ou à l'Afrique. Qu'ils soient riches ou pauvres, les peuples ont les mêmes préoccupations, les mêmes rêves et, à ce niveau, il est difficile de parler d'âme noire ou d'âme blanche.[21]

> [Why did I begin with folk tales? I wanted to show that our folk tales, if they were well written and well presented, could equal Western folk tales. I am struck by the similarities that exist between folk tales, whether they originate from the USSR, Japan or Africa. Whether people are rich or poor they share the same preoccupations, the same dreams, and, at this level, it is difficult to talk about a black or a white soul.]

Here, of course, Dadié's essential respect for other cultural traditions is expressed in a literary argument about the universal significance and value of a particular genre: the folk tale. However, the remark also raises the point that if the universal significance of an African oral genre is to be truly appreciated by other cultures then it will first have to be converted/adapted successfully to a written form. This is not a comment about the inherent superiority of written genres but rather a desire to show that the African tale is a culturally adaptable genre. By the same token, it is possible to see how Dadié might argue that an African can adapt the travelogue, which has traditionally belonged to a Western literary tradition, in order to highlight the genre's universal significance and its ability to underline a shared humanity. This may not involve a wholesale conversion from written to oral conventions – as in the example of Dadié's written adaptations of oral folk tales – but this generic adaptation or appropriation will nevertheless incorporate aspects of the oral tradition in order to take account of its new context. For example, Michael Syrotinski singles out as evidence of a residual orality in *Un Nègre à Paris* the 'use of the present tense, the direct address neatly achieved by using a letter form, the inclusive *nous*, the exclamations, the digressions, the rhetoric embellishments, and the insistent rhetorical questions' (one could also mention here the text's episodic as opposed to linear structure).[22] Just as important as identifying these features is the idea that Dadié's incorporation of orature's journey motif could also be said to underline the presence of a literary tradition that exists outside Western written forms and where travel is always already in evidence. Also, if it is '*bien écrit*', as Dadié argues, the African travelogue will presumably be worthy of standing alongside other 'well written' French texts, such as those by Montesquieu and Daninos. Of course, it is also possible to argue that, like many of the other Negritude writers with whom he is associated, Dadié's choice of the French language and a Western literary form in *Un Nègre à Paris* is proof of an inability to rule out Africa's need for the mediating intervention of the West in its attempts to assert its cultural 'modernity'. However, I believe that levelling the argument of 'colonial mimicry' against Dadié fails adequately to take account of the subversive strategy governing his travel text.

In his reading of Dadié's text, Michael Syrotinski also convincingly argues for the inclusion of *Un Nègre à Paris* (and Dadié's other travelogues) within a broader tradition of non-fictional travel writing. However, Syrotinski is equally careful to demonstrate that Dadié's use of the genre has a far more important purpose than merely proving his ability to master a Western literary form. For him, Dadié's ironic reworking of the rhetoric and ideology of travel writing is intended to '[unmask] the complicitous manner in which European travel writing served the ideology of colonial imperialism'.[23] Syrotinksi insists that it is this, and not any notion of a genuine 'outsider' status, that distinguishes Dadié from Montesquieu. What is crucial is that the African is 'both inside and outside', and his deliberate and ironic intertextual nod to *Les Lettres Persanes* must thus be read as 'mimicking colonial mimicry' and 'interrogating not just the foundations of Western civilization and its humanist values but the very strategies it employs to represent and contain others'.[24] Identifying Dadié's 'inside/outside' position, which was alluded to with regard to the issue of his relationship to the French language, is crucial because in this otherwise 'cheerful' text it links him to the psychological and exilic drama we have come to recognize as being central to other African experiences of travel to the colonial centre. It is this particular position that also lies at the heart of his text's structure and which emerges more clearly once his particular brand of satire, with its 'two simultaneous and contradictory positions', is explored.[25]

If, as Charles A. Knight proposes, satire is 'not a genre in itself but an exploiter of genres', then it has been particularly effective, as Dadié clearly knows, when its ironic tones align themselves with narratives of travel and cultural encounter.[26] In the case of *Un Nègre à Paris*, however, irony and gentle satire not only allow him to encode subversion and provocation in the manner generally associated with this mode – and which we will look at in more detail below – it also reflects the very position in which he, as an African traveller in Paris, finds himself. By using irony for the purpose of saying one thing and meaning another, Dadié reveals how his double vision (and 'double-voicedness') can be exploited more effectively to question fundamental features of European travel writing – assumed superiority of Western culture, direction of ethnographic gaze – and deftly to correct the images of African inferiority codified in the genre. This double perspective also highlights the question of split readership discussed in the introduction. Whilst the text's use of the epistolary form plainly indicates its destination for an African (albeit francophone) readership, it seems clear, too, that Dadié's essentially Christian-inspired message of cultural tolerance is also targeted at the colonizing people and culture he is describing: the French. The indirect nature of any negative view of French society and the preference for gentle rather than excoriating satire also appear to be carefully designed to lead metropolitan French readers into critical reflection about the 'welcome' this African traveller receives in their own country. In addition, the double-sidedness of Dadié's irony transforms what initially appears to be a generically compliant text into a challenge to literary authority, and seemingly uncritical admiration of Western culture into an exposé of its contradictions.

Finally, it should be stressed that Dadié's use of irony is, as Linda Hutcheon stresses, 'a risky business': 'even while provoking laughter, irony invokes notions of hierarchy and subordination, judgement and perhaps even moral superiority'.[27] Of course, as Dadié himself notes, travel is also frequently associated with risk, especially physical risk. Hence, the African tradition of providing a 'bénédiction [...] lorsque nous entreprenons un long voyage' (*NP*, p. 115) ['a blessing [...] when we're ready to set off on a long voyage', p.78]. In the case of *Un Nègre à Paris*, however, the risk is primarily discursive but is also heightened by the geographical context of Dadié's writing: he has quite literally travelled to the heart of the empire in order subtly to criticize it. Any accusations of misplaced moral authority and insurgency will arguably render this colonized author even more vulnerable than had he criticized from 'home'. However, carefully crafted and well-written, irony's double use will in fact serve to protect him: it can help to circumvent problems posed by perceptions that this colonized African traveller is daring to speaking from an 'authoritative' position. Irony's double use, and the uncertainty surrounding its intentions, also cancels the need for any ingratiating apology for daring to adopt the conventions of the travel writing genre. In this way, Dadié can proceed safely to reverse the ethnographic gaze in order cleverly to expose the unjust connection between power and knowledge structuring the relationship between the West and Africa.

Travel and time

We have already seen that Dadié's identity as a tourist prompts him to visit what he considers – or what he has been told constitute – culturally significant sites. In addition, our discussion of genre has highlighted a distinctly subversive intent in his writing that is meant to provoke reflection on the part of the reader. But what exactly does Dadié visit and observe? And what, if any, is the 'moral' or ideological argument at the heart of his text? Although *Un Nègre à Paris* presents no clear linear trail to enable the reader to follow Tanhoe Bertin's itinerary precisely, it is possible to establish a list of some of the sites visited during the course of his short visit to the French capital. Unsurprisingly perhaps, several of the 'usual suspects' of a standard tourist visit feature: the metro, Notre Dame, Montmartre and Sacré-Cœur, Pigalle, Les Invalides. Nonetheless, when it comes to establishing a moral centre to Dadié's narrative, one could be forgiven for seeing in the author's overwhelming tolerance and generosity an almost bland, middle course that refuses to condemn the blatant racism of his reception by certain French hosts.

Closer inspection, however, shows a far more complex approach to the cultural encounter of travel and to the 'moral' agenda of this traveller. Although Dadié visits various important cultural monuments, he is not simply interested in glancing at their surface appearance, but is more concerned with interpreting their deeper symbolism and significance to French culture and history. Also, in the wider context of the text, the space devoted to these monuments is minimal compared to the substantial amount of commentary devoted to behaviour and to French history. Although Dadié's humour undermines any 'scientific' quality to his observations, it is clear nonetheless that his 'reverse-ethnographic' approach is meant to provoke reflection both on the nature of ethnographic discourse and the problematic distinction between 'anecdotal' travel writing and 'scientific' ethnography.

Of the several consistent thematic threads running through *Un Nègre à Paris*, one stands out as revelatory of how Dadié approaches and reinforces the moral issue that lies at the heart of his text. For Dadié's treatment of the question of time offers a subtle demonstration of the way his text exposes and questions the asymmetrical power relations between blacks and whites and between France and her African colonies. Before Tanhoe Bertin leaves African soil, he is warned that Parisians' relationship to time is not quite what he is used to as an African. Of course, a curious feature of his subsequent attempts to present time as a crucial element of intercultural understanding is that it depends on the temporal luxury of tourism: 'Tout ici est sujet à réflexion *pourvu qu'on en ait le temps* (*NP*, p. 80, my emphasis) ['Everything here is worth contemplating – *providing, of course, you have the time*', p. 59]. In other words, it is the specific temporal dimension of his way of travelling that permits him to contemplate the issue. Bertin, however, is less interested in the temporal qualities of tourism and more concerned with examining the contrast between what he sees as the slow, measured pace of life in his own country and the frenetic tempo of the daily routine in Paris. For Parisians, time is money and they slow down, as Dadié observes, only to look at their watches. Time, for them, is also 'une maladie incurable. Tous accrochés aux secondes, livrant au temps la plus exténuante des courses' (*NP*, p. 182) ['an incurable disease. They can't keep their eyes off the second hand; and as a result they're forever running an exhausting race against time', p. 128]. This race against the clock is evident in other areas of Parisian life – notably in women's various attempts to defy the ageing process, and the reliance on the speed and efficiency of the metro – but emerges most significantly in the link established between the hectic pace of life, increased productivity and materialism, and an apparent concomitant decrease in social values. Despite, or as we argued earlier, because of Dadié's gentle irony, wry comments regarding an obsession with flowers, pets and physical appearance means human relations in Paris appear less meaningful and seem to be in danger of being replaced by a regime of accumulation and alienation:

> Les machines, lancées, tournent et tout le pays avec elles, comme pris de vertige. Le mal du siècle est de tourner, de produire le plus possible, de créer des richesses. L'homme est devenu un rouage; et on lui donne tout juste ce qu'il faut pour jouer son rôle, tourner aussi.
>
> Je suis révolté quand je pense aux valeurs humaines qu'on a étouffées sciemment pour le plus grand malheur de l'humanité. (*NP*, p. 195)

> [But the machines keep turning and turning, and the whole country with them. It's like one big dizzying joyride. The great evil of this century is this constant push to produce as much as possible, to get richer and richer. Man has become nothing more than a cog in a wheel and he's provided with everything he needs to play that role, to keep spinning.
>
> I get absolutely livid when I think of all the truly important human values that have willingly been sacrificed to the utter detriment of all mankind.] (pp. 137–38)

Whilst such observations are clearly part of Dadié's reverse ethnographic project, they are also part of the lessons of travel, its 'field of usefulness' as was discussed in the introduction, which, we shall see, becomes a central feature of another seemingly conventional travelogue in this study, *L'Africain du Grœnland*. For if Dadié's observations of temporal reality provide him with an important insight into Paris and Parisians, they are just as relevant to imminently independent African colonies that, in their own way, are facing the dilemma of the traveller tempted to integrate into a Parisian (Western) way of life. Dadié's stopover in Dakar has highlighted the fact that Western cultural and economic models will continue to be imported into Africa. The Ivorian traveller notes that the Western-inspired bureaucratic practices and technological developments of the Senegalese capital point to a clear desire for 'progress'. However, as Dadié advances further on his route he becomes ever more aware that such progress will increasingly result in choices that reflect the dilemma of some travellers: will Africa adopt this model wholesale? Or will it manage to maintain its own identity in the face of a 'more progressive' foreign culture?

In a lengthy passage that is exemplary in this respect, Dadié switches from an emphasis on the Parisian 'they', and introduces the first-person plural 'we' in order to link a collective African dilemma to his own dilemma as a traveller-tourist. He has just described the French habit of saving for the future, for retirement and the next generation's education, and has seemed to suggest that this is a practice that Africans, with their penchant for living in the present, might be advised to emulate. However, as can be seen below, he subsequently reveals himself to be acutely aware that Africa, as it faces independence, is in a state of profound transition, where traditions are being lost and where there is insufficient reflection on what should replace them. The danger, in such a context, is that Africa will embrace values that are culturally unsuitable. For this reason, Dadié cautions against rushing headlong into the *adoption* of French practices for, as he argues, Africans are resolutely not French. Instead, he implies that Africa's relationship to France should be that of the astute, detached traveller who, through *critical observation*, comes to distinguish between what aspects of another culture can be *adapted* to benefit, enhance or revitalize the values of his/her own culture. (This explains his wish that 'Dieu fasse que nous profitons des leçons que nous donne Paris' (*NP*, p. 195) ['God grant that we benefit from the lessons Paris provides', p. 138].) Consequently, what Dadić advises is not emulation of the lifestyle or material values of Parisian society, but learning, as the traveller does, from the French capital's age-old valuing of its strengths and traditions. Clearly, Africa must be prepared to move forward. But, as Dadié emphasizes here, the continent's 'modernizing' project must be a self-conscious and critically comparative negotiation of its own values as well as those from which the continent would seek to learn:

> Face aux difficultés [auxquelles nous sommes confrontés], nous risquons d'adopter des mœurs que nous n'avions pas [...]. L'essentiel pour l'instant est de prendre hardiment position sur ces problèmes cruciaux, de retrousser les manches et de bâtir rapidement la nouvelle société, telle qu'elle pourra sauvegarder la chaude communauté d'hier et les exigencies actuelles d'une nation civilisée. Nous naissons dans un monde trop vieux qui voudrait nous faire adopter ses lenteurs, parce qu'il est convaincu que c'est la seule façon de créer durable, d'évoluer sûrement. [...] Nous aurions pu naître à Paris nous aussi et hériter des valeurs acquises, accumulées. La société nous aurait donné tous les moyens pour étudier, cultiver nos capacités. Dans le choc des valeurs, les nôtres résisteront-elles? Comment nous y prendre pour leur donner de la force. (*NP*, pp. 117–18)

[Given the difficulties [we face today], we risk adopting another's customs [...]. What we must do immediately is take a stand on the matter, roll up our sleeves and get busy constructing a new society, one that safeguards the warm community of yesterday and at the same time deals with the actual concerns of a modern civilized nation. We were born in a world that is now out-of-date, one, however, that continues to want us to move slowly. It's still convinced that crawling along inch by inch is the only way to create something lasting, the only way to evolve and progress. [...] We too could have been born in Paris, inherited all those values acquired and accumulated over the years. And society would have given us everything we needed to continue our education, to improve ourselves. What will happen to our own values? Will they endure as these cultures clash? What will we do to strengthen them?] (pp. 79–80)

For Dadié, it is travel, and particularly travel to Paris, that provokes such critical reflection on where he (Africa) has come from, and where he (Africa) is going. For the French capital appears to provide a model for Africans both to admire and to strive to emulate:

Cette ville [Paris] vous pousse à réfléchir. Il a connu toute une série d'invasions, d'occupations et chaque fois, il s'est retrouvé tel qu'il est: le même Paris. Il a toujours eu assez de force, de caractère pour faire face aux orages sans être emporté. Nous avons, ici, l'exemple d'un peuple décidé à rester lui-même. (*NP*, p. 119)

[Paris forces you to think. The city has faced one invasion and occupation after another, and yet it's still the same. Paris has always had the strength of character necessary to weather the storm and endure. Here we have an example of a people determined to remain true to themselves.] (p. 80)

The above discussion of a specifically Parisian tradition of self-belief and endurance also raises a complex temporal issue of another kind: the question of history, and its bearing on the present and the future. In certain respects, *Un Nègre à Paris* can be read as a form of potted history more usually associated with the travel guide book. From the moment Dadié arrives in Paris on the French national holiday of 14 July, the reader is immersed in the capital's history, and travels through time as the African tourist returns again and again to what appears initially to be the 'glorious' French past. Over the course of his text, this 'time travelling' functions to reinforce the sense of cultural transformation and evolution that is commonplace when describing Western history. However, what is notable in Dadié's case is the way in which he cleverly writes his own continent into this vision of sequential time. Most interesting, perhaps, is that in keeping with the understated tone of his book, this is not done in any contrived way, but through subtle and ironic asides.

Before dealing with Dadié's particular reinscription of Africa into the Western paradigm of evolutionary time, it is appropriate to recapitulate very briefly the temporal dimension of the West's appraisal of the Other as examined by Johannes Fabian in his well-known study of the eighteenth- and nineteenth-century development of Western anthropological praxis. For the influential ethnographer, Western anthropology is historically guilty of the distancing of those being observed from the time of the observer. This practice, Fabian argues, fed into political and economic discourses justifying the colonial enterprise:

> [Anthropology] promoted a scheme in terms of which not only past cultures, but all living societies were irrevocably placed on a temporal slope, a stream of Time – some upstream, others downstream. Civilization, evolution, development, acculturation, modernization (and their cousins, industrialization, urbanization) are all terms whose conceptual content derives, in ways that can be specified, from evolutionary Time. They all have an epistemological dimension apart from whatever ethical, or unethical intentions they may express. A discourse employing terms such as primitive, savage (but also tribal, traditional, Third World, or whatever euphemism is current) does not think, or observe, or critically study, the 'primitive'; it thinks, observes, studies *in terms* of the primitive. *Primitive* being essentially a temporal concept, is a category, not an object of Western thought.[28]

For Fabian, current anthropological discourse is still engaged in time-distancing practices, both in its disciplinary tendency to temporalize and chronologize, but more significantly in its exercise of allochronism, or what he refers to as the 'denial of coevalness': 'a *persistent and systematic tendency to place the referent(s) of anthropology in a Time other than the present of the producer of anthropological discourse.*'[29] In the context of contemporary Western travel writing, Debbie Lisle similarly notes the persistence of 'an important temporal distance between [the] factual observations [of Western travel writers] and their imagined destinations, between their "civilized" homes and "backward" destinations'. Tellingly, however, she also illustrates how the nostalgia inherent in this distancing project ultimately fails to 'secure a progressive, teleological and evolutionary account of history' because even the most 'backward' destinations show 'abundant signs of modernity'.[30] Lisle's specific critique of the unstable foundations of travel writing's timeline also leads her to conclude that travel writers 'can no longer act as unreconstructed anthropologists who situate foreign subjects back in the queue of history to be gazed upon and documented'.[31]

Initially, it would seem that Dadié's particular strategy for countering the Western view of history's 'queue' is a gentle, largely uncontroversial absolution of Western cultural and historical evolution conducted on the basis of relativization. As he observes with regard to the competing and contradictory historical descriptions of the fall of the Bastille: 'cela démontre surtout que comme nous, chacun présente une histoire selon son optique, son milieu' (*NP*, p. 28) ['it shows that each of us sees the past in our own particular way given our own particular upbringing', p. 18]. However, as Dadié journeys further into the French past, and ponders on the African future, it is clear that the 'stream of time' he envisages is more complex than it first appears. Whilst this visitor clearly admires French pride in their historical achievements he does not accept uncritically the notion of a simple linear narrative of French (and by extension Western) progress beginning with 'de pauvres gens qui habitaient de pauvres huttes' (*NP*, p. 97) ['a race of poor people who lived in poor huts', p. 65] and culminating in the sophisticated lifestyle practices of the modern city he is visiting.

Dadié's strategies for countering anthropological modes of thinking about time and evolution are subtle and varied. His repeated insistence on the similarities between Parisians and his own people – be it with regard to behaviour or history – suggest a simple denial of allochronism in favour of the argument that all human societies, regardless of important cultural differences, have undergone a long process of evolution and change. In other instances, Dadié is keen to stress the recursive – as opposed to sequential – nature of temporal influence. To take the question of cultural production, for example, Dadié stresses that the true origins and genius of French writing derive from an oral tradition that is not unlike that of vast parts of 'primitive' or non-developmentalist Africa. This argument is not premised on the notion that French writing is somehow more 'advanced' than African oral forms, but that ideas and cultural practices ebb and flow in time, as well as travelling across space. Failure to acknowledge this fact leads to the kind of judgments by the French on contemporary written African culture that are based at best on misinterpretation, at worst on ignorance (*NP*, p. 191 [p. 135]). Another effective strategy employed by Dadié to counter Western notions of temporality is to question the Western acceptance of a view of time governed by the teleology of scientific progress. We have already seen how Dadié exposes the underside of Western progress and modernity by emphasizing the accompanying decline in social values. However, his constant returns to the French past are also important reminders that the 'stages' leading to their notion of modernity have blinded the French to the exact nature of what was involved: progression to freedom and democracy certainly, but progression also through a series of arguably ever more violent and oppressive eras that hardly provide a temporal model worthy of emulation:

> Ce qui m'a inquiété, c'est que des Parisiens trouvent que nous voulons brûler les étapes. Cet illogisme au pays de la logique m'a terriblement effrayé de prime abord. Or à bien réfléchir, je soutiens que c'est le poids des ans qui leur fait tenir un tel langage. Un langage de vieillard. Où serait le rôle de flambeau que joue Paris s'il nous fallait repartir d'un haut Moyen âge, reviver les croisades, un siècle Louis XIV, des guerres sans fin? (*NP*, p. 192)

> [What disturbs me, however, is the fact that some Parisians think we want to race into the future without making the necessary stops along the way. Such statements on the part of an otherwise logical people scared me at first. But after mulling it over, I've come to the conclusion that the burdens of their own past make them think that way. It's the way an older person thinks. After all, how would Paris look if she forced us to return to the Middle Ages and relive the Crusades, let alone the age of Louis XIV and all those wars that form part of her history.] (p. 135)

Finally, Dadié's most controversial, or 'risky', strategy for questioning Western temporal thinking is to reposition the principal players on anthropology's stream of time. As ever, Dadié's comments are presented in his unmistakable ironic tone, but their implications are never in doubt. Whilst he accepts that Parisians may be 'ahead' of his own people in certain respects, in others he argues they are behind or are simply not as 'ancient' – as 'evolved' according to Western temporal logic – as they would have their colonized subjects believe. Sometimes, this process involves simply questioning, with characteristic wit, the label 'primitive' that is applied to certain African customs. For example, the rules of etiquette surrounding the African practice of eating with one's hands are described as being too sophisticated for the French to master (*NP*, p. 154 [p. 107]). Instead, Dadié suggests that the French have been forced to adapt to eating with cutlery, and devising a table etiquette that is more hierarchical than the social way of eating favoured by Africans (*NP*, p. 175 [p. 122]). At other times, Dadié is more explicit in his restaging of the Western slope of time. In the following quote, the travelling author unusually acknowledges the 'risk' he is taking in redirecting the ethnographic gaze. However, the risk is even greater here because not only is Dadié suggesting cultural similarities with Africa, he is also questioning the very foundations upon which Western temporality is built. Progress and evolution, he seems to argue, are not determined by how far you have travelled and where you have arrived, but by how long you have managed to survive. The humorous logic deployed to support the argument about the 'oldest' people on earth is not what matters here. Instead, Dadié is making a vital point about the need to reconceptualize time so that travel, whether of people or ideas, between Africa and the West can take place against a background of mutual respect:

> Plus je me penche sur [l'histoire] de ces gens, plus je trouve que leurs ancêtres en certains de leurs comportements, avaient beaucoup de points communs avec les nôtres. Ils vont se récrier, je le sais. Il ne le feront pas parce que cela peut avoir du vrai, mais parce que je semble les ramener à notre niveau, en arrière, oubliant du coup les millénaires d'efforts, le chemin qu'ils tracent au monde. [...] Qu'ils ne me fassent pas rire! S'ils étaient aussi vieux qu'ils le prétendent, ils auraient eu la peau noircie par le temps. Or à peine sont-ils bronzés! Ils ne peuvent pas soutenir être les plus vieux du monde, qu'ils se regardent tout de même! (*NP*, p. 126)

> [The longer I study [the history] of the Parisians, the more I realize how much their ancestors resembled ours. The Parisians would like to strongly argue the point, but they won't, not because it just might be true, but because I seem to be taking them backward, forgetting in one fell swoop the thousands and thousands of years of hard work they've put in to get to the place they've carved out for themselves in the world. [...] It's enough to make me laugh! If they were as old as they think they are, their skin would have darkened with age. But they're barely even tan! There's no way in the world they can say they're the oldest people in the world; they only need to look at themselves!] (pp. 85–86)

Also linked to the particular examination of Western temporality in *Un Nègre à Paris* are Dadié's observations on the significance of religion in the French capital. Given Dadié's boldness in challenging and deconstructing the temporal mainstays of Western notions of its own superiority, one might expect a similar undermining of Western religious practices. However, readers expecting a subtle exposé of the double standards of the Christian missionaries in Africa or a defence of indigenous religious practices will be disappointed. From the very opening pages, Dadié reveals himself to be a devout Christian who is clearly well versed in the doctrine and history of French Catholicism and is unwilling to question its essential premises. If there is an ideological foundation to his thinking, it would appear to be closer to New Testament-inspired morals of tolerance and equality than the radical politics of Marxism or anti-colonialism. Nonetheless, Dadié's observations on religion in Paris lead the reader to important conclusions regarding French society and its particular relationship to temporality.

First, the decline in social and moral values that Dadié regularly bemoans as a feature of Parisian life is seen to be as much a consequence of the religious hypocrisy of the French as a corollary of scientific progress. Essentially, the abandonment of religion and the growing sense of alienation in the French capital are seen as evidence of the divorce in French culture between religious theory and praxis. These double moral standards are also evident in the very fact of colonization that promotes a sort of 'house angel street devil morality' that leads to differential treatment of black Africans in the 'Christian' metropolitan centre and the more unlawful, wayward colonies:

> Ces Parisiens nous gardent, intacte, l'affection que leurs ancêtres avaient pour nous du temps où la mode était que chacun eût son négrillon. C'est vraiment un plaisir pour eux de nous recevoir. Mieux, ceux qui, chez nous, n'auraient jamais osé nous invité à leur table, ici, sont les premiers à le faire. Ils veulent prouver publiquement leur largeur d'esprit et donner le change aux leurs. (*NP*, p. 182)

> [The Parisians retain the same affection for us their ancestors had when it was fashionable for everyone to have a Negro servant. I can assure you it's truly a pleasure for them to welcome us. Even more, those who, back home, wouldn't dare to invite us to dinner, here, on the other hand, are the first to do so. They want everyone to see how broadminded they are and, at the same time, show those others how wrong they've been.] (p. 127)

In certain respects, it is possible to view this development as an illustration of the Western view of time that moves away from the sacred towards the secular. However, closer examination of *Un Nègre à Paris* reveals that such a rupture is not completely supported by the abundant signs of 'backwardness' in the 'modern' destination of Paris. In this way, Dadié aims to prove, in reverse, the inherent failed logic of Western travel writing's distancing project as identified by Debbie Lisle above. As Dadié's observations of Parisian society remind his readers, residues of a more 'pagan' time clearly remain, linking the French to an African view of the world, and disputing, once again, the simple notion of linear progress. In support of this argument Dadié cites the persistence in French secular life of superstition and irrational thought – evident, for example, in the special powers attributed to 'la branche de coudrier [...], le chat noir et la poule noire' (*NP*, p. 135) ['hazel tree [...], black cat and black chicken', p. 92] – as well as the French tendency to mix fact and fiction in accounts of events and characters of historical and religious importance:

> Aimant les légendes, les récits fabuleux, ils donnent à leurs héros des origines surnaturelles. Le naturel leur paraît trop simple pour convenir à leurs grands hommes. Ils affirment que l'arrière-grand-père de Clovis eut pour père un monster marin. Vraiment on peut être Parisien et raisonner comme un Agni... (*NP*, pp. 32–33)

> [Since they adore myths and fairy tales, they always give their heroes supernatural origins. The natural ones are too simple and, therefore, unsuitable for those whom they consider great and glorious. They maintain, for instance, that the great-great-grandfather of Clovis was a sea monster. It seems you can be a true Parisian and still reason like an Agni.] (p. 21)

The second point that emerges from Dadié's account of French religious practice is less obviously emphasized but nonetheless contributes to the overall politics of time explored in the text. Ultimately, by stressing the French mania with speed and progress, and the resulting hypocritical denial of the relevance of the 'irrational', the travelling African is making a subtle and powerful point about the so-called evolutionary sequences of France's culture. For, like the evolutionist anthropologists discussed by Johannes Fabian, the French tendency to make sense of their 'modern' culture and society in terms of 'evolutionary stages' is fundamentally reactionary because 'little more [has] been done than to replace faith in salvation by faith in progress and industry'.[32]

Clearly, the travelogue format of *Un Nègre à Paris* raises difficult questions for French readers whose history Dadié systematically
analyses from the outside. However, the value for a French readership of reading themselves as the 'Other's other' is also perhaps more
clearly underlined by the text's form than it is in *Mirages de Paris*
and *Kocoumbo, l'étudiant noir*. By forcing the French to look at their
culture and society through the eyes of a colonized traveller Dadié
succeeds in underlining France's achievements and failings in such
a way as to prompt the French to reflect upon their moral imperative with regard to Africa and its black colonial subjects. In this
way, Dadié clearly hopes to turn French superiority against itself and
thereby encourage the colonial power to accept responsibility for the
blatant injustices of its imperial policies.

It would be wrong, however, to see Dadié's observations as
applying uniquely to a French context. Dadié's essential 'humanism'
and tolerance refutes such a reading. On one level, his vision appears
to tie into a more generalized fear regarding the gradual erosion of
basic Christian values which, as we shall see in the next chapter, is
further explored in his representation of American capitalism as a
type of 'hypermodernity'. Dadié's African roots, as well as comments
explicitly directed towards an African readership, also return us to
the question of the split readership of francophone African textualizations of travel and the relevance of his travels (or its 'usefulness') to his fellow Africans. In *Un Nègre à Paris*, the primary goal
of Dadié's observations, I would argue, is the rethinking of how Africans and their former colonizers are to relate to each other in a post-
independence world. As his stopover in Dakar illustrates, aspects of
the frantic pace of modern, industrialized Paris are also evident in
the Senegalese capital, showing that colonial history has instigated
a contact that presents enormous challenges for a continent about
to embark on the process of postcolonial nation-building. Despite
the brutalizing history of colonial domination, Dadié's travels to the
heart of colonial power raises vital questions for the postcolonial
future. Are there things that Africa can learn from France, both from
its achievements, but also its failings? Does moving forward mean
rejecting the African past and embracing Western codes of living?
For Dadié, as for other African travellers of this crucial period in
the continent's history, it would appear that the self-reflective and
comparative dimensions of travel must constitute the cornerstone of
any thinking on these issues.

CHAPTER FOUR

Atlantic Travels:
Beyond the Slave Ship?

The proliferation in recent decades of critical work devoted to the cultural and political life of inter-war 'black France' attests to a growing recognition of the role of transatlantic travel in the rise of an international black movement.[1] Scholars of Negritude and African American literature and culture of the period from the 1920s to the 1950s have focused on the French capital in particular so as to elucidate the manner in which dynamic transnational interaction and cultural and intellectual exchange contributed to new versions of black identity during this period. For Brent Hayes Edwards, the transnational and 'translated' perspective afforded by the emphasis on 1920s 'Paris noir', for example, permits an important shift away from the 'U.S-bound themes of cultural nationalism, civil rights protests, and uplift in the literary culture of the "Harlem Renaissance"' that characterizes much of the critical work on African American culture of this period.[2] Indeed, as Edwards points out, attending to the particular nature of Paris-based black internationalism reveals the Harlem Renaissance to be 'merely the North American component of something larger and greater'.[3] In his book, *Black France: Colonialism, Immigration and Transnationalism*, Dominic Thomas also underscores the defining role played by Paris as a nexus for a diverse range of ideas that led not just to new ways of conceiving blackness but also to new conceptions of national boundaries and identities.

Undoubtedly, this convergence on Paris as a crucial point of intersection for black culture is an important critical development. However, although references to a vital criss-crossing of the Atlantic in the development of black political and cultural sensibilities are not excluded, the overwhelming emphasis is split between the type of Europe-bound African American travel highlighted in the title of Michel Fabre's study, *From Harlem to Paris* – this axis of movement also includes Antillean travel to Europe – or the north-bound journey of Africans to Paris. Whilst the absence of critical attention to other travellers and directions of travel is entirely understandable – the preceding chapters have already highlighted the complex centripetal allure of Paris for Francophone Africans, but geographical and financial considerations also played their part in the small number of texts devoted to other axes of travel during this period – it does not tell the whole story. Indeed, impressive as the growing body of scholarship on 'black Paris' is, converging on the French capital in order to explore the complex transnational network of black relations arguably threatens to reinforce at some level a colonial geography of political and cultural domination. Of course, operating exclusively within this framework also risks the creation of a reductive topography that excludes other networks of exchange that either bypass or extend beyond the European centre. For example, frequently overlooked in studies of the rise of black internationalism are the 'vagabond' trajectories of francophone figures such as René Maran, Prince Kojo Tovalou-Houenou and Frantz Fanon.[4]

My interest in this chapter, however, is more specific than the trajectories just mentioned or the extensive topic of African, Antillean and African American interaction with Europe. Instead, a primary concern of the following pages will be two texts that present a black transnational Atlantic exchange emanating from west-bound transatlantic travel and focusing on an American point of intersection. Despite the very different style and form of Lamine Diakhaté's *Chalys d'Harlem* and Bernard Dadié's *Patron de New York*, both these texts provide an important theoretical impetus for reconceptualizing African intercontinental travel as more complex and geographically diverse than the dominant accounts of European journeys would suggest.[5] In their way, they contribute to the complex genealogies which Agustin Lao-Montes sees as crucial to the project of '[mapping] the myriad of histories, identities, cultural-intellectual currents, and political projects that compose the African Diaspora and the Black Atlantic'.[6] The focus in these texts on Africans in America also points to a critical failure – understandable perhaps because of the paucity of relevant examples – to devote attention to African cultural influences in America beyond those that have survived from slavery, or been romantically and ideologically projected onto African American dreams of a return to the 'mother continent'.[7] Likewise, studies of the influence of American culture in African countries tend to provide a focus for the question of 'return journeys' made by the descendants of African slaves rather than any sustained engagement with how Africans themselves view America and its culture.[8]

Diakhaté's 1978 text *Chalys d'Harlem* is a fictionalized biography of the Senegalese-born but naturalized American Chalys Leye. Leye is a former sailor who settles in Harlem in 1919 where he becomes a recognized political activist and, later, owner of a well-frequented diner, the 'Leye-Lunchonett' (sic).[9] Despite what could be construed as a cumbersome style, frequently incoherent plot and largely unconvincing attempts to create page-turning suspense, *Chalys d'Harlem* holds significant cultural and historical interest for the contemporary reader. Set against the historical, political and economic background of 1920s–1950s Harlem, Chalys's story is a rare example of a return journey amongst African representations of intercontinental travel. From Chalys's Atlantic crossing as a crew member aboard a steam ship to his successes and failures in Harlem, and finally to his return visit to Senegal more than forty years later, the text plots in particular the entrepreneurial successes of Chalys, his wife and daughters as they overcome the racial, political and especially economic challenges of the time. However, the text is not simply a biography of Chalys but also links, through the voice of its Senegalese narrator, Omar Fall, the American adventure with political developments in a newly independent Senegal. Although never explicitly stated, we are led to believe that Fall's presence in New York in July 1959, where he chances to meet Chalys, is not just linked to a 'holiday' but may be in some way related to an unspecified role at the headquarters of the United Nations.[10]

Like *Un Nègre à Paris*, Dadié's account of a 1963 six-month trip to the United States, *Patron de New York*, appears to be inspired by the structure of a conventional Western-style travelogue. The distinctive ironic tone of the American text also ties it to the earlier Parisian text. Yet in its account of American life and culture *Patron de New York* is decidedly more impressionistic and frustrates more explicitly the imperatives of chronological and spatially linear narrative normally associated with travel narratives of this kind.[11] Like Diakhaté, Dadié is also acutely aware of America's image as a place where individual endeavour is respected and rewarded. However, whereas Diakhaté sees this fact as providing a positive spur to social and economic advancement, Dadié's particular perspective is more attuned to the ambiguities of America's rhetoric of progress, as well as to the pitfalls of its capitalist work ethic. Another important difference in

Dadié's text concerns the portrayal of Harlem: Diakhaté's emphasis on Harlem as a black 'ghetto' in fact highlights the district's role as a close-knit, ethnic haven that somehow tempers issues of inequality and discrimination. On the other hand, Dadié's fleeting, almost superficial references to the New York neighbourhood reveal his desire to focus on a more global view of American society in order to highlight the all-pervasive issue of racial inequality. For this reason, his American travelogue can be read as a counter view to Diakhaté's upholding of the American way as a social and economic model for newly independent African nations.

Reading the texts back to front and following the chronology of the two narratives rather than the dates of publication, this chapter will focus on the respective portraits of American society as revealed in *Chalys d'Harlem* and *Patron de New York*. I am especially interested in examining the significance in both texts of the means of transport used for transatlantic travel. Consequently, in the two sections of this chapter ships and planes will be used as critical tropes that permit a figurative understanding of the very different ways African travellers relate to America and its culture in the era leading up to, and immediately succeeding, independence.

Chalys d'Harlem: *The economics of travel*

Before examining the question of a black Atlantic community in *Chalys d'Harlem*, it is worth devoting some space to the text's unusual emphasis on the question of economics. In the introduction to this study, reference was made to the unspoken economic power of Western travellers, and the impact of material comfort on the practices and textualizations of travel. In this respect, African narratives of travel were also said collectively to make a crucial point about the ways in which material conditions affect the attitudes and itineraries of travellers from that continent. However, *Chalys d'Harlem* arguably goes further than this by building its narrative of cultural encounter almost entirely around the question of labour and economics. Certainly, the privileging of economic questions can hardly be said to be surprising given that the text deals largely with 1920s and 1930s America, a notoriously unstable period in that country's social and economic history. Moreover, the resonance of the middle passage within the framework of transatlantic studies, the critical approach broadly underpinning this chapter, means that questions of trade and capital should not be neglected in favour of more abstract notions of cultural translation and exchange. Finally, it is also reasonable that in any discussion of a former colony's attempts to assert itself as an independent nation there should be some mention of economic issues. What seems unusual in Diakhaté's text, however, is a certain underplaying of the heady cultural and political activity that tends to predominate in common perceptions of Harlem of this era. Ultimately, despite brief references to jazz and to 'New Negro' literature, it is the blunt question of economic survival – on an individual but also a community level – that supplants cultural and political preoccupations and emerges as key to understanding Harlem's distinctive identity.[12]

Despite the atypical thematic focus of *Chalys d'Harlem*, the question of economics, focused as it is on Harlem, proves to be an exceptionally effective means for understanding black American life and culture as seen through the eyes of the main protagonist, but also as lived by him. More than anything, the economic life of Chalys and his family – his trajectory from steamship crew member to employee in a white-run restaurant, associate in a black-run supermarket and finally owner, along with his wife and daughters, of their own diner and tailoring businesses – emerges as part of a general picture of one of the major tenets of the 'American dream': the acquisition of material success and economic stability. However, if the focus is on the 'self-made man', it is in order to examine the travelling *homo economicus* as a practical model for successful cultural and economic integration not just for African Americans but later for an independent, self-sustaining Senegal seeking to find its place in a globalized world.

Given that Chalys lives and works through the economically unstable 1920s and subsequent Great Depression, the achievement of personal economic stability is not a smooth-run course. For example, discussion of the 1927 Pan-African Congress in New York – an event that represents a focal point in the early stages of Chalys's narrative – highlights the amount of attention devoted to unemployment and its repercussions for black Americans. Throughout, the spectre of a stalling economy, joblessness and decreased purchasing power looms large, providing a backdrop to the challenges faced by Chalys, but also by black political leaders of the time. It is, therefore, all the more remarkable that in the declining economic situation leading

to the 1929 stock market crashes Chalys decides to resign from a
secure restaurant position in order to play a full role in a demonstration coinciding with the end of the Pan-African Congress. Diakhaté's
failed attempts at building suspense are most evident here when we
learn that the city authorities, due to an alleged threat of violence,
have cancelled the demonstration. Over several chapters – which
amount to just several hours in real time – the reader's attention is
maintained through the build-up of a will-they-won't-they tension
surrounding the decision to march. The issue is eventually resolved
in an understated pronouncement by local black activists who accept
the ban and propose instead a series of individual meetings to take
place in Harlem's various districts and to be attended by Congress
leaders. A triumphant, festive atmosphere characterizes these meetings but any sense of the political significance or ideological defiance
motivating this strategy seems undermined in the text by a sudden
shift in focus to the personal and professional dilemma of the by-now
redundant Chalys.

Once again the foregrounding of economics in the text compen-
sates for any disappointment the reader may feel at the apparent
neglect of cultural and historical contexts. For careful attention reveals
that what Diakhaté wants to highlight are not the facts surrounding
the failed demonstration, but rather what he sees as the economic
direction underpinning post-1927 African American and pan-African
ideology.[13] Chalys's description of this new-found conceptual 'matu-
rity' is centred on a speech given by one of the Congress leaders to his
district, where it is announced that the pan-African movement is now
ready to move beyond a merely oppositional role in order to provide
concrete solutions to the questions of civil rights, black identity and
economic disadvantage, issues which, it is stressed, are profoundly
imbricated.

The concern for Chalys's professional future that preoccupies
disappointed militants on the evening the march is banned should
not then be seen as a deferral to the purely personal and apolitical by
Diakhaté. Instead, Chalys's dilemma becomes a means to explore how
practical solutions to the situation of America's black population, and
later newly independent Senegal, might be configured. Significantly,
Chalys's ability to weather the storm of economically depressed
America can be said to stem first from the importance of travel to his
own identity. A descendant of a people believed to have travelled by
boat to the Senegalese coast and who subsequently settled there, Chalys

frequently suggests that his destiny has been profoundly shaped by a life spent in close proximity to the Atlantic.[14] His character thereby provides an excellent opportunity to examine the distinctive effects produced when the experience of travel is framed by the history and politics of the black Atlantic. 'Je suis fils de la mer Atlantique' [I am a son of the Atlantic] (*CH*, p. 47), he observes, suggesting that this heritage has provided him with a venturesome spirit and instinctive seafaring skills which make him more than suitable for his first chosen profession as crew member aboard a transatlantic steamship. Intuitive awareness, too, of Europe's weakened post-war economic status – gleaned from travelling between the continent's main ports – and the potentially negative effects of rationalization and the amelioration of technology in the maritime transport industry finally prompt Chalys and his Senegalese companions to abandon a life on the sea in favour of a life on the American Atlantic coast.

In earlier chapters, the symbolic importance of the ship in colonial African accounts of intercontinental travel was highlighted as a means of thinking figuratively about African experiences of intercontinental travel. However, in *Mirages de Paris* and *Kocoumbo*, the African traveller's status as passenger served predominantly to frame a nascent awareness of a debilitating double consciousness, and the hierarchical pattern of his travel conditions on board the ship was also seen both to link back – albeit in a highly complex manner – to the uprooting of slavery and forward to the displacement of mass immigration. *Chalys d'Harlem*, on the contrary, provides another way of looking at the ship's significance that reminds us of the dangers, outlined by Paul Gilroy, of 'viewing black people's experiences of displacement and relocation exclusively through the very different types of travelling undergone by refugees, migrants, and slaves'.[15] Thus Chalys's early professional experience emphasizes the fact that not all transatlantic routes have imperial connections, nor are they necessarily routes of power. In addition, despite the former sailor's subordinate role within the professional ranks of the ship, and his awareness of the implications of his 'racial' identity, his transatlantic travel provides him with a sense of the economic opportunities arising from a life of mobility. In this way we see how he exploits his contacts in shipping – made through the connecting practices of travel – to source ingredients for his restaurant trade, and how he uses his encounters with Atlantic cultures to design an international menu that proves highly successful. Ties of friendship made during his time on the sea have also stood the test of time and of personal economic trials, and aspects of Chalys's political and ideological beliefs are also shown to have been directly informed both by solidarity with fellow seamen and by struggles to improve working conditions aboard the steamship.

Put succinctly, it is Chalys's seafaring experiences that have taught him to survive during times of economic and professional uncertainty. For Tom Nissley, this capacity for self-sustainment is fundamental to defining the American notion of the self-made man, and reaches back to the trajectory followed by former slaves such as Benjamin Franklin and Frederick Douglass.[16] Clearly, however, a significant divergence between Chalys's self-making process and the trajectories of those such as Franklin and Douglass emerges where the issue of slavery is concerned. As Nissley describes it, the figure of the self-made man in African American literature hinges on a fundamental paradox: owning oneself depends on the ability to sell oneself – or at least the part of the self constituted by labour. The resulting threat of a re-enslavement of sorts, as well as the potential anxiety stemming from 'the problem of the self being represented by something outside of the self – money for example', creates an undeniable drama of alienation.[17] (A sense of alienation is not entirely absent from the Senegalese version of the American Dream but emerges for very different reasons as I will demonstrate below.) In addition, Nissley's emphasis on the problematic dependency of many self-made former slaves on the figure of the patron sheds light on another fundamental difference in Chalys's economic fortunes. For where Nissley seems to suggest that the labour relations between former slave and patron constitute a form of Marxist alienation, Chalys is seen, first, to abandon wage labour, and, subsequently, to apply his entrepreneurial skills and his ambition as much to the benefit of the wider black community of Harlem as to reasons of purely personal economic advancement. In return, it is his friends and advisors, rather than patrons, who are seen to assist him in a relationship that allows all concerned to profit from a mutually beneficial form of economic progress.

Despite these crucial differences, *Chalys d'Harlem* is nonetheless clearly influenced by the American model of the self-made man. This is most evident when one looks more closely at the heuristic value attributed to Chalys's efforts for economic success. In this respect, *Chalys d'Harlem* can be seen to fulfil an important 'exemplary' function of the autobiographies of former American slaves outlined by Nissley:

The writer's representation of his life story constructs an implicit or explicit prescription for the labouring black population, as well as an exhibition for a larger, mostly white, public of the qualities that those blacks should be assumed to possess. [...] The conditions of their narrative self-presentation – of intimacy, sincerity, and reputation – are much the same as the conditions that govern the labour contract and the accumulation of capital under the system of free labour, and their narrative position, no less than their own careers as labourers, stand as representatives for how the freed people of the South might negotiate the conditions of their own work.[18]

As Nissley sees it, being representative in this context does not mean 'merely to be an example but to be exemplary [...]; to be ideal rather than merely typical'.[19] And this is precisely how Chalys is seen, if not always by himself, then by his friends in Harlem who clearly see his professional decisions as having economic significance beyond the mere potential for individual upward mobility. Thus, for example, the disappointment of Chalys's Harlem friends at his decision to resign from his post in the restaurant can be understood in terms of the negative repercussions arising from what they perceive initially to be a less than 'exemplary' choice. Not only does Chalys, an important 'representative' role model in the community, risk unemployment and, therefore, his reputation, he is also abandoning any possibility of securing employment for others within his community in the restaurant trade.[20] Ultimately, however, Chalys's decision to resign proves to be an astute one that copper-fastens his standing as a model of integrity and economic success. Further forays with his close friend Davidson into the burgeoning supermarket business during the economic uncertainty and deteriorating racial relations of the Great Depression and Roosevelt's New Deal prove to be an unqualified success. This eventually leads to the establishment of his own restaurant business, an entrepreneurial venture that he sees as being rooted in the values of community and friendship.

If Chalys's propensity for 'staying afloat' can be understood within the context of the American self-made man, then the continued relevance of transatlantic travel in Chalys's life story suggests a more international significance for this quality, a significance that takes into account the place of Chalys's relationship with his native Senegal as the country moves from colony to independent nation. Illuminating in this respect is William Boelhower's analysis of the influential eighteenth-century autobiography of former slave Olaudah

Equiano.[21] Focusing on one key scene in the narrative, Boelhower describes the surprise of a certain Captain Pascal who, having previously sold Equiano into slavery for a second time and returned him to the Caribbean, meets the by now free African thanks to a chance encounter in London. Upon being asked *how* he returned to Europe, the former slave curtly replies, 'in a ship'. For Boelhower the answer illustrates Equiano's determination to buy his freedom and, as Douglass and Franklin will later do, become 'the sole determinant of [his] labour and its products'.[22] However, Boelhower, like Paul Gilroy in *The Black Atlantic*, also sees the former slave's enigmatic reply as pointing to the ship's broader figurative value, i.e. as a means of understanding the particular nature of the ebb and flow of transatlantic cultural and intellectual movements: 'By linking the earlier scene of Equiano's departure with his return, the ship stands for the principle of reversibility itself. For an ex-slave, learning how to flow literally means learning how to loop one's way across the Atlantic both as ocean and as the heuristic surface of a new order.'[23]

In a similar way, Chalys's return journey to Senegal can be viewed as evidence of a belief in an emerging new order, one that he places 'de l'autre côté de la mer Atlantique, là bas' [on the other side of the Atlantic, over there] (*CH*, p. 167) but which is intimately connected with black America as he has experienced it. In effect, it is a system underpinned by movement and exchange, where trade, travel and economics remain vital elements, but where the significance of African transatlantic journeys is being profoundly reshaped. Returning once again to the symbolic role of the ship, but this time in relation to Chalys's eastern-bound return journey to Senegal, it is possible to see how travel is conceived as 'a field of usefulness' for post-colonial African economies. However, unlike the above mentioned 'exemplary' narratives by former slaves that seek to establish the economic credentials of America's black population for a predominantly white American audience, Diakhaté's aim is arguably more ambitious, at least in its geographical reach. Thus, in the final section of *Chalys d'Harlem*, Chalys's own trajectory, and his seafaring experience, become the basis upon which to build an 'exemplary' economic model that can launch independent Senegal on to the global stage.

Although Chalys shows an interest in the country of his birth throughout the text – sometimes from the nostalgic perspective of one who has no sense of its evolution during the period of his absence – it is the advent of independence that finally prompts him to return.

In contrast to an America paralysed by the seemingly intractable problem of racial inequality, newly independent Senegal appears to Chalys to have donned the mantle of economic and ideological ambition that was so seductive to him as a young man newly arrived in Harlem. However, for this 'marin de formation' [sailor by training] (*CH*, p. 191) the decision to return is one based not on simple curiosity, but on the belief that his personal trajectory is 'exemplary'. Once again, the image of the ship is linked to economic progress, but this time travel and the shipping trade are directly cited as activities that can contribute to Senegal's nation-building process. Indeed, Chalys quite literally imagines his country of origin following the sea routes he has already traced in order to assert itself economically in a postcolonial, globalized world:[24]

> Il accordait une importance toute particulière aux problèmes de la navigation maritime. Il voyait déjà des paquebots battant pavillon sénégalais refaire la route qu'il fit jadis, lui-même, à plusieurs reprises autour du monde. Peut-être, pensait-il, le pays aura besoin de son expérience. (*CH*, p.167)

> [He saw the issue of maritime navigation as being of crucial importance. He could already imagine ships flying the Senegalese flag and following the route he himself had taken on several occasions around the world. Perhaps, he thought, the country will benefit from my experience.]

Whilst there can be no doubting Chalys's commitment to Senegal, the final section of his life story, describing his return journey, also highlights an undeniable sense of alienation that has been largely absent from the Harlem section of the text. The question 'what will Chalys do?' raised by the Harlem community in reference to his economic plight is replaced in Senegal by a determination to 'décéler le mal dont [il] souffrirait' [to discover what could be wrong with him] (*CH*, p. 209). In effect, the complex, and often ambiguous, feelings provoked by the rediscovery of his country of origin awaken in Chalys a profound sense of unease that displaces the text's focus from the resolutely economic to the psychological. Indeed, the self-reflective tendencies that have come to be associated with travel only come to the fore when Chalys realizes he has become a first-world 'traveller' observing and interpreting his former African 'home'. (Needless to say, this shows once again how de Certeau's notion of Western travel writing's historical frame needs to be rethought in the context of African practices and textualizations of travel.) Feeling increasingly isolated and distanced from people and cultural habits that have either evolved in his absence or become alien to his own philosophy, Chalys admits to himself that where his relationship to Senegal is concerned, 'il n'était pas loin de se croire un modèle, une manière d'archétype' [he hadn't been far from believing himself to be a model, a sort of archetype] (*CH*, p. 198). However, this sense of his personal travelling trajectory as 'exemplary' has also, he finally realizes, been tinged by a subliminal superiority complex that has made him blind to the necessity of fusing local knowledge and traditions with the lessons of his own travel experiences. Once again, it is travel's self-reflective propensities that offer a first important step towards correcting his distorted perspective:

> Chalys s'émerveillait de constater que le bon sens, la logique et l'expérience constituaient la dalle de ce qu'il est convenu d'appeler la 'sagesse populaire' dans tous les pays. Sans le vouloir, il s'était senti, à son arrivée, quelque peu supérieur [...].
>
> Au fil des jours, il se convainquit qu'il lui fallait descendre de son piédestal, se mêler plus intimement à ses parents et amis qui l'assiégeaient journellement. (*CH*, pp.198–99)

> [Chalys was amazed to discover that everywhere common sense, logic and experience were the foundations of what is known as 'popular wisdom'. Without meaning to, he had felt a little 'superior' on arrival [...].
>
> As the days went by, he became convinced that he needed to come down from his pedestal, and mix more closely with the relatives and friends who besieged him on a daily basis.]

This is a rare admission of the negative aspects of unreflective travel practices and of prolonged stays in the West that in many ways mirror the alienation of Senegal's colonial, and soon to be ruling, elite: a distancing from the culture of origin, and an uncritical belief in the value of the colonizer's culture. In the specific geographical context of *Chalys d'Harlem*, this is also the only suggestion that the 'American way' may not contain all the answers to the challenges facing newly independent Senegal. Indeed, until this point, there has been no critical awareness of the shortcomings and inherent social injustices of an economic system built on free market trade and meritocracy. In addition, Chalys never questions capitalist modes of industrial development and international trade nor their historically exploitative and colonial origins.[25] The text's portrayal of Harlem, and the

United States more generally, underplays the inequality unleashed by an unquestioning belief in capitalism, an issue that forms the basis for some of the canonical works of American literature.

This final comparison of Chalys's 'return' with Senegal's emergence from colonial rule provides an opportunity in the text to discuss some of the political and artistic opportunities available to the alienated and travelled elite who wish to participate in rebuilding the nation. In particular, the beliefs of the proponents of Negritude and those supporting 'engagement politique' [political engagement] (*CH*, p. 203) are examined, with the text revealing a clear bias in favour of the former. Despite this, however, the focus on Chalys could be said to represent a possible 'third way'. The self-reflective nature of his return journey convinces him that he is not the 'toubab' [white man] some of his Senegalese friends and family believe him to be. Nor is he the person he was when he first left his native country to sail the Atlantic. Instead he has been shaped by his travels, by hard work and by the largely successful integration of his African identity into the particular cultural and economic identity of Harlem. However, the key to his identity, and by extension to that of newly independent Senegal, is hinted at in a sort of epiphany that takes place in the text's closing pages. Standing by the Atlantic shore, and watching the tide ebb and flow, Chalys is reminded that this is where his ancestors have come from: this is, then, the space that has defined his life, and arguably that of America and Senegal. Chalys's decision to return to Harlem cannot, therefore, be seen as a final abandoning of his country of birth but as an acknowledgement that he belongs to both sides of the Atlantic. As he flies once more back across the ocean his professed commitment to a continued to and fro relationship with Africa underscores the central role the continent will continue to play for him. At the same time, his acknowledgement of the fundamental role of transatlantic travel, both to his past and to his future, is a powerful evocation of the intertwined histories and destinies of Africa and America.

Patron de New York: *Aviation and the new world order*

In the closing pages of *Chalys d'Harlem* it is the aeroplane that replaces the ship, thereby subtly linking aviation with a new era in American-African transatlantic dialogue. This fact provides a felicitous point of departure for discussion of Bernard Dadié's 1963 visit to America as the Ivory Coast's first minister of culture.[26] For Dadié, Atlantic airspace is 'cet autre océan' (*PNY*, p. 20) ['that other ocean', p. 10] with its own travel symbol, or chronotope, the aeroplane, crystallizing the nature of cultural, political and economic forces that flow back and forth across it in an emerging new world order. The aeroplane also forms part of a broader metaphorical emphasis on machines in *Patron de New York* that, for Michael Syrotinski, suggests 'an increasing mechanization and technologization of life as a fundamental characteristic of American society'.[27] Needless to say, the particular function of the aeroplane also emphasizes its role as a *travelling* marker of 'Americanness' as it carries its African passenger westwards. It is important to note, however, that in *Patron de New York*, the cultural coding of the aeroplane differs slightly to that attributed to this same mode of transport in *Kocoumbo, l'étudiant noir*. In Loba's text, the aeroplane pointed to French, and broadly Western, values and practices that, ultimately, were seen as desirable for Africans. In *Patron de New York*, such certainty about the American values symbolized by the aeroplane and air travel does not exist. On the contrary, the sense that America and Americanization constitute a menace as much as a positive force is never quite contained. The following section will focus, therefore, on the text's opening description of the flight to America in order to examine how Dadié seizes upon the aeroplane as a means of introducing the salient features of an internationally travelling American culture.

Quite apart from his prescient comments on the penchant of airlines for stripping away the personal, transportable luxuries of travel and revealing a less client-friendly attitude, Dadié's description of the transatlantic stage of his journey is particularly concerned with passenger interaction, or lack thereof, within the tight space of the aeroplane. Certainly, the relationship between technology and travel, the emphasis on comfort and service and the use of an international yet comprehensible gestural language by the flight crew all seem to point to a concerted effort to introduce the intimacy and familiarity of 'home', or the local, into this global travelling space. However, with characteristic irony, Dadié notes that, in fact, everything is arranged to promote a retreat into the self and an avoidance of interaction with other passengers:

> Un siège profond dans lequel je me noie. Des prises d'air et des lumières individuelles. Vous pouvez tout faire sans déranger le

voisin. Chacun est chez soi. Me voici dans l'avion de la liberté et de l'individualité. Un monde de voyageurs séparés par des fauteuils. (*PNY*, p. 16)

[I sink into a deep seat, noticing air vents and individual lights, set to do everything without disturbing my neighbour: each person is at home. Here I'm on the plane of freedom and individualism separated by seats.] (p. 8)

Dadié's aim in this description, and later in his account of a brief conversation with a fellow passenger, is not primarily to highlight the fleeting, arbitrary encounters of late twentieth-century travel practices.[28] Rather, the travelling author's emphasis on air travel's promotion of an unashamed individualism provides a stepping stone for delving into what he sees as the many negative consequences of America's ambiguous pursuit of progress. Thus, the luxury of air travel is later revealed to be a reflection of the country's general wealth and abundance. However, rather than leading to greater social interaction and cohesion, this affluence has given rise to growing loneliness and alienation, even in the most social contexts:

On a beau réunir les citoyens dans les bureaux, les mêler dans les cafeteria, le subway, les usines, ils paraissent demeurer étrangers les uns aux autres, chacun poursuivant ses rêves et cherchant obstinément son étoile dans la bannière nationale. (*PNY*, p. 133)

[It's useless to get Americans together in offices, mix them in cafeterias or the subway; they remain strangers, each one tenaciously pursuing his own dreams, each one stubbornly trying to make it.] (p. 71)

In direct contrast to *Chalys d'Harlem*, where hard work is seen as the cornerstone upon which to build the American dream, Dadié's *Patron de New York* emphasizes the dystopian aspects of this unqualified faith in grafting: a relentless capitalist work ethic that promotes individualism and self-interest. In addition, unlike certain African-American representations of the self-made man mentioned earlier, where re-enslavement of capitalist labour practices is seen as a threat to America's black population, Dadié sees *all* Americans at risk from becoming 'asservi à la machine et à l'argent' (*PNY*, p. 294) ['enslaved to machines and money', p. 157]. In this country of excessive consumerism, of which Dadié gives innumerable examples, it is suggested that the dollar reigns supreme, and an individual's worth is measured by the size of his or her bank account. However, if

Dadié is at pains to stress America's near veneration of the individual, he also points to an ambiguous feature of this tendency: an over-whelming sense of conformity.[29] In his repeated reference to one-way systems, including interminable airport corridors, Dadié evokes the image of a society marshalling its citizens towards the same goals and aspirations.[30] Indeed, the 'assimilative power of affluence', as Richard Kuisel terms it, ensures little deviation from the norm and a mentality that considers it to be '[du] mauvais ton que d'être hors du circuit, du courant, de ne pas faire comme les autres' (*PNY*, p. 96) ['bad taste to be out of sync, different', p. 51].

An effective metaphorical function of the aeroplane and air travel practices is also discernible in Dadié's strategy of using them to examine the significance of speed to American life. Needless to say, one of the most distinguishing consequences of the growth in air travel has been time-space compression, a development that has accentuated Western travel writing's rhetoric of planetary exhaustion and travel's increasing 'artificiality' as airborne travellers are said to skim the surface of a world that has already been 'discovered'. As with the other texts examined here, Dadié's text in fact reveals the endless worlds and possibilities travel continues to open up. Likewise, although Dadié appears largely uninterested in the relevance of air travel's speed and 'artificiality' to a specifically travel-related discourse, he explicitly links the invention of the aeroplane with America's need to save time (*PNY*, p. 172 [p. 92]) and thereby, he seems to suggest, immerse itself in mere surface experience. If he were more interested in speed's relationship to the evolution of travel practices, Dadié might comment upon the fact that, in contrast to Chalys's 1919 maritime journey, the speed of his transatlantic flight immediately evokes the possibility of return and indicates an important shift in new mean-ings and directions for intercontinental travel. His previously noted gift for prescience might also prompt him to foresee a link between growing acceleration and greater numbers travelling for recreational purposes. However, what interests Dadié is extrapolating the notion of air travel's speed to America's devotion to the culture of speed more generally. For example, within the plane itself, a passenger with a copy of the *Reader's Digest*, 'un consommé de nouvelles' (*PNY*, p. 16) ['a condensation of the news', p. 8], fascinates Dadié:

> Notre lectrice, à l'exemple de ses collègues, n'aime pas gaspiller son temps dans les détails que l'on trouve certainement inutiles et encombrants. Économie! L'Amérique ne paraît pas un pays de

poètes, de rêveurs. Des spécialistes apprêtent pour leurs compatriotes le peu qu'ils doivent savoir pour briller dans les salons et brûler
les étapes. Un pays très pressé de se hisser on ne sait à quel niveau
dans le monde et dans l'esprit des gens. Un Reader's digest! N'est-ce
pas mettre des œillères aux lecteurs, cultiver leur paresse mentale,
tuer en eux la féconde curiosité? (*PNY*, p. 17)

[Our reader, like her compatriots, dislikes wasting time on details she
would certainly find useless and cumbersome. Waste not! America
does not seem to be a country of poets and dreamers. Specialists
prepare for their fellow citizens the minimum they must know to
shine at parties and get ahead. A country in a great hurry to climb
to who knows what level both in the world and in the hearts and
minds of her people. A Reader's Digest! Is that not putting blinkers
on readers, cultivating mental sloth and killing their pregnant
curiosity?] (p. 8)

The suggestion here is that, consistent with their predilection for
speedy methods of travel, Americans prefer hasty outcomes and
uncomplicated choices that lead them to skim over the surface of
issues. Thus, in political life, the uncluttered choice between Demo-
crats and Republicans is described as a *Reader's Digest* system, and
in commercial and economic life, the price of success is an ability
to 'gallop', stopping only to 'prendre du carburant' (*PNY*, p. 164)
['refuel', p. 88]. Indeed, speed of mobility – subways, air travel and
the numerous references to American highways and one-way systems
– is said to be the means by which America not only dazzles newly
arrived immigrants, but succeeds in integrating them by creating
a kind of sensory confusion that eliminates less desirable cultural
characteristics (namely idleness and, by extension, lack of speed) and
facilitates integration:

Elle leur offre [à ses communautés d'immigrés] ses magnifiques
autostrades afin de les brasser, les étourdir, les griser de vitesse pour
les amener à se débarrasser elles-mêmes des scories qui pourraient
les empêcher d'être des dignes enfants des United States of America.
(*PNY*, p. 132)

[She offers them her magnificent highways to stir them up, to deafen
them, to dazzle them with speed so that they will get rid of the traces
that could prevent them from being worthy children of the United
States of America.] (p. 71)

Linked also to America's cult of the individual, speed and haste are
seen to discourage more meaningful social interaction. Thus Dadié

sees the absence of café and restaurant terraces (p. 95 [p. 51]) as proof of a desire to prevent people from slowing down, relaxing and communicating. Likewise, for Dadié, language and communication appear to have developed in a way that reflects a preference for speedy, uncomplicated formulae that minimize interaction. Hence the preference for 'hi' rather than 'hello' (p. 278 [p. 149]), succinct letter endings rather than convoluted but, in Dadié's mind, respectful, French conventions (p. 41 [p. 21]), and finally the growing importance of telephone communication (artificial presumably because conducted through a machine), as opposed to face-to-face interaction or less hasty letter writing (p. 270 [p. 145]).

Yet another figurative use for the aeroplane and air travel in *Patron de New York* involves highlighting its links to American military power. Returning once again to the description of the outbound transatlantic flight to America, it is significant that this stage of the journey provides Dadié with an occasion to note the importance of aircraft to modern armies and warfare. Interestingly, his first discussion of this subject is in the context of Portuguese suppression of anti-colonial resistance in Angola.[31] In a highly unusual example of travel's arbitrary encounters that occurs during a Lisbon stopover, the Ivorian appears to see Portuguese soldiers boarding military aircraft as 'anges exterminateurs' ['exterminating angels'] leaving for their African colony in order to 'semer la mort dans d'autres foyers' (*PNY*, p. 20) ['sow death in other homes', p. 10]. Needless to say, the reference to colonization on this European stopover is not coincidental. It allows Dadié at once to raise the spectre of America's neo-colonial tendencies while at the same time linking them to the old European world to which he sees America as inextricably tied.

Dadié, however, is less concerned with the specifics of American overseas military policy than with a broad-strokes look at the significance of its military might and its links to other key elements of the country's culture, notably devotion to speed. Thus the obsession with stockpiling weapons and building ever bigger and *faster* military aircraft is seen as the expression of 'le caractère essentiel de l'Amérique. Compétition entre les hommes, compétition entre les buildings, compétition entre les compagnies! Qui arrivera le premier?' (*PNY*, p. 258) ['the essential character of America, competition among men, buildings and companies! Who'll get there first?', p. 138]. This competitive edge may appear to be innocent, or at best limited to the economic sphere, but, as Dadié subtly suggests, it does not quite hide a domineering, even bellicose, spirit that makes the desire to win appear far more menacing. As he argues, where America needs to defend its interests, economic or other, it will not hesitate to deploy its military might, its 'bombardiers supergéants, ses milliers de soldats' (*PNY*, p. 139) ['gigantic bombers and her thousands of soldiers', p. 75]. Notably, it is the use and domination of air space through fighter jets and technologically advanced airborne missiles that Dadié sees as characterizing American military might and defining a form of modern warfare that '[laisse] [l]es mains propres et la conscience tranquille' (*PNY*, p. 238) [leave[s] their hands clean and their consciences free', p. 127].

For all that Dadié is intent on presenting what he sees as specifically American characteristics, his emphasis on France, and his repetition of cultural features and failings already raised in his earlier travel book on Paris, remind the reader that what the African traveller observes is not entirely unfamiliar to him. America may be at pains to distinguish itself as a 'new world', but air travel has not so much connected it as *re*connected it to its true progenitor: Europe. Read in conjunction with *Un Nègre à Paris*, then, it is possible to argue that what Dadié is attempting to draw out in his numerous references to France, and in particular that country's gift of the Statue of Liberty, is not so much America's role as a new international civilizing force but as a reincarnation of all the ambiguous, even hypocritical, propensities of colonizing Europe. Unusually, Dadié is explicit when he makes this connection. For him, America is not the 'wayward child' of so much anti-American discourse but is dutifully following the imperial footsteps traced by France, Spain and Great Britain:[32] 'elle veut brûler Moscou [...] reconstituer l'Empire, créer la dynastie des Amériques' (*PNY*, p. 228) ['she wants to burn Moscow [...], rebuild the empire and create the American dynasty', p. 122]. This results in America emerging from the text as a version of the Europe Dadié is familiar with, but with its failings intensified. In this respect, *Pax Americana* and the country's self-appointed role as international guardian of 'freedom' are, like France's *mission civilisatrice*, revealed to be less the policies of a people wishing to share the benefits of its technologically advanced civilization than the hubristic actions of a nation impervious to the destruction of which it is capable. The emergence of America as a European-inspired 'neo-colonial' superpower would thus suggest that, even if Africa has entered a postcolonial age, its former European colonizers are not to be exonerated.

Crucially, where America can appear powerful and united in its ability to galvanize 'sa couvée [...] pour les injustices qu'elle estime devoir combattre chez d'autres peuples' (*PNY*, p. 70) ['her brood to crusade against injustices she deems necessary to combat elsewhere', p. 38], sustained discussion of racial inequality in *Patron de New York* sheds light on the deep divisions at the very heart of the nation. It is this subject, more than any, that reveals Dadié's unquestionable talent for figurative language and, once again, he effectively resorts to the question of air travel to raise some of the key issues in America's 'race' debate.

The presence of 'blacks' on American airlines initially seems to imply that this population's star is rising. Gaining access to travel and becoming airborne appears to suggest that African Americans are finally breaking free of their enslavement by landowners and benefiting from America's desire to render them more visible:

> Il y a tellement de Nègres qui voyagent sur les lignes américaines! Une véritable invasion. L'Amérique paraît promener d'autres nègres par toutes ses villes pour s'habituer à ses nègres. Certains ainsi pourront se rendre compte que le nègre américain, produit du sol, n'est pas un phénomène insolite. (*PNY*, pp. 172–73)

> [There are so many blacks travelling on American airlines! A true invasion. America seems to parade other blacks through all her cities in order to get used to them. Some people will thus be able to realize that American blacks, products of the land, are not a strange phenomenon.] (p. 93)

In his typical linguistically ludic mode, Dadié suggests that the development of air travel in America, to the detriment of train travel, is proof of a concerted effort to remove the rail tracks that discriminate against those born on the wrong side (*PNY*, p. 176 [p. 94]). (Although clearly not a fluent English speaker, Dadié proves to be as entertained by language, and 'language travels' in this text as he is in *Un Nègre à Paris*.) However, despite air travel being apparently invested with a fundamentally democratic ethos, as well as with the potential for delivering a more racially harmonious society, elsewhere Dadié's observations appear to confirm the persistence of a racially based discrimination that shows no signs of abating. It is impossible to do justice here to Dadié's frequently powerful evocation of this distressing feature of American society. However, from a purely travel-related perspective it is worth noting that Dadié's discussion of this issue reveals him to be well informed prior to arrival, and nothing in his American travel experience seems to suggest that his preconceived notions were inaccurate. To summarize briefly, there may well be no black in the Stars and Stripes, as Dadié notes, but otherwise and more generally the American landscape is seen as overwhelmingly mono-chromic. Everywhere and everything, from the White House, to the national preference for milk, to black-tarred roads and the colour sensitive retina of white Americans, provide Dadié with an opportu-nity to observe how the concept of 'race' remains a key structuring element in American culture and social relations. For him, it is this, more than anything, including foreign policy and ruthless economic expansionism, that is seen to make America's discourse of liberty and equality sound as hollow as the New York statue devoted to these principles.

However, if this subject provides inspiration for some of Dadié's most potent imagery in *Patron de New York*, there is no sense of how the traveller comes to his conclusions. Unusual in a travel narrative of this kind, lack of anecdotal evidence gives the impres-sion that Dadié is himself guilty of a surface reading of this and other crucial features of American culture of the time. For example, repeated references to Harlem give little sense of its cultural, political and economic life. Where Dadié does promise unusual insights, such as noting the predominance of funeral homes in Harlem's business world or the importance of music and dance, the reader is frequently rewarded with glib analysis or none at all. More significantly, unlike *Un Nègre à Paris*, where Dadié's own ethnic identity is constantly reflected back to him, there is very little mention in this text of human encounters and no reference to how he is perceived as an African either by black or white Americans. (Indeed, this peculiar absence in Dadié's text deserves comparison with Omar Fall's experiences in *Chalys d'Harlem*. Fall's first human contact with Harlem takes place when he meets some lively religious proselytizers who claim to have met him on the first day of creation and proceed to welcome him to black Africa. Quite apart from underlining the role religion has played in African-American politics and culture, what emerges here is an example of an African traveller who journeys to the West and is welcomed, albeit in a very specific context, on the basis of recogni-tion and the assumption of a shared past.)

If Dadié has any identity when travelling in America it is as a non-English speaker, and as Michael Syrotinski notes it is precisely moments of linguistic mishap that provide the rare examples of subjective experience in *Patron de New York*. This in itself is significant, pointing perhaps to America as a destination where the African traveller has at last transcended the politics of visualization that so dominates the journeys of Africans to Europe. However, the considerable amount of space devoted to the question of 'race' in *Patron de New York* would seem to suggest that Dadié could not have travelled as an invisible and disembodied observer. Moreover, any sense of black America and Africa forming part of a complex continuum framed within the Atlantic is lost in Dadié's unwillingness to delve deeper into the bonds that undoubtedly link them.

Of course, the array of criticism Dadié levels at American culture and society is complex, particularly as it can be tempered with undeniable respect and admiration. In addition, apart from the brief Portuguese stopover, Dadié does not travel through Europe, yet many of his observations are filtered through a European, and more particularly French, perspective that makes it difficult to untangle a specifically 'African' point of view. More worrying perhaps is the notion that decentred travel becomes questionable given the persistent relevance of France and French culture as crucial points of reference for this African traveller. However, given the political context of his journey, it is possible to argue that certain aspects of Dadié's undoubted anti-Americanism are not French-inspired but products of post-independence African nationalism, an ideology which, as two commentators on 'Third World' anti-Americanism argue, can give rise to a 'hypersensitivity to foreign inroads and influence, real or imaginary'.[33] (Such a perspective could be supported by Dadié's brief Dakar stopover at the beginning of the text where the city's adoption of an 'American' architectural style is seen to create parallel neighbourhoods of poverty and deprivation that have no place in the particular vision of progress defined by anti-colonial nationalism.) In addition, even if it is possible to identify clear elements of a Gallic anti-Americanism in Dadié's comments (not least in his perception of the importance of the English language as a threat), his view could also be seen as an international take on the hegemony of a Western techno-consumer social model. As Richard Kuisel points out, the global nature of late twentieth-century cultural, political and economic exchange means that vast swathes of the globe, including Africa, have been transformed along the lines of some vaguely American model. [...] There is a kind of global imperative that goes by the name Americanization. Although the phenomenon is still described as Americanization, it has become increasingly disconnected from America. Perhaps it would be better described as the coming of consumer society. Whatever the case, the phenomenon [of anti-Americanism] to be observed in post-war France has parallels all over the world in recent decades.[34]

Ultimately, much more troubling than the difficulty of identifying a national or ethnic perspective in *Patron de New York* is the decontextualization of its arguments. Unlike *Un Nègre à Paris*, the text itself provides no clear indication of the length of time spent on American soil, there is no notion of any clear itinerary followed in this vast country, and geographical knowledge is strangely absent.[35] Although some historical context is provided through references to slavery and the fate of native American Indians for example, they appear more superficial than the particular historical discussion of *Un Nègre à Paris*. (Even if the earlier text is also largely impressionistic I would argue that it provides a clearer sense of place than *Patron de New York*.) Moreover, by divorcing criticism of America's cultural and social norms from its history, and from the type of anecdotal evidence normally found in travelogues, Dadié contributes significantly to what David Allen Case rightly refers to as the text's many 'crude generalizations'.[36] (I am not suggesting here that anecdotal evidence is reliable, merely that the personal travel experience it highlights can contribute to a sense of place.) Dadié's only concession to the issue of contextualization, his acknowledgement of the sheer size of America, merely contributes to the impression that he has simply skimmed the surface in order to confirm a small number of preconceived ideas. In addition, what Dominic Thomas accurately identifies in *Un Nègre à Paris* as the 'acknowledgement and expression of awareness of the dangers of assuming a position of authority in the analysis of other cultures' is less obvious in *Patron de New York*, despite the characteristic deployment of satire and irony to temper any accusation to the contrary.[37]

Nonetheless, however disquieting this tendency to impose generalized patterns on American society, it would be inaccurate to align such features with the ideological processes of colonial travel narratives. For both *Chalys d'Harlem* and *Patron de New York* register an important shift in tone and perspective that is clearly rooted both in the optimism of newly achieved African independence and the geographical context of their travels. That both authors should be guilty of omissions and inaccuracies should certainly not be ignored. But nor should it surprise the reader. As we have seen, written accounts of travel and cultural encounter, from whatever perspective, are invariably subjective and selective, and consequently guilty of errors and misconceptions. What is more important where the American-based texts of Dadié and Diakhaté are concerned is the undeniable confidence both authors reveal in their efforts to engage with this other culture as equals. Viewed in this way, we can see how *Chalys d'Harlem* and *Patron de New York* provide an important step towards the elaboration of a sophisticated African literature of travel, and propel it towards exciting and unexpected destinations.

CHAPTER FIVE

L'Africain du Grœnland: 'Primitive' on 'Primitives'

Having raised the issue of the geographical diversity of African travel literature in the previous chapter, in the following pages I will develop it further by looking at Tété-Michel Kpomassie's *L'Africain de Grœnland*. This intriguing account of a journey to the Arctic was published in Paris in 1981 but recounts a journey that begins late in 1958 on the eve of African independence, when, at the age of 16, Kpomassie takes a 'taxi-brousse' from his home in Togo to his aunt's house in the then Ivory Coast capital, Abidjan. Here he takes up the first of many posts that will fund his ambition to travel beyond the African continent. Eight years later, after slow but eventful progress through various African and European countries, the author finally arrives for a sixteen-month stay in the Danish colony of Greenland.

Certainly, by reversing the story of European colonial travel to Africa and journeying 'back' to the European 'centre', Tété-Michel Kpomassie's *L'Africain du Grœnland* retains a key element of the predominant travel paradigm studied here. From the text's title, however, it is clear that Kpomassie's account of his journey is somewhat at odds with what we have come to expect. Most notably, even if Kpomassie travels through the colonial centre, it is not his final destination. And whilst politically, and also from the point of view of travel logistics, the centre still holds in this text, the unprecedented emphasis on the periphery – both as point of departure and destination – tentatively points to the potential for a new network of travel relations in the postcolonial world that move beyond the African and French topographies that so dominate the corpus of francophone African literature. In addition to the text's geography, the dynamic nature of Kpomassie's journey and his enthusiastic embracing of travel's potential marks it out from other accounts of African travel to the West where displacement, exile and at times stasis dominate the experience of travel. Indeed, Kpomassie's way of travelling appears to bear significant resemblances to Western recreational travellers for whom travel itself is the primary motivation and objective. In formal respects, Kpomassie's text also distinguishes itself from other accounts of African travel with its description of a linear, horizontal and implied circular journey immediately evoking more conventional Western travelogues.

Nonetheless, although Kpomassie's text appears both to borrow familiar templates of Western travel literature and to be rooted in Western travel practices, closer examination will demonstrate that, as with the African travellers examined in preceding chapters, the traveller's origins cannot be ignored, for they help explain the far more dynamic and culturally specific techniques that operate beneath instances of apparent emulation. In the different sections of this chapter, I will consider the interrelation between key features of *L'Africain du Grœnland* – literary travel companions, ethnographic writing practices, comparative observational paradigms and the quest for authenticity – and the cultural contexts of the epic journey described. I will focus in particular on the complex ways in which the domestic and political territories of both Africa and Greenland converge in the text and impose the necessity of thinking doubly (at least) about how Kpomassie travels and how his text is read.

Travel and reading

As Frances Bartkowski notes, Tété-Michel Kpomassie's obsession with travelling to the Arctic is initially formed following a textual encounter with this region.[1] This impetus for travel is not unusual, and Kpomassie's enthusiastic response is a reminder of the eternally interdependent and complex relationship that exists between travel and reading.[2] As with the colonial literature that shaped images of Africa for European readers and inspired them to embark on their own discoveries of the 'dark continent', Kpomassie's reaction to Robert Gessain's *Les Esquimaux du Grœnland à l'Alaska* illustrates the ways in which literature can induce and transform readers into travellers/tourists and influence their attitudes towards, and expectations of, other places.[3] Whether it transports the aspiring traveller to other imaginary destinations, or returns the real traveller back temporarily to their point of departure, reading, as David Scott demonstrates in his analysis of Michel Leiris's literary companions in the African jungle, is 'a spatial as well as a temporal activity'.[4] Kpomassie's first encounter with Greenland suggests that he is no different to other travellers who mobilize 'the fantasies' associated with what Graham Huggan and Patrick Holland refer to as the 'complex textual zones' constructed and deployed by Western travel writing.[5] As we have already seen, reading – especially the creative writing and historical accounts encountered in the context of a colonial education – frequently provides the initial motivation for colonial/postcolonial African travellers (real or would-be) to Europe.

However, if certain reactions to the literature of other places might be said to be universal – e.g. the ability to 'escape' to the elsewhere of the text or to have expectations of other places confirmed or challenged – it is important to remember that reading is a situated practice, and the particular nature of Afro-European relations means that other factors must be considered where the particular reading practices of colonized Africans are being considered. Literary exchange – or the 'travelling' book – is, of course, one of the most abiding aspects of cultural encounter in the context of colonialism. However, this has largely been an unequal, and often one-way, transaction. Crucially, during the colonial era, the texts read by aspiring African travellers were more often than not chosen by European educators in order to convey to African students the colonizers' own view of the superiority of their 'home' and culture. As we saw in *Mirages de Paris*, *Un Nègre à Paris* and *Kocoumbo, l'étudiant noir*, Africans who travelled – or harboured desires to travel – to Europe did so with their expectations coloured by the ideological assumptions and cultural geography of classical European literature. In addition, if this literature moved readers imaginatively closer to Europe, it also facilitated a distancing from their own cultural origins. It is also important to stress that although Western literature unquestionably acted as a promoter of the metropolitan centre, Africans' possibilities for travel were as limited as the social mobility thought to be conferred by a Western education. Still today, the prerequisites of financial means and access to leisure time mean that for many African readers the desire to travel and experience a geographical elsewhere are rarely put into practice. Finally, whilst the imaginative impact of such travel across the pages is part of an undeniably complex creative act of transference and transformation, it also explains the feelings of isolation, disappointment and exile that emerge when reality for the traveller fails to correlate with fictional descriptions of place.

In many respects, the mesmerizing effect of Gessain's text on

Kpomassie is not unusual. What is more telling is the fact that his literary inspiration is not sanctioned by the colonial educational establishment but is found in a bookshop in Lomé amongst texts 'qui n'étaient point lus dans nos classes' ['that were never on our school syllabus'] but which found their way, 'comme par erreur' (*AG*, p. 62) ['as if in error', p. 47], on to the shelves of the otherwise largely religious and educational stock. The unusual circumstances explaining Kpomassie's reading thus explain the atypical choice of destination but they also reveal an independence of spirit that is translated into Kpomassie's steadfast resolve to transform the literary-inspired '*idée* d'aller au Grœnland' (*AG*, p. 64, my emphasis) ['*idea* of going to Greenland', p. 49] into reality. Interestingly, books remain his travelling companions as he heads northwards, and study through reading is described as an ideal method of learning for the traveller:

> Je choisis donc de m'instruire seul, ce qui semblait mieux répondre au cas de l'instable que j'étais et j'entrepris sérieusement de lire tous les classiques français en commençant par le seizième siècle. Mes grosses valises, en fin de compte, renfermaient plus de livres que de vêtements. (*AG*, pp. 71–72)

> [I decided to teach myself, as this seemed to be the best answer for a wanderer like myself, and I embarked on a thorough study of all the French classics, beginning with the sixteenth century. My large suitcase eventually contained more books than clothes.] (p. 56)

Clearly, like other African travellers, Kpomassie is proud of his literary knowledge. What is noteworthy, however, are the consequences of Kpomassie's independence from the reading context of colonized African travellers examined earlier. Detached as he is from the formal structures and political and cultural ethos of the colonial educational system, Kpomassie does not appear to allow literature – or a particular way of reading – to influence the manner in which he anticipates his European destination. Indeed, in his conversation with a former French colonial administrator in Paris it is clear that Kpomassie sees formal higher education as leading to the stifling of initiative and a spurning of adventure. In his brief discussion of literature, Kpomassie, unlike Tanhoe Bertin for example, feels no need to demonstrate his learning. Titles of books and names of characters are never mentioned, and when the Togolese traveller finally does reach Europe no comparisons are made between textual depictions of place and his own observations of reality. As soon as he gets to

Greenland, literary works and reading habits are no longer mentioned (apart from one telling observation where the presence of a shelf of Danish translations of European classics in a home for elderly Inuit subtly points to the erosion of indigenous cultural knowledge).[6] For Kpomassie it would seem that the experience of Greenland afforded by physical travel is a better substitute for flights of imagination to a destination on the page. As the following description suggests, it is almost as if the value of reading becomes redundant in the context of travel, and the individual's sublime visual encounter with a real landscape ultimately exposes the inadequacies of printed worlds:

C'est le soir du jour où la première neige est tombée que j'ai été effrayé par un phénomène bizarre. Je rentrais seul, la nuit était silencieuse. Levant soudain les yeux, je vois au-dessus de ma tête de longues traces blanches que le vent fait tournoyer. On dirait la lueur de quelque foyer invisible. [...] Il y a des changements continuels dans l'intensité, la marche, le chatoiement et les ondulations de cette curieuse voile démesurée qui flotte dans l'atmosphère. [...] Je rentre vite et en parle à mes hôtes qui, sans daigner sortir, m'apprennent que je viens de voir une aurore boréale. Je ressors pour l'observer de nouveau, tant cette première vision a été plus impressionnante que tout ce que j'ai pu lire sur ces aurores polaires. (AG, p. 160)

[On the night of the day the first snow fell I was frightened by a bizarre phenomenon. I was walking home alone and the night was still. Suddenly, looking up, I saw long white streaks swirling in the wind above my head. It was like the radiance of some invisible hearth. [...] There were continual changes in the intensity, the motion, the iridescent play of colors and the ripplings of this strange, gigantic veil that floated through the night sky. [...] I rushed home and babbled something about it to my hosts, who didn't bother to go outside but informed me that I had just been watching the aurora borealis. I went out to watch it again for a long, long time, so much more impressive was it than anything I had ever read about these polar auroras.] (p. 145)

Reading and writing ethnography

One of the most significant outcomes of Kpomassie's reading of *Les Esquimaux du Grœnland à l'Alaska* is, of course, his decision to treat Europe as a stepping-stone to another destination. Certainly, he is impressed by what he sees and experiences of Europe: he claims to be intrigued by the metro in Paris and to be enchanted by his first experience of the French capital's historical monuments. However, at no time does one get the impression that he is in awe of what he sees, or that he is convinced by Europe's supposed cultural and technological superiority and, by implication, Africa's inferiority. In short, the journey across Europe to Denmark highlights essential differences with Africa, but because these differences are never presented on a hierarchical scale the impression is that of an interesting and noteworthy, albeit protracted, stopover en route to the main destination.

Nonetheless, moving beyond the European centre does not mean that the young African traveller has moved entirely away from Western ways of seeing others and other places, particularly so-called 'primitive' societies. For Debbie Lisle, one of the most significant aspects of Kpomassie's decision to write about his Greenland journey is that he disrupts 'the automatic transposition of an identity/difference logic onto a colonizer/colonized framework: [he occupies] *both* sides of the identity/difference logic'.[7] It is worth returning to the initial motivating text for the Greenland journey to understand this point. Unlike the typical reading of other African travellers to Europe, Kpomassie's first imaginative encounter with the Inuit culture he decides to visit is mediated through the particular vision and practice of Western ethnography. This fact is crucial in several respects. First, Kpomassie's relationship with this text transforms him from a typical subject of ethnographic inquiry into a reader of ethnography and, as we shall see, arguably, a producer of ethnographic writing. In a more general sense, Gessain's text is also an important reminder of the historical context and discursive practices of a particular Western way of travelling and of seeing and interpreting others.

Despite the development of a more reflexive approach to ethnographic writing, examined most notably in the critical writing of James Clifford, Talal Asad forcefully reminds us that the origins of social anthropology – the broader field in which ethnography is located – mean that any claims for the discipline's objectivity and value-free observations need to be closely examined:

> It is not a matter of dispute that social anthropology emerged as a distinctive discipline at the beginning of the colonial era, that it became a flourishing academic profession towards its close, or that throughout this period its efforts were devoted to a description and analysis – carried out by Europeans, for a European audience – of non-European audiences dominated by European power.[8]

Without wishing to deny the diversity of anthropological research, nor to underplay the significance of the discipline's laudable struggle with the epistemological crisis engendered by its colonial legacy, it is also true that anthropology's tendency to produce exoticism frequently led to other cultures being seen as monolithic and primitive, and implicitly inferior to Western cultural norms. In addition, as Nicholas Thomas argues, anthropology's historical insistence on cultural difference means that the discipline's recent wave of collective autocritique has not halted the

> scope for slippage from the appropriate recognition of difference [...] to an idea that other people *must* be different. Insofar as this is stipulated by [...] anthropological rhetoric, the discipline is a discourse that magnifies the distance between 'others' and 'ourselves' while suppressing mutual entanglement and the perspectival and political fracturing of the cultures of both observers and observed.[9]

L'Africain du Grœnland can by no means be qualified as a meta-narrative on ethnographic writing, or indeed travel writing. Indeed, the novelty of Kpomassie's journey, and his own subversive status within the ranks of travel literature and exploration, is highlighted more explicitly in Jean Malaurie's introduction than it is in the main narrative. Nonetheless, the text's various allusions to ethnographers and explorers who have preceded Kpomassie to Greenland – Gessain, but also Knud Rasmussen and Malaurie himself – implicitly draw attention to the author's own place within this tradition of writing. The influence of Western ethnographic travel literature also makes itself felt in the text's two opening chapters, with their dual ethnographic and autobiographical features combining to create a sort of autoethnography that is used to set up the cultural logic that will later inform Kpomassie's comparisons between Africa and Greenland. (Here I use 'autoethnography' simply to describe the manner in which Kpomassie emphasizes his own cultural background as much if not more so than autobiographical facts.)

The influence of ethnography also makes itself felt in Kpomassie's implied intention to treat his travels in Greenland as a type of project where fieldwork is carried out and experiences recorded. Although his camera appears to be an unsolicited gift from his generous French benefactor, he himself purchases paper before leaving Copenhagen, and later we also learn that he has a tape recorder, although we never learn where he has acquired it, or to what extent or for what purposes he uses it. (Of course this equipment also implies a process of intention regarding the textualization of his journey, a fact that also aligns his text with 'scientific', factual travel writing, as opposed to 'anecdotal' and fictional travel literature.) The inclusion of eighteen photographs of his travels, and in particular those depicting traditional pursuits such as fishing and hunting, could also be seen as confirmation of a scientific dimension to his project. Although there is no real interplay between the text and the photographs, they nonetheless underscore the authenticity of his experience by providing visual proof that his written observations are real, and his participation in this other community genuine. The photographs, with their overwhelming emphasis on tranquillity, harmony and community life, might also be interpreted as idyllic representations of Greenland life that in turn imply the nostalgia and yearning for a pristine past that has been criticized in much Western travel and ethnographic writing.

In addition to these recording devices, the recurrence of a decidedly scientific tone in the text also suggests that not only do ethnographic texts prompt Kpomassie's initial desire to travel and later form part of his essential preparation, they also influence the way he narrates his experiences. For example, the following extract from a lengthy description of indigenous female dress illustrates perfectly the detached style and authority that are immediately recognizable as the rhetorical features of ethnographic reporting:

> Ce costume féminin de la côte sud-ouest, véritable chef-d'œuvre de la patience, est composé de trois pièces: les *kamiks*, le *sirkenak* et l'*anorak*.
>
> Cet anorak des femmes se distingue de celui des hommes en ceci qu'il ne comporte pas de capuchon. C'est une sorte de tunique en toile, à carreaux clairs et foncés comme un damier. Il est doublé extérieurement par le *sabangouantak*, grand collet fait uniquement de perles multicolores qui recouvre les épaules, la poitrine et le dos. Une savante opposition des couleurs en fait des motifs réchampis, réguliers, superbes. Ces motifs diffèrent non seulement d'une région à l'autre, mais dans un même village, voire au sein d'une même famille. C'est l'invention de l'ouvrière qui recherche son propre effet décoratif. [...] Le haut de l'anorak se termine par un *iloubakosit*, bande de peau noire qui entoure le cou et que l'on retrouve aux poignets. (pp. 113–14)

[This women's costume from the southwest coast, a real masterpiece of patient handicraft, is composed of three pieces: the *kamiks*, the *sirkenak* and the *anorak*.

The women's anorak is distinguished from the men's by not having a hood. It is a sort of cloth tunic, checkered with dark and light squares like a chessboard, and decorated on the outside by the *sabanguantak*, a broad band covering the shoulders, chest, and back, made entirely of multicoloured pearls. Subtle colour contrasts produce motifs with superb regular patterns. These motifs differ not just from one region to the next but even within the same village, sometimes within the same family. They are invented by the crafts-woman, who develops her own decorative effects. [...] The collar and cuffs of the anorak are bordered with an *ilubakosit*, a band of black skin.] (pp. 99–100)

In addition to such descriptions, which recur in other passages relating to eating habits and social and religious customs, the use of footnotes providing translations of indigenous terms, or historical, geographical and cultural information also points to a certain scien-tific tone and authority reminiscent of ethnographic literature. But more problematic perhaps is the presence of what Tim Ingold identi-fies as the 'ethnographic present',

> that style of describing forms of life other than our own as though what people say and do now they have always said and done, and always will. [...] To represent people as existing forever within that moment, caught – as it were – in suspended animation, is to consign their lives to a time that, in the experience of the ethnographer, has already been left far behind.[10]

In Kpomassie's text, this notion of an 'ethnographic present' is evident in the unattributed sentences or instances where the author ascribes generalized or 'subjective states' to Greenland culture, a tendency that James Clifford sees as evidence of an ethnographic aspiration to 'a Flaubertian omniscience that moves freely throughout a world of indigenous subjects'.[11] Thus we are frequently told about the ubiqui-tous Greenland hospitality, the 'mœurs des habitants' (*AG*, p. 124) ['Greenland morality', p. 110] that begin to disgust him, and that 'si les Grœnlandais aiment railler, ils craignent cependant le ridicule' (*AG*, p.2 53) ['although Greenlanders love to make fun of others, they fear ridicule themselves', p. 245].[12]

Whilst the above rhetorical features clearly reveal the influence of a certain form of authoritative Western ethnographic writing, it would be inaccurate nonetheless to ally Kpomassie unconditionally to this tradition. First, as I discussed in the introduction, specific material circumstances invariably distinguish Kpomassie from the particular

travel and representational practices of Western ethnographic expe-
ditions. In this respect, it is notable that as soon as Kpomassie decides
to act on the inspiration provided by Gessain's ethnographic account,
concrete, material reality forces him to switch to a specifically African
framework to find a solution to the very practical question of how
to travel. Consequently, his working to travel solution is modelled on
the semi-nomadic practices of the African Hausas who, he explains,
travel between countries in stages, 'trouvant dans chaque pays un
travail quelconque pour un an ou deux' (*AG*, p. 65) ['finding some
sort of work for a year or two in each country', p. 50]. Although
Kpomassie continues to receive financial support from a generous
French benefactor, material circumstances continue to distance him
from the travel practices of the Western ethnographer throughout his
journey, a point he makes in his telling desire to be less dependent
on Greenland hospitality and to have 'comme la quasi-totalité des
ethnologues dans l'Arctique, un logement à part et à l'écart des habitants' (*AG*, p. 223) ['what nearly all Arctic ethnologists have – an
isolated house to himself', p. 216].

Although distinctions between related observational modes are
always tenuous, Kpomassie's narrative is, in the final analysis, a
subjective account that also distances him from what David Scott
identifies as the rational and analytical 'discours scientifique' [scien-
tific discourse] that has come to distinguish ethnology from the imaginative 'discours de découverte' [discourse of discovery] of the type of
non-fictional travel writing exemplified by *L'Africain du Grœnland*.[13]
In addition, 'expressive conventions', as James Clifford stresses, are
only one of several factors impacting on ethnographic writing, and
Kpomassie's relationship to other determinants – generic, institutional, contextual, political, historical – means that there are crucial
divergences in his particular representation of Greenland culture.[14]
In the introduction we have already looked at the negative effect
of literary taxonomies – particularly those governing the writing of
other places and people – on the categorization of African writers.
Furthermore, despite Kpomassie's undeniable interest in the history
of ethnography, it is clear that his travels and (written) observations are undertaken outwith any official institutional and scientific
framework which necessarily limits his access to the discursive structures of ethnography. Indeed, it is possible that the absence of any
scientific training allows Kpomassie to enter into a non-professional
dialogue with Inuit culture and ultimately reinforces a reciprocity

that, according to Huggan and Holland, tends to remain elusive to the Western travel writer and professional ethnographer.[15]

As significant as institutional issues is the relevance of the political and historical contexts of Kpomassie's narrative which we have already identified as framing his reading practices. Needless to say, these contexts also have considerable bearing on his representational practices and mean that his writing interacts in a far more complex way with the power imbalances that underwrite much – though I stress not all – Western ethnographic writing. Principal amongst these issues of inequality between observer and observed is, of course, the question of the 'authority to represent cultural realities', which, according to James Clifford, 'is unequally shared'.[16] Crucially, the 'authority' of the Western ethnographer – and also the travel writer – is based on social and geographic location, and an assumption of cultural and intellectual superiority can insinuate itself into the judgements of even the most cautious. On the contrary, both Kpomassie's colonized background and 'racial' identity immediately cast him as the primitive whose travel credentials and any intellectual authority he might possess are attributed by one French colonial administrator not to any African influence but to an intrepid, independent spirit that has been nurtured and developed by an exemplary *French* colonial education. If Kpomassie is to be conceded any authority in his observations then the following quote would suggest that it will be located in his ability to learn and reproduce the colonizer's way of seeing:

«Ainsi, dit mon hôte [...], vous voulez relier le Grœnland à l'Afrique. C'est en effet une entreprise peu banale pour un Africain. Vous qui venez d'un pays qui dépendait de la France il y a encore trois ans à peine, vous serez bien placé pour établir un rapprochement entre ce que nous avons pu réaliser en Afrique pendant un demi-siècle et ce qu'on a fait depuis pour les Esquimaux... Je suis d'avance persuadé que nous avons accompli des œuvres efficaces, ne serait-ce que dans le domaine de l'alphabétisation. Et la preuve vivante de ce que j'avance est vous-même: non seulement vous vous exprimez dans un français correct, mais vous faites aussi preuve d'une grande ouverture d'esprit sur le monde extérieur, fruit d'une remarquable instruction». (*AG*, p. 78)

["Well now", said my host [...], "so you want to link Greenland with Africa. That's an unusual ambition for an African. Coming from a country which scarcely three years ago was still a French colony, you are well placed to compare what we were able to accomplish during half a century in Africa and what has been done since for the Eskimos. I am convinced that we managed to achieve some good things, if only in the field of literacy. And you are living proof of that: not only do you express yourself in correct French, but you also show great open-mindedness towards the outside world – the result of a remarkable education."] (p. 63)

Aside from correcting for the reader the factual inaccuracy of the above observation – by stressing that he is largely self-educated – Kpomassie's development of his own individual way of observing provides subtle proof of the emergence of what James Clifford sees as an ambivalent and counter-hegemonic tendency in ethnographic work, which, by extension, can also be evinced amongst the forms of representation developed by the multiple voices of travellees turned travellers.[17] First, Kpomassie's own radical physical difference – height and skin colour in particular – from native Greenlanders tends to undermine any impression that his observations are those of a detached, unreflexive and disembodied outsider. Invariably, the largely respectful curiosity of his hosts with regard to his ethnic identity – as opposed to the racism encountered by earlier African travellers to France – means that the differences he represents are as important as the differences he observes and, as the following quote illustrates, serve as a constant reminder of his status as 'the Other's other', to borrow Dennis Porter's expression quoted in the introduction:

> Le futur patron de Chris nous emmena chez lui boire de la bière. Tous les enfants abandonnèrent leurs parents et nous suivirent. Il en sortait de chaque maison […]. La scène me fit penser aux Lilliputiens entourant Gulliver. Parti pour découvrir, j'étais moi aussi une découverte. (*AG*, p. 98)

> [Chris's new employer […] took us to his house for a beer. All the children left their parents' sides and followed us. More of them came out of every house […]. The scene made me think of the Lilliputians surrounding Gulliver. I had started on a voyage of discovery, only to find that it was I who was being discovered.] (p. 83)

The ambivalence of Kpomassie's ethnographic 'methodology' is also evident in his relationship to the significance of difference, 'anthropology's enduring rhetorical form' according to Nicholas Thomas, and traditionally the basis for using 'one stable and distant culture to relativize cherished and unexamined notions imputed to culture at home'.[18] Initially, Kpomassie's pre-travel reading and preparations colour his expectations and more than attune him to the presence, and relevance, of cultural difference. Indeed, in his reaction to aspects of his hosts' sexual behaviour, difference not only forms the basis of his judgement but is also presented as a barrier to real intercultural dialogue: 'Mon comportement et notre manière de voir doivent refléter assez en ce moment deux mondes, le leur et le mien, inconciliable en ce domaine' (*AG*, p. 124) ['My behaviour at this time, and my own way of seeing things, must have been a fair reflection of our two worlds, theirs and mine, in this respect irreconcilable', p. 110]. What is crucial in this comment, however, is the use of the temporal adverbial construction 'en ce moment' ['at this time'], which suggests a subsequent divergence from this way of seeing. Indeed, hints of Kpomassie's distrust of a lazy recourse to stereotype and unqualified statements on cultural difference are already evident in his observations on the French:

> Lorsqu'on a été reçu comme je l'ai été, il est difficile de se mettre aveuglément du côté de ceux qui considèrent que le Français est peu accueillant. Certes, j'ai connu comme n'importe qui des mésaventures dans une ville aussi grande que Paris; mais elles furent largement rachetées par les excellentes dispositions de deux hommes dont la bonté du cœur et la simplicité des mœurs m'ont rendu plus optimiste que jamais. Et c'est dans cet état d'esprit que je continuai mon voyage à travers l'Europe. (*AG*, p. 81)

> [When one has been made as welcome as I was, it is hard to agree with the common sweeping judgement that the French are not very hospitable. Certainly, like anyone else, I ran into occasional trouble in a city as large as Paris; but this was amply compensated for by the two men whose goodness of heart and simplicity of manner made me more optimistic than ever. It was in this state of mind that I continued my journey across Europe.] (p. 66)

The true epistemic and heuristic benefits of Kpomassie's journey come to the fore, however, when we analyse the changing nature of the significance played by cultural difference in the context of his travels in Greenland. It is notable that as the text and the journey progress the generalizations mentioned above become increasingly rare. Although difference never becomes inconsequential for Kpomassie, the overwhelming impression the reader gains is that of the progressive development of an observational style that progresses from an emphasis on difference to a recognition of shared cultural practices or, to use Johannes Fabian's term, *wiedererkennen*. This is not to absolve

Kpomassie of certain double-standards regarding sexual behaviour (whilst he claims to be disgusted by the sexual mores of his Inuit hosts he is not averse to taking advantage of them). Similarly, an unwillingness to review certain culturally informed prejudices regarding gender difference means his views of women remain circumspect (although this too is perhaps evidence of a cultural similarity). Nonetheless, the emergence in the text of a preoccupation with the identification of cultural and political similarities between Africa and Greenland is of crucial importance. For it provides evidence that Kpomassie appears to be aligning himself with Nicholas Thomas's notion of a comparatist ethnographic approach 'that does not take the radical form of alterity in a gulf between observers and observed' and where ultimately difference is 'historically constituted, rather than a fact of cultural stability'.[19]

Comparing colonies

Although Kpomassie cannot be described as apolitical at the outset of his journey, it would seem that he takes only a superficial interest in African political developments of the time. Increasingly, however, as Kpomassie's journey progresses, the narration becomes more finely balanced between seemingly neutral description and a nascent awareness of such explicitly political concepts as imperialism, internationalism and social development. By the end of his narrative, when faced with a choice between remaining in Greenland – where, by now, he feels accepted and culturally integrated – or embarking on a slow return journey to his native country, Kpomassie announces:

> Mais de quelle utilité serait ma vie, si je la passais dans l'Arctique, pour mes compatriotes, pour mon pays? Après avoir tenté et réussi l'aventure polaire, est-ce que je ne me dois pas d'être auprès de mes frères restés en Afrique le 'conteur' de cette terre glaciale [...]? Après l'avilissement de la colonisation et la lutte pour l'indépendance, est-ce que la tâche principale ne reviendra pas aux éducateurs, afin qu'ils ouvrent au continent des horizons nouveaux? Est-ce que je ne devrais pas, moi aussi, participer à cette tâche, apporter à la jeunesse africaine ma petite contribution à son ouverture d'esprit sur le monde extérieur? (*AG*, pp. 303–04)

> [Having tried and succeeded in this polar adventure, was it not my duty to return to my brothers in Africa and become the 'storyteller'

of this glacial land of midnight sun and endless night? After the degradation of colonization and the struggle for independence, wasn't it the task of educators to open their continent to fresh horizons? Should I not play my small part in that task and help the youth of Africa open their minds to the outside world?] (p. 293)

What has happened in the meantime to transform Kpomassie from an apparent recreational traveller into one who not only acknowledges the heuristic benefits of his own international experience but also begins to see travel, with its propensity for encouraging critical thinking, as a 'field of usefulness' in itself? What exactly has he learned from Greenland culture and tradition to make him more committed to his own origins? The answer almost certainly lies in the larger political and historical context of Kpomassie's travels that comes to serve as an interpretive background for the young traveller's growing recognition of the ties that bind Africa and Greenland. In 1960, by the time Kpomassie has left Togo and is working in the Ghanaian capital, Accra, the number of independent African states has risen to 26. Thousands of miles away, Greenland is beginning to feel the first effects of the Danish colonial government's post-Second World War policies of development. It is precisely this political context that is key to an understanding of Kpomassie's stance towards Greenland culture. Indeed, this shared history of colonial domination and its effects on 'traditional' indigenous culture are undoubtedly what tie Kpomassie to his Greenland hosts and underwrite the nature of the comparisons he is eventually drawn to make. As Jean Malaurie reminds us in his introduction to the original French text:

> Dans les réactions des Grœnlandais et de l'auteur, on notera aussi un lien essentiel, une évidente similitude. Les racines de leurs cultures, leurs archétypes de pensées sont non chrétiens et non blancs. Mais toute leur éducation, qu'elle soit danoise ou française, parle de la "grandeur blanche", de "mission civilisatrice" et de "métropole". (p. 11)

> [An essential link and obvious similarity is noticeable in the reactions of both the Greenlanders and the author. Their cultural roots and their intellectual paradigms are neither white nor Christian. However, their entire education, be it French or Danish, speaks of the 'greatness of white culture', the 'civilizing mission' and the 'metropolitan centre'.]

Interestingly, the crucial importance of the colonial encounter appears to be belied initially by the opening chapters of *L'Africain du Grœnland*. Here, any political and historical realities appear to be subsumed by an uncomplicated, almost Negritude-like view of traditional, 'primitive' rural African society. (Later, this issue of an untainted, pre-colonial culture will figure in Kpomassie's search for traces of 'authentic', pre-colonial Inuit life.) From the outset, the reader is plunged into the hierarchies imposed not by colonial society but by the polygamous marriage of the author's father. Prolonged accounts of different initiation rites and cultural practices also tend to reinforce an image of a timeless Africa governed by unchanging social and cultural structures. This image is further strengthened by the second chapter that examines in detail traditional treatments for an injury the author sustains during a traumatic encounter with a snake. Kpomassie's father tries varies traditional potions and rituals – including an animal sacrifice – to heal his son, and when these fail he takes the adolescent Kpomassie to an isolated forest community who live according to the purest forms of traditional, animistic practices. When their methods prove successful Kpmossaie's own future is decided by his parents who promise to hand over their son as an initiate to this cult.

As with other ethnographic-style openings to African accounts of travel examined earlier, this picture of a pure, eternal and homogenous rural idyll is misleading. A more careful reading of Kpomassie's adolescence and the subsequent African stage of his journey to Greenland serve to underline that his strategy is not to contrast a 'primitive' Africa with a more 'modern' Europe. Instead, it highlights the difficulty of extricating a reading of this cultural landscape from the history of colonization and introduces the reader to the competing cultural and political realities that exist *within* colonized African societies. Just as French/Western culture has incorporated itself into Africa – leading, much later, to Kpomassie being mistaken in Greenland for a Frenchman – the Togolese traveller's Arctic journey will reveal that Greenland cannot simply be presented as Denmark's opposite. What is also notable in these opening Togolese chapters is the subtle emphasis on the growing local conflict between traditional practices and the newer forms of medicine that are clearly associated with white European culture, and, therefore, with the cultural interaction brought about by colonization. So, whilst Kpomassie's parents may be loth to take their injured son to a hospital where 'les médecins n'entendent rien à nos coutumes' (*AG*, p. 39) ['the doctors know nothing of our customs', p. 24], the 'culte des serpents', with its almost hermetically sealed reality and jealous protection of the integrity of tradition, is hardly presented as a viable alternative. True, the cult members are afforded the respect that their unusual status and lifestyle deserve, but they are also feared, and joining them is not a decision that is taken lightly or by many. This is not to suggest that Kpomassie's decision to travel away from – or escape – the life for which his father has destined him is a simple rejection of a traditional way of life. On the contrary, what is noteworthy in *L'Africain du Grœnland* is Kpomassie's respect for the Inuit's 'traditional' way of life, his understanding of what is happening to it, and the way in which this interest subsequently leads him back to his own cultural origins. What Kpomassie does reject is the stifling, stagnant form of tradition to which his father has destined him and which his aunt, with her insistence on the value of a local marriage, also sees as his future.

In light of the above, it is clear how travel not only becomes a way of leaving this behind, but is itself the antithesis of such a perception of tradition in its refusal to become rooted to one place, to adhere to one view of how life should be lived. What Kpomassie will ultimately come to embrace is a form of tradition that has the courage to recognize values of its own in the face of a more dominant and powerful colonizing culture. Finally, Kpomassie's method of comparing colonies emphasizes once again the need to revisit Michel de Certeau's understanding of travel writing's tripartite structure (a structure that, unlike many of the other texts studied here, is reproduced in *L'Africain du Grœnland*). For de Certeau, the 'departure' element of travel writing underlines a search for the strange, thereby establishing the *a priori* of difference and its resulting rhetoric of distance. Kpomassie certainly goes in search of difference, but ironically, the greater the distance he travels, the closer he feels, culturally, to his Inuit hosts. To be sure, reason, information and reliability, the three conditions of the travel narrative's testament as de Certeau identifies them, are also present in Kpomassie's narrative. But the implications of Kpomassie's relationship to home, the ambivalent relationship to questions of authority due to ethnic and colonized identities, and the crucial emphasis on similarity and *wiedererkennen* means that ultimately de Certeau's mutually empowering framing structure does not quite function.[20]

Although the 'African' stage of Kpomassie's journey is largely glossed over, it offers, nonetheless, an interesting insight into the author's perception of the political direction newly independent Africa is taking. Leaving Togo in 1959, on the eve of that country's independence, Kpomassie remarks upon the dynamism and optimism of this period when 'un curieux vent de fraternisation, inconnu jusque-là, soufflait sur l'Afrique (*AG*, p. 68) ['a strange new wind of brotherhood was blowing through Africa', p. 53]. No doubt Kpomassie is here referring to the discourse of pan-Africanism which was in its heyday at the time he is travelling northwards through the continent.[21] Unusually, but also revealingly, Kpomassie's view of the predominant ideologies of this period is seen purely in terms of how they facilitate or impede travel progress. Of course it is possible that the internationalist spirit of the pan-African movement may have inspired Kpomassie's own transnational approach to travel. But whilst this theory must remain at the level of conjecture (as must any discussion of the extent to which he has absorbed the various ideological discourses surrounding the construction of cultural and national identity), it is certainly true that the contemporary sense of Africa's new international role does allow the young traveller to avail himself of various educational and professional possibilities and to use his linguistic competence to work as an interpreter and translator in embassies in both Accra and Dakar.[22] However, in his brief description of this African 'stage', it is also evident that Kpomassie is unimpressed by the limited horizons of newly independent Africans who judge things according to financial gain as if, he claims, 'toute entreprise ne devait avoir qu'un but lucratif' (*AG*, p. 72) ['the only reward could be in cash', p. 56]. More damning perhaps are Kpomassie's comments regarding bureaucratic impingements on free movement and travel that ultimately belie the grand vision of anti-colonial and pan-Africanist discourses. Rather than embrace freedom and strive towards a truly postcolonial vision of continental space, post-independence African nations appear more intent than ever on retreating behind the artificial national boundaries of the colonial era.[23] In other words, as newly independent Africa attempts to move away from the narratives of colonial discourse and forge a new way of being seen, Kpomassie seems to be pointing to a concomitant failure to develop new ways of seeing:

> Dans ces deux villes [Casablanca et Alger] tout passager africain qui désirait simplement mettre pied à terre pour quelques heures pendant les escales était tenu de remettre son passeport à la police du port [...]. Ceux qui n'en avaient pas se virent catégoriquement

refuser l'autorisation de descendre du navire, dont la passerelle resta
sous bonne garde. Apparemment, l'entrée libre des Africains dans
d'autres pays du continent n'était pas prévue au programme de la
fameuse unité qui, il fallait bien se rendre à l'évidence, n'existait que
dans le discours des dirigeants! Comble de l'ironie, nous passions
plus librement les frontières au temps de la colonisation...Main-
tenant, par un nationalisme absurde entre pays dits frères, chaque
territoire exigeait de ses voisins passeport et visa, inventions des
Blancs, tout en calomniant ces mêmes Blancs dans l'esprit des
peuples. (p. 73)

[In those two cities [Casablanca and Algiers] any African passenger
who just wanted to go ashore for a few hours was required to hand
in his passport to the police [...]. Those who didn't have a passport
were categorically forbidden to leave the ship, whose gangway was
never left unguarded. Apparently, freedom of entry to other African
countries had not been laid down in that ambitious programme
for unity; it soon became obvious that it existed only in leaders'
speeches! Ironically, we could move across frontiers more freely in
colonial times. Now, because of an absurd nationalism springing
up between supposedly brotherly neighbors, each country in Africa
insisted on passports and visas, inventions of the whites, while denigrating those same whites to their people.] (p. 58)

Whilst Kpomassie does not embark on his journey with the explicit
intention of undertaking a political comparative project, it is clear
that, as he progresses, this becomes an unavoidable consequence of
his experiences. The pleasure and 'innocent observation' of the recreational traveller give way to cogent analyses regarding the challenges
faced by colonized cultures as they deal with the transition from
'tradition' to 'modernity'. Increasingly, Kpomassie's opinions are
established using his African origins as a yardstick, and the further his
journey progresses the more sophisticated his comparisons become.

Although the question of Danish influences on Greenland culture
figures in the text from the moment Kpomassie leaves Copenhagen
it is not an issue that, initially at least, is subjected to any critical
scrutiny. Thus the reader is informed through matter of fact and
non-judgemental comment that Danish builders are importing their
'modern' construction skills to Greenland, a Greenland beautician
will import Danish-trained notions of beauty to her homeland, motor
boats are replacing Kayaks and elderly Inuit are being fed Danish
food under the pretext that it, and not their usual diet, will build up
their strength. When criticism does begin to creep in, it is initially

based, as we saw, on moral objections to sexual mores, treatment of the elderly and alcoholic behaviour. In addition, much of this criticism sounds a false note given Kpomassie's own participation in some of the behaviour he condemns. Ultimately, however, Kpomassie comes to understand that a more complex interpretation of Greenland cultural norms is necessary, and moral condemnation slowly gives way to awareness of the political and historical factors shaping Greenland life at the time of his visit.[24]

Critical works on the Danish colonization of Greenland largely concur that the first significant effects of colonial policy on Inuit society and culture did not make themselves felt until the early part of the nineteenth century.[25] At this time, climate change persuaded the Danes that a transition from the subsistence economy of hunting to the more lucrative returns of the fishing industry should be encouraged. This kick-started the erosion of hunting knowledge that appears to be in terminal decline by the time Kpomassie reaches K'akortoq (Julianehåb) more than a century later. However, more significant than this nineteenth-century development is the change in attitude of the Danish government following the Second World War. Realization of Greenland's strategic position in the new global era forced the Danes to reassess their isolationist policies and encouraged them to embark on a process of 'modernization', the social consequences of which are patently obvious to the African traveller. Again, fishing was targeted for major investment, industry was concentrated in specifically targeted urban districts in the south and west, schools encouraged the learning of Danish as part of modernization and people were encouraged to move to towns for jobs and an improved benefit culture. Kpomassie's observations on the nature of Greenland society in the 1960s clearly support the conclusions of critics with regard to this particular period of colonial rule. Although we shall see that the African's obsession with discovering an 'authentic' hunting community is problematic, it nonetheless reflects the consequences of centralization and urbanization which led, according to David Sugden, to the abandonment of villages, the decline of nomadic lifestyles and the damaging dependency on welfare payments described in *L'Africain du Grœnland*.[26] Even more destructive, however, are Kpomassie's conclusions regarding the cultural consequences of this period. Danish colonial policy has clearly introduced a hierarchy that means Danes have better housing, are better paid and have a higher social standing whereas the Inuit population are not only denied access to their own culture through education, but appear to have internalized, in Fanonian manner, negative assumptions about the 'primitive' nature of their own cultural heritage:

> On met des enfants à l'école mais on ne leur apprend rien des activités traditionnelles. Mieux encore: on déprécie devant eux cette vie qui est pourtant la leur. Devenus adultes, ils ne savent même pas chasser en kayak. Voilà les Grœnlandais actuels de cette côte méridionale.
>   —Mais y a-t-il encore des localités où vivent des chasseurs de phoque, avec des chiens, des traîneaux et des kayaks?
>   —*Avannamoût*! (il faut aller plus au nord).
> [...]
>   —C'est là-bas que tu verras les Esquimaux.
>   Et ces Grœnlandais civilisés du Sud, descendant d'Esquimaux, prononcent à leur tour, comme jadis les Algonkins, ce mot «Esquimaux» avec mépris. (pp. 126–27)

> [Children are sent to school but are not taught anything about the traditional activities. Even worse, that way of life is disparaged to their faces, although it is their own. When they grow up, they can't even paddle a kayak. That's how things are for the Greenlanders on the southern coast.
> "But are there still places with seal hunters and huskies, sledges and kayaks?" I asked.
>   "*Avannamût*!" (You must go further north!)
> [...]
>   "That's where you'll see the Eskimos!"
>   And these civilised southern Greenlanders, descendants of Eskimos, now spoke the word "Eskimo" with contempt, as the Algonquians used to!] (pp. 112–13)

In certain respects, Kpomassie's impatience with the attitude of west coast Greenlanders and his determination to journey ever northwards in search of what he imagines will be a more authentic cultural reality allows him to rehearse what Holland and Huggan identify as the 'most obvious temporal attribute' in Arctic travel literature: deferral.[27] The faltering progress of Kpomassie's search for authentic versions of Greenland culture could also be said to be linked to the other more generalized temporal attributes of much Western travel writing: belatedness and nostalgia. For if Kpomassie is determined to find his imagined Greenland there is also an underlying suspicion that he has arrived too late to find it – indeed, this is precisely how Jean Malaurie sees it in his introduction. Although no clear definition of what will prove to be an elusive 'authenticity' is provided in the text, Kpomassie's disappointment with aspects of the Greenland he does find initially appears to bear some of the hallmarks associated with nostalgic Western travel literature, most notably in a seemingly unqualified tendency whereby, according to Charles Forsdick, 'transformation is cast crudely as death or loss' and the glorification of the past involves 'the freezing of a culture in time [and therefore] outside the processes of history'.[28] Aside from the not insignificant financial and climate considerations that dictate the means of transport he uses, Kpomassie's views of the mechanization of modes of transport also suggest that he is to some extent seduced by a wistful view of past traditions. This is most evident in his preference for travel by sledge but, curiously, it also emerges in a subtle, but instantly recognizable association of technological advances with more superficial travel practices. In the following quote, for example, the causal link implied between flying and the decline of 'authentic' travel immediately evokes an elitist Western anti-tourist discourse that associates accelerated travel – and its concomitant time–space compression – with the idea of interchangeable space and passive, usually mass, travel practices:[29]

> L'éventualité d'un voyage de Christianshaab à Thulé par hélicoptère est tout de suite exclue, non pas à cause de mes ressources qui du reste ne me le permettraient pas, mais simplement parce qu'une telle liaison par hélicoptère n'est point établie dans le pays. Et, même s'il existait, où est l'intérêt de survoler un paysage? Ne vaut-il pas cent fois mieux naviguer dans cette nature grandiose, se sentir écrasé par elle? Émotion supérieure à la superficielle admiration éprouvée d'en haut. (p. 277)

> [Travelling from Christianshåb to Thule by helicopter was immediately ruled out, not because of my own finances, which would not have stretched so far in any case, but simply because no such link had been set up in the country. And even if it had been, what's the point of flying over a landscape? Wasn't it a hundred times more worthwhile to sail through this natural grandeur, to feel its overwhelming power? Such feeling was far superior to the superficial admiration experienced from the air!] (p. 268)

In many respects, once Kpomassie achieves his first goal of reaching Greenland, it is this quest for authenticity – or the defeat of belatedness – that begins to propel his journey. Be it the possibility to travel in a 'traditional' manner or the encounter with non-Western ways of living, with each step further north he believes himself closer to the reality that corresponds to his preconceived ideas. Thus, upon reaching the town of Jakobshavn, where he is not too late to witness aspects of a subsistence economy based on traditional hunting methods, Kpomassie comments on the true Greenland identity of this community:

> Cette agglomération est la plus grœnlandaise de toutes celles que j'ai connues jusqu'à present à cause du nombre de kayaks, de chiens robustes et de traîneaux plus grands que ceux de Sisimut. On voit une quantité impressionnante de séchoirs où pendent des poissons, de la graisse de phoque, des peaux de renards. Si, avec ses 1 750 habitants, Jakobshavn possède une vingtaine de petits bateaux pour la pêche à la crevette et une usine modeste pour le traitement et la mise en boîtes, cette conserverie n'emploie qu'un nombre restreint de gens. La plupart des habitants vivent de la chasse, les parages du fjord glacé étant très giboyeux. (p. 185)

> [This community was the most authentically Greenlandic of all those I had seen so far: there were plenty of kayaks, strong huskies, and sledges bigger than those at Sisimut. On an impressive number of drying racks hung fish, seal blubber, and fox skins. Though with its 1,750 inhabitants, Jakobshavn possessed about twenty fishing and shrimp boats and a small cannery, this industry employed relatively few people. Most of the inhabitants lived by hunting, for the frozen fjord and its surroundings teemed with game.] (p. 179)

Once again, however, to read Kpomassie's narrative within the critical framework normally applied to Western travel literature is to ignore both his own cultural origins and the transformations in his thinking engendered by his travel experiences. First, despite the importance of waiting and deferral in *L'Africain du Grœnland*, it would be inaccurate to see this temporal trope as '[hypostatizing] into lyric poem, into crafted meditation on the motionless' in the way that the Western Arctic travellers discussed by Holland and Huggan do.[30] As with Kpomassie's views on Greenland morals, his views on the halting progress of his journey northward and the procrastinating tendencies of his hosts are transformed as his journey progresses. Comparisons between Africa and Greenland begin to impose themselves, and the search for an 'authentic' Greenland reveals itself to be doomed. Thus, instead of lyrical meditation, we initially find a sense of impatience, frustration and, at times, sheer boredom with the endless drinking, dancing and all-round partying. This, in turn, gives way to a more nuanced understanding of the reasons behind the particular rhythm of the Greenlanders' 'vie inactive' (p. 128) ['idle life', p. 113]. Climate conditions and long months of darkness clearly play a significant role, but Kpomassie also comes to realize that colonial policy – especially welfare payments and the development of fishing – has radically shaped people's attitudes, and that the poetic motionless analysed by Holland and Huggan can also be interpreted as the more socio-economic reality of idleness. Clearly, dependency on Denmark has extended beyond the economic and political and has infiltrated other areas of activity to such an extent that cultural and social life have literally become stagnant and Greenlanders' responsibility for their own activity has been deferred, or worse, relinquished: 'Pour ceux des Grœnlandais qui n'ont d'autres activités que celles que leur procurent les Danois, ces longues journées de fin de semaine s'annoncent affreusement vides' (p. 131) ['For those Greenlanders who have no other activity than what the Danes provide, the long weekend days are appallingly empty', p. 117].

Just as the notions of deferral and motionlessness are coloured by the historical and political context of *L'Africain du Grœnland*, the text's apparent nostalgia and belatedness also need to be analysed according to a more complex framework. First, the original meaning of nostalgia as homesickness becomes redundant in a text where the young traveller admits that 'je me suis à ce point adapté aux conditions d'existence de cette contrée que plus rien ne pourrait m'empêcher, je pense, d'y passer le reste de mes jours' (p. 303) ['I had adapted so well to Greenland that I believed nothing would stop me from spending the rest of my days there', p. 293]. More importantly, for Patrick Holland and Graham Huggan the nostalgia evident in so much Western travel writing – and of which there are undeniable traces in Kpomassie's writing – is better qualified by Renato Rosaldo's notion of 'imperialist nostalgia' as it describes 'the elegiac modes of perception through which the West mourns the passing of a world it itself has irrevocably altered'.[31] However, as an African travelling during a period of profound political change in his own country, Kpomassie's outlook might perhaps be more accurately described as both a backwards look to the future and a realistic appraisal of the present. The solidarity Kpomassie feels with his Greenland hosts is born not just of certain shared cultural practices such as the importance of orature and respect for the natural world. It also emerges from a recognition that, along with Africans, Greenlanders are emerging from a world which has, to paraphrase Rosaldo, been altered largely without their consent. It is Kpomassie's travel experiences that force him to reassess the nostalgic, and backward-looking quest for authentic culture and slowly accept a more complex reality. If the ubiquitous warmth and hospitality of his hosts show the persistence of aspects of traditional society, the loss of hunting skills, the fragmentation of kin-based groups and the lack of respect for elders suggest that other important elements have indeed been irretrievably lost. Other experiences, such as a rare refusal of hospitality, a racist exchange and the contemptible treatment by locals of the impoverished Thue family suggest a far less rose-tinted view of traditional society or emphasize a universal shared humanity, some aspects of which are more palatable than others: 'Je suis maintenant convaincu que je vis au milieu de gens qui ne sont pas différents des autres hommes de la terre et dont on a simplement exagéré le penchant communautaire' (p. 215) [I was now convinced that I was living among people no different from any other men on this earth, and that their communal spirit had simply been exaggerated', p. 208]. However, the most influential encounter in Kpomassie's slow journey to understanding the 'real' Greenland is his meeting with the elderly Robert Matâk.

In Frances Bartkowski's largely psychoanalytically influenced reading of *L'Africain du Grœnland*, Kpomassie's decision to reject the future his father has destined for him with the sacred Togolese cult is seen as the central factor motivating the young African's journey northwards. Viewed in this way, Kpomassie's journey becomes a form of 'transgression and flight from paternal authority' with Matâk attributed the role of a transferential father figure who allows the African to reconnect with his past and to decide finally to return to his country of origin.[32] Bartkowski's analysis certainly provides a more than plausible explanation for the undoubted bond of affection that exists between the two men as well as Matâk's role in persuading Kpomassie to return to Africa. However, it is also worthwhile examining the cultural significance that the Inuit's distinctive lifestyle represents and its influence in convincing Kpomassie of the broader significance of his travels for his homeland. For Matâk seems to represent for Kpomassie a form of viable cultural 'authenticity' that can in some way compensate for the disappointment of his failed quest for the 'real' Greenland. By 'authenticity' I do not mean an idealized, romanticized and ultimately unrealistic way of life. Clearly, aspects of Matâk's lifestyle are far from ideal, most notably the undeniable poverty and social isolation experienced by him and his family members. Instead, what is significant for Kpomassie is the way in which Matâk embodies a relationship to tradition that is at once respectful of the past without shutting itself off to outside and 'modern' influences. This dynamic view of tradition is in many ways mirrored by the appearance of Matâk's home: a rare surviving example of traditional wood and turf construction methods, the house is nonetheless capped with a 'cheminée anachronique faite en maçonnerie' (*AG*, p. 278) ['anachronistic masonry chimney', p. 269]. Similarly, the cramped interior is described as having the intimate sleeping arrangements of tradition but is nonetheless insulated against the cold with pages from Matâk's collection of contemporary periodicals of world affairs. The tiny hut thus becomes a personalized library with references that this sedentary old man, who is quite literally 'at home in the world', can consult in order to inform himself of other traditions. At the same time, he himself becomes a significant source of wisdom to which the outside world, in the shape of Kpomassie, can come to consult for insights on Inuit cultural traditions. (In this way one could also argue that his home successfully combines the features of both oral and written traditions.) Perhaps most importantly of all, however, is that Matâk's respect for the outside world and cultural difference appears to be colour-blind. Upon learning that Kpomassie is francophone, Matâk duly goes to his 'library' to look for a photograph of one of his African visitor's 'compatriots'. This turns out to be the French president, de Gaulle, and provides a rare example of an African traveller's 'difference' being perceived primarily through language rather than skin colour.

By the time Kpomassie decides to begin what inevitably will be the long journey home to Africa he has not just gathered factual information but has come to see life from the perspective of another tradition and has in turn assimilated it into his African view of the world. His particular method of comparison, I believe, does not simply consist of arrogantly converting difference into something assimilable to the configurations of his own culture of origin. Nor does it lead to an uncritical notion of some idyllic, harmonious postcolonial reality. Instead it has allowed him to discover travel's 'field of usefulness': the heuristic and epistemic benefits derived from the failed quest for authenticity and from Matâk's ability respectfully to combine the past with the future and outside influences. For Kpomassie, these lessons of travel must ultimately transcend the pages of a travel account and be applied concretely and usefully in order, as he says, to open postcolonial Africa to 'des horizons nouveaux' (*AG*, p. 303 [p. 293]). This, it is implied by the text's comparative methodology, will underline the ways in which so-called 'primitive' societies have value systems and ideologies to offer the wider world and need not, therefore, blindly succumb to a notion of progress based solely on 'Westernization'. In travel terms, then, it could be said that Kpomassie has abandoned an aimless sense of wandering in favour of a concrete purpose.

CHAPTER SIX

Le petit prince de Belleville, Maman a un amant: Immigrants and Tourists

Migrant mobility occupies an important space within postcolonial criticism. From Homi Bhabha's influential writings on the liminality of the migrant experience to the numerous critical works on diasporic cultural production, a range of conceptual terms has evolved to enable new ways of thinking about the experiences and consequences of mass postcolonial travel practices. However, this critical vocabulary, a corollary of contemporary theory's mobility turn, has often been the subject of heated debate, particularly when the movement concerned has been abstracted from important social and cultural variables. For example, in her important study of the different uses of travel-related language in post-modern discourse, Caren Kaplan speaks of the tendency of 'Euro-American discourses of displacement [...] to absorb difference and create ahistorical amalgams'.[1] Janet Wolff's judgement on the 'vocabularies of travel' that have saturated recent critical discourse identifies them as '*gendered* [and] just as the practices and ideologies of *actual* travel operate to exclude or pathologize women, so the use of that vocabulary as metaphor necessarily produces androcentric tendencies in theory'.[2] And in his discussion of the nomad, 'the geographic metaphor *par excellence* of postmodernity', sociologist Tim Cresswell warns against theoretical generalizations that flatten out difference and transform this travelling figure into 'a remarkably unsocial being – unmarked by the traces of class, gender, ethnicity, sexuality and geography'.[3]

Literary criticism of travel has been relatively successful in historicizing and rescuing Western women's textualizations of travel, and challenging the notion of travel discourses as being exclusively masculinist. For example, Sarah Mills sees the 'complexity of the way women are constituted as producers of texts' as resulting in the unstable 'discursive position' of colonial women travel writers who simultaneously repeat and undermine the prejudices of their male counterparts.[4] Patrick Holland and Graham Huggan also focus

on certain peculiarities of women's travel writing and are particularly attuned to the restrictive implications of gender on women's
travel practices. However, they also underline the more transgressive ways in which 'women have historically used travel writing to
cut across gender conventions' and 'to fashion a space in which to
explore their own identities'.[5] In Susan Bassnett's view, this journey
to self-discovery evidenced in women's travel writing also impacts on
form and content. Although Bassnett is careful to stress the dangers
of essentializing women's travel writing, she none the less suggests
that gender differences are discernible where the selection of material
is concerned, in the privileging of the personal and in the more intimate relationships many women travel writers establish with their
readers.[6]

Critical theory has arguably been less effective at using examples
of mass travel, especially economic migration, to challenge received
ideas on mobility.[7] For example, textualizations of migration are
still not given due recognition for their contribution to the development of travel literature, and the figure of the economic migrant, in
particular, can often become trapped within a homogeneous form
of alterity that underplays his/her contribution to, and commentary on, contemporary cultural realities. This failure on the part of
literary criticism systematically to contextualize new forms of travel
and mobility is an important reminder of the subliminal thinking
governing the abstracted use of travel metaphors. According to Tim
Cresswell, such substraction of the material and sociological factors
shaping new travel practices obscures the fact that it 'is always
predicated on the definition of other mobilities as threatening, transgressive and abject'.[8] For this reason, Paul White's contention that
migrant movements provoke 'altered or evolving representations of
experience and of self-identity' provides a useful thesis for identifying how mass forms of travel contribute to the development of new
cultural artefacts including, as White argues, 'new forms of literary
production'.[9]

Calixthe Beyala's literary diptych, *Le petit prince de Belleville*
and *Maman a un amant*, is the enormously successful portrayal of a
Malian immigrant family residing in the Parisian *quartier* of Belleville.
As with many of the texts already examined here, the centripetal pull
of Paris is still at the heart of the journey undertaken by the texts'
African characters, even if it is now dictated by economic factors.
Consequently, themes such as the ambivalent relationship with

'home' and 'destination', the resulting feelings of exile and alienation and the complex negotiation of identity persist. However, what
distinguishes *Le petit prince de Belleville* and *Maman a un amant*
from the texts examined previously is that the negotiation of *female*
identity provides the key impetus for plot development. Given that
this issue appears to be triggered by events that take place after the
actual intercontinental journey of the main female character, M'am,
discussion of her fate can lend itself to the metaphorical, abstracted
use of travel mentioned above. However, closer inspection reveals
that the development of M'am's epistemological journey does in fact
rest upon physical travel between different geographical locations,
and on a distinct spirit of adventure of the sort that can be elided by
'abject' definitions of migrant mobility. In the first instance, M'am's
journey from Mali to France exposes her to new cultural perceptions of female identity that prompt a consideration of where she
has come from and how her cultural origins shape attitudes to travel
and mobility. This particular cultural encounter/clash forms the focus
of *Le petit prince de Belleville* and leads, in *Maman a un amant*, to
a more sustained and novel exploration of migrant mobility when
M'am's family, the Traorés, become tourists and head southwards
from Paris for a two-week holiday

   A prolific and controversial author who has been in the literary
limelight for almost two decades, Beyala has produced works that
straddle, or explicitly espouse, different established literary forms.[10]
Where *Le petit prince de Belleville* and *Maman a un amant* are
concerned, frequent references to these popular texts within the
context of emerging francophone immigrant writing implies their
relationship to new forms of literary production. However, the French
literary establishment's tendency to cast Beyala at times as an African
writer and at others as an immigrant writer attests to the futility of
categorizing her work according to established literary taxonomies.
Consequently, this chapter will not impose a clear-cut generic identity for the Loukoum texts. Instead, the prime aim is to use White's
notion of '*altered* representations' as a fruitful way of examining the
particular portrayal and significance of travel and mobility in *Le petit
prince de Belleville* and *Maman a un amant*. My discussion of the
texts' various journeys will also adhere to the principle governing
Tim Cresswell's use of 'mobility': 'Mobility is the dynamic equivalent of place. [...] Within geographical theory and philosophy it has
come to signify meaningful segments of space – locations imbued

with meaning and power.'[11] This approach will permit an analysis of the texts' travel practices that sees them as linked to an intricate network of power relations that attempt to contain and police access to mobility. For this reason a crucial element in this chapter will be the influence of gender, especially female identity, on attitudes to travel and ways of travelling. Another key point of critical discussion here will be the realignment of migrant identity as the Paris-based Malian family in the texts studied become Western-style tourists or holiday-makers in the south of France. Finally, discussion of the symbolism of dress in both texts will be shown to illuminate the particular trans-formation of female identity provoked by immigrant travel.

Immigrant travel: a female perspective

Establishing the travelling identity of M'am, the central female character in *Le petit prince de Belleville* and *Maman a un amant*, is arguably less straightforward than it was in relation to the fictional protagonists examined earlier. This, as I shall demonstrate, can be explained in part by gender issues. However, it also derives from the specific context of immigration, the structure of the texts and the particular portrayal of the confined, controlled spaces that Beyala's female immigrant characters tend to occupy. Unlike textualizations of travel examined in previous chapters, the framing device of travel's descriptive narrative – departure and return – is also more obviously undermined in Beyala's Loukoum texts. Where M'am is concerned, the absence of an anticipated return to Africa ('home') means that a fundamental prerequisite of travel narratives is missing. For even when the more conventional travelogue is not structured according to a circular journey, the notion of an eventual return to the point of departure remains implicit. However, in Beyala's Loukoum texts, the central characters' African home is barely mentioned, and when it is, it is in terms of simplistic idealization of a fixed, unchanging space of tradition (the overwhelmingly male perspective) or outright hostility (the overwhelmingly female perspective). Indeed, the provocative association of home with oppression and poverty means that the original journey from Mali to France is seen less as an adventure than as a forced upheaval that approaches conditions of exile. As Abdou, M'am's husband explains, even if he wanted to leave, the notion of a voluntary departure is problematic:

Je suis venu dans ce pays tenu par le gain, expulsé du mien par besoin. Je suis venu, nous sommes venus dans ce pays pour sauver notre peau, acheter le futur de nos enfants. Je suis arrivé, nous sommes arrivés par ballots avec, enfouie au fond des cœurs, une espérance grosse comme la mémoire. (*PPB*, p. 20)

[I came to this country in the grip of material gain, expelled from my own land by need. I came, we came to this country to save our skin, to buy our children a future. I arrived, we arrived in bundles with a hope as enormous as memory itself, hidden deep in our hearts.] (p. 11)

On one occasion, Abdou fleetingly implies a sense of the stages of his journey to France as well as underlining some of the micro-processes that police immigrant travel: 'Jai immigré. J'ai franchi des frontières. J'ai laissé des empreintes digitales' (*PPB*, p. 51) ['I've immigrated. I've crossed frontiers. I've left fingerprints behind', p. 29]. However, despite the indication that more than one national border has been crossed, there is no account of the original journey to France: when it took place, how it was financed, what mode of transport was used and what itinerary was followed. This, coupled with the absence of any detailed description of the African point of departure, means that Beyala's Loukoum texts appear to hang less clearly together with those that present a more obvious record, or history, of migrant mobility through their description of a journey's stages.[12] This suppression of travel's linear or horizontal structure also tends to suggest a centripetal relationship to Paris and the West that reinforces the mythic status of the French capital examined in earlier colonial texts: getting to this Eden is all that matters and how this journey is achieved becomes unimportant. In the case of M'am, her relationship to travel and travellers is more acutely compromised given that the only explanation for her presence in Paris appears to be her identity as Abdou's wife. Nonetheless, despite all the evidence to the contrary, M'am is indeed a traveller and recognizing her as such should not be seen as a critically convenient strategy to include female or migrant experiences in discussion of African textualizations of travel. Indeed, it is precisely the singular nature of her travel experience that both justifies M'am's inclusion in this study and underlines the continued diversity of postcolonial African travel practices.

    The first crucial point to be made concerns M'am's role in underlining the limited access of African women to travel and in highlighting the paucity of examples of female travellers in African literature. Of course, the relatively late arrival of female voices onto the African literary scene explains the absence of a female travelling voice in the crucial period leading to and immediately succeeding independence when, as we have seen, key male-authored textualizations of travel appear.[13] However, this is not to say that women's roles are insignificant in such representations of travel. Even if discussion is limited to the texts studied in the present volume, it becomes clear that women, where they are mentioned, are clearly identified with 'roots', and men with 'routes'. In both *L'Africain du Grœnland* and *Kocoumbo*, mothers remain removed from any major decisions governing their sons' futures, and marriage to a woman is seen either as a means to stymie travel projects (as in Kpomassie's text) or to mark the conclusion of the international journey and the definitive return home of the male traveller (as suggested in Loba's text). In *Mirages de Paris* and *Chalys de Harlem*, marriage to women from the host culture, whether successful or not, is also clearly seen as marking an end to travel and a potential means of 'rooting' the African male within a new cultural context.

Not insignificantly, then, M'am's intercontinental journey is as a dependant. As we have seen, the 'independence' of certain male African travellers is in part undermined by their financial situation and their dependence on other, usually Western, sources of material and financial support. Nonetheless, once they 'arrive', these male travellers retain an important amount of control over their itineraries, whom they meet, what they see. M'am, on the other hand, seems to move from one sedentary and bounded space to another, where patriarchal norms remain unchanged and unchallenged. Moreover, in M'am's case, the family apartment in Belleville appears, initially, to illustrate both the sessility of women as construed by certain discourses of travel, and the double marginalization of African women as highlighted by elements of feminist postcolonial theory. Indeed, the two rooms she occupies with her husband, his second wife, Soumana, Loukoum (Abdou's biological son and M'am's adopted son) and Soumana's three daughters clearly function as metonymic references for restricted space and mobility. Moreover, the overwhelming association of M'am's personal drama (Abdou's infidelity, the arrival of Loukoum's biological mother, Aminata, Soumana's fatal illness, the legal consequences of polygamy) with this reduced space serves to oppose her sedentariness with the seeming dynamism of the male characters who are seen to move constantly between home, café, neighbourhood, various public spaces (schools, mosque, swimming pool, public park), and other parts of the city. M'am's spatial alienation and sedentary domestic reality are further reinforced by the narrative construction of *Le petit prince de Belleville* which largely excludes her subjective opinion in favour of an overwhelmingly male-controlled perspective. Loukoum's informal first-person narrative and *faux naïf* perspective dominate the narration. Brief confessional passages in formal, almost poetic tones provide Abdou's perspective. The female perspective is suggested through dialogue reproduced by Loukoum. This, then, suggests a silent, silenced image of the female immigrant, marginalized both by the patriarchal values of her own cultural origins and by the host society with whom she appears to have little meaningful opportunity to interact.

However, M'am's relationship to Paris differs significantly from that of her husband. Abdou clearly equates immigrant life in Belleville with interminable, disabling exile, and, as time passes, becomes increasingly sedentary, almost dissolving into the family couch by the end of *Maman a un amant*. M'am, on the other hand, retains a more stoical outlook that eventually transforms into optimism and increased physical mobility. For her, this new 'travelling-in-dwelling', even with its clear resonances of exile, becomes an opportunity to engage with another culture. It is evident, too, that this adventurous outlook predates her arrival in France so that even if the main motivation for her journey appears to be joining Abdou, she nonetheless admits that 'je voulais partir. Abandonner cet horizon de boue et de suie […]. Je voulais partir, acheter ma liberté' [I wanted to leave. To abandon that muddy, sweaty horizon […] I wanted to leave and buy my freedom] (*MAM*, p. 49). As M'am's adventure progresses, her interpretation of the meaning and potential of travel to France begins to diverge further from that of her husband. Of course, Beyala's attempt here to distinguish attitudes to travel along gender lines is problematic because of the danger of essentializing the issue. However, I believe that in these texts, that elsewhere are guilty of caricature and a certain schematic approach to plot, the attempt to delineate a specifically female experience of migrant travel and mobility is, in the main, successful. This success stems largely from a refusal to deal with the question of the main characters' changing identities as though they were a rigid linear continuum that evolved smoothly without periods of doubt and uncertainty. The complex 'movement' of the texts, as well as the consideration of male, female and generational relationships to mobility and space, further contributes to the complex portrayal of travel practices in the context of migration.

In this regard, it is worth revisiting the restricted space of the apartment and its role in exposing M'am to alternative views that enable her to question the patriarchal system restricting her mobility. Indeed, if certain nineteenth-century European colonial travellers were guilty of 'sedentary' practices as they moved through vast colonized spaces, then M'am's apparent sessility proves, in the end, to be far more dynamic and 'nomadic' than her husband's apparent mobility. This echoes Janet Wolff's assertion that any attempt to establish connections between female identity and what she identifies as an intrinsically masculine travel discourse must avoid 'inappropriate' and 'simple metaphors of unrestrained mobility'. For Wolff, any destabilization of patriarchal systems of thought 'has to be from *a location*'.[14] Accordingly, the Traoré family apartment is slowly transformed from a space where Abdou's wives appear willing to remain and play the submissive, fixed roles of 'tradition' to 'a location', in Wolff's sense of the term, that is open to alternative views of female identity. Such views are represented not just by the French 'feminist', Madame Saddock, but also by other African women who are introduced into the confines of the Traoré home in various contexts. In this way, the fixed location of home is transformed into a place of transit that forces M'am to re-evaluate her role as woman, wife and mother.

With regard to motherhood, for example, M'am has clear maternal responsibilities both as the 'official', legally recognized mother of Abdou's children and as a type of 'assistant' or adoptive mother within the polygamous structures of her own household.[15] Nonetheless, her cultural origins have taught M'am to place an inordinate value on women's ability to bear children. Failure to do so, therefore, is the ultimate stigma, both in her husband's opinion, but also, more damagingly, in her own view: 'L'absence d'un enfant. L'horreur que rien n'égale. [...] J'étais un arbre desséché, ou un animal inconnu mi-homme mi-femme qui s'accouplait avec Abdou et emprisonnait ses forces males' [The absence of a child. An incomparable horror [...] I was like a withered tree or an unidentified animal, half man, half woman, who slept with Abdou and entrapped his male strength] (*MAM*, p. 75). In the context of the Loukoum novels, travelling to France means exposure to new, and sometimes conflicting, concepts of female identity that challenge African views and force M'am to find worth in her own role; a sort of 'travelling to theory' as opposed to travelling theory. Thus, she discovers that biological mothers can sell their bodies (the prostitutes in both texts), abandon their children (Loukoum's mother, Aminata), have sexual relationships with other women (Mathilde), and verbally defy patriarchal authority (the prostitutes in the café, albeit with varying degrees of success). In addition, the successful shared responsibility and solidarity of M'am and her co-wife, Soumana, attest to an alternative view of polygamous arrangements that underlines the specific nature of Beyala's feminist discourse: one that refuses to capitulate to the supposed universal relevance of Western feminist discourse.

In relation to issues of physical travel and mobility, however, the apartment's true significance emerges when Abdou, betrayed to the police by Madame Saddock, is finally arrested for polygamy. This ultimate restriction on the patriarch's mobility propels M'am into the position of head of household (Soumana, rather too conveniently in terms of plot, dies following an unexplained illness and Loukoum, nominally head of household because of his gender, is too young to assume the responsibility). At this point, M'am shows remarkable entrepreneurial initiative by identifying the potential in Loukoum's efforts to make money by making and selling African bracelets to his French friends. In a similar fashion to Fara and Ambousse following the 1931 Exposition coloniale, M'am seizes on a consumer niche that has almost certainly been created by the cosmopolitan and 'exotic' tastes of Western travellers and establishes her own kitchen table business, importing materials from Africa to produce presumably 'authentic' ethnic jewellery. However, unlike Fara's limited foray into business, M'am succeeds beyond all expectation. Restricted still in her access to mobility, no doubt because of household responsibilities, she employs a white man to distribute her products. It is she too, in a remarkable reversal of roles, who 'directs' and controls Abdou's contribution to the business when he is released from police custody. In this way, M'am concludes an important 'stage' of a journey that has seen her subtly challenge, and invert, perceptions of female identity informed by gendered travel practices.[16] Indeed, by exposing the true dynamism of the supposedly static reality of the family home, women's place *par excellence* in the masculinist discourse of travel, M'am restates the emphasis on the personal traditionally associated with women's textualizations of travel and also proves herself more than ready to take to the road in order to explore the possibilities of physical travel in the form of tourism.

Immigrants to tourists

That tourism has a close relationship with migration is perhaps a self-evident fact, even if this connection can prove disquieting. Given tourism's association with recreational travel and pleasure, any comparison with the harsher socio-economic forces governing migration seems at best simplistic, at worst hypocritical. However, the overlaps between these very different forms of mobility and travelling figures reveal important issues related to postcolonial practices of, and attitudes towards, travel. Not least amongst the critical insights provided by examining the migration–tourism nexus is the light it sheds on globalized consumer capitalism and the way in which it makes these very different forms of mobility mutually dependent. For example, the growth of Western tourism in developing countries can be said to generate labour migration to provide services for tourists. In turn, migrants returning home or receiving visits from family left behind generate new forms of tourism that can, in turn, give rise to new motivations for migration.

In general, discussion of migration and tourism views these different forms of travel as interconnected yet retains a clear separation between the travelling figures of immigrant and tourist. When migrants are said to participate in tourism, it is usually as workers providing services (legitimate and illicit) for wealthier Western travellers. *Maman a un amant*, however, draws attention to a more unusual congruence between immigrant and tourist discourses by highlighting the potential for crossover between the two identities. Indeed, by reversing the orientation of the Africans' immigrant journey, Beyala questions the framework that construes immigrant mobility as geographically restricted and dominated by purely economic considerations. The holiday sequence also reinforces the dynamic view of identity construction at the heart of both Loukoum texts by illustrating the progressive building of migrant experience that, as Paul White stresses, contributes to divergent labels and 'perceptions of what [immigrants] may become'.[17] In addition, the exploration of the Traoré family's tourist experience develops another important theme of this study: the particular insights that African travellers provide into the society and culture of their Western destination, in this case provincial France.

The fact that M'am's family is going on a holiday that she finances suggests first that her status as an independent woman and traveller has been consolidated and, secondly, that the family have taken an important step towards integration into French society and culture. The historical and cultural significance of the annual *congé* [holiday] for French citizens, in particular Parisians, should not be underestimated. Indeed, although holidays, in the sense of a temporary relocation outside the home for rest and leisure, are not legally enshrined as a 'right', paid time off work, *congés payés*, have since 1936 under the Popular Front government been politically secured and, as Ellen Furlong explains, have come 'to be understood as a right of citizenship bound up within a European standard of living'.[18] The issue of the holiday destination chosen by the family also suggests that they clearly understand, and adhere to, the unspoken rules governing certain tourist practices. By falsely informing their immigrant neighbours that they are to spend the holiday in the Mediterranean town of Cannes they are indicating that they have understood that holidays mean being on the move in more ways than one, and that choice of destination is a crucial marker of social position. In addition, the Traorés' own reactions to their actual destination, the isolated and unknown village of Pompidou, are also underwritten with positive and negative stereotypes that suggest they have bought into oversimplified French discourses of rusticity criticized by Jean-Didier Urbain as 'des discours, qui prêtent aux lieux et aux usages un sens qu'ils n'ont pas et qui parlent à l'envi de "simple maison de pays" ou d'un "environnement-nature" alors que rien n'est simple ni vraiment naturel dans cette affaire' [discourses that attribute to places and customs a meaning they do not possess and that appeal to the desire for a 'simple provincial house' or an 'environment close to nature' when there is nothing either simple or natural about this issue].[19]

It would not be excessive I believe to suggest that the particular discourse of rusticity represented in the Loukoum texts is evidence of a highly complex reconfiguration of the type of 'imperialist nostalgia' mentioned in the previous chapter. Indeed, in his fascinating and perceptive study of the effects of decolonization on French tourist trends, Jean Viard provides an unconsciously postcolonial interpretation of the nostalgia evident in France's post-1960s *aménagement du territoire* [regional planning]. Noting that decolonization was accompanied by a relationship to space that was no longer defined by outward expansion, Viard explains how the French 'rediscovered' and 're-colonized' their own country through various spatial practices, including tourism, and thereby sought to redefine its metropolitan spaces and their meanings. In this way tourist destinations came to satisfy a wistful desire for the spaces and 'traditional' lifestyles associated with the former colonies.[20] However, identifying Rosaldo's specific notion of 'imperialist nostalgia' in the Loukoum texts is complicated given the uncertain position from which the family speaks: are they urbane Parisians who might be said to view the countryside through an 'elegiac mode of perception'?[21] Or are they African immigrants on holiday whose own marginalized position within the dominant society makes it difficult to imagine how they might see the French countryside as a type of 'static savage [society]' that operates as 'a stable reference point for defining [their] civilized identity'.[22] In fact, the Traorés shift between both identities and this is evidenced in the ambivalent way in which they relate to certain aspects of rural life. For example, comments by various family members regarding the superior quality of air and fresh vegetables available in provincial France and the timeless, unchanging simplicity and solidarity of human relations suggest a nostalgic view of the countryside as some lost paradise that can be accessed temporarily on holiday. On the other hand, the negative and, at times, crass observations regarding the lifestyle of Pompidou's full-time inhabitants (such as behaviour suggestive of madness, internecine disputes over seemingly petty issues, frustrated bachelorhood) suggest a form of rurophobia that casts the rural population as savage and their urban counterparts as sophisticated.[23] However, the comparison drawn by Loukoum between the socializing habits of 'toute la tribu française' [all the French tribe] in the local café and those of African immigrants in Belleville (*MAM*, p. 86) ultimately suggests an unexpected overlap between rural French and African immigrant communities. Indeed, this comparison suggests that Loukoum recognizes the villagers as representing, for a certain section of French society, a form of marginalized and exoticized identity that, within a Parisian context, is shared by Belleville's residents of African origin.

Nonetheless, there are important features of the Traorés' holiday experience that belie the image of solidarity between these rural and immigrant populations. For all the 'comedy' of Loukoum's narration, local reaction to ethnic identity is the primary indication that several decades after Fara travels to the Colonial Exposition the politics of visualization regarding black–white encounters persists. Even before leaving Paris, the Traorés are reminded that the way they travel is, for certain French observers, inextricably linked to their ethnic identity.

Failing to start the car in a traffic jam and move with the flow, Abdou and his family are treated to an explicitly racist insult from an irate driver: "'Avancez! braille un automobiliste. Nous ne sommes pas à Ouagadougou, ici! Nous sommes dans un pays civilisé, nous!'" ["Move it", yells a driver, "this isn't Ouagadougou. This is a civilized country!"] (*MAM*, p. 25). But whereas the technologically inferior movement and apparently nonchalant stalling of the African family appear entirely logical, even natural, to the Parisian driver's racist politics of mobility, later the notion that this family should be on holiday in rural France is construed as somehow unnatural. Thus, their first encounter with their hostess, Madame Trauchessec, sees them treated with incredulity when the true identity of this African 'tribu' [tribe] (*MAM*, p. 33) is revealed. For the French hostess, an African family on holiday in the countryside is clearly an anomaly, and their presence, therefore, only makes sense if they are either thieves as she first suspects, or lost, as Monsieur Tichit, another guest and M'am's future lover, initially believes. The reactions of these characters also suggest that in the minds of France's white population African immigrant bodies have become urban bodies that are alienated from 'natural' and rural landscapes.

On another level, it is also possible to see in these reactions to the Traorés' rural sojourn elements of the much commented post-war European narrative of travel's decline. According to Ellen Furlong, the lament of mass-tourism's inexorable rise by such illustrious figures as anthropologist Claude Lévi-Strauss and sociologist André Siegfried presented 'inauthentic' tourist practices as superseding 'authentic', elite travel and thereby provided 'the framework for contemporary stereotypes of mass tourists as herd-like [and] lacking internal social distinctions'.[24] Nonetheless, subtly disdainful comments by Monsieur Tichit concerning the size of M'am and Abdou's family, and their effect on the peace and tranquillity of the rural destination where he himself has also chosen to holiday suggest a more complex expression of this particular anti-tourist sentiment that converges with aspects of an anti-immigrant discourse. Indeed, throughout both texts, comments are made concerning the negative effect of immigrants on French life and culture that repeat criticism of the tourist's intrusion into the exclusive spaces and practices hitherto reserved for a pure, 'authentic' elite. In addition, the perception of the Traorés as a 'threat' reveals an antipathy towards migrant mobility (with its perceived ethnic character and associations of uncontrolled flux) that echoes fears of the

seemingly unrestrained democratic nature of tourism and its promotion of mass travel. In this way, the holiday context of *Maman a un
amant* could be said to point to the emergence of a new form of travel
hierarchy that opposes the French holidaymakers with the immigrant
tourists.

In a complementary way to the above reading, Nicki Hitchott
argues that the reception of the Traoré family by Pompidou residents
points not just to the persistence of racial stereotypes in African
experiences of travel in the West but also to a complex notion of
performance that sees the immigrant tourists cast as 'a kind of travelling spectacle or freak show'.[25] This point returns us once again to
unsettling similarities with *Mirages de Paris* which appear to suggest
that African postcolonial travel practices have come full circle since
the heyday of the French colonial era. Indeed, as with Ambrousse's
performance of his 'primitive identity' at the 1931 Colonial Exposition, Loukoum appears happy, indeed proud that his family actively
parade and perform their 'exotic', African identity. Likewise, the local
population appear willing to play the observing spectators of this
staged 'exoticism':

> Les jours suivants, on s'est vraiment amusés. [...] On a visité les
> environs. Nous portions nos gueules de Nègres en porte-drapeau,
> on marchait dans la ville. Ça en faisait une tribu! Les gens sortaient
> de leur maison, exprès. Ils nous regardaient, ils fouillaient nos
> tronches de garnison exotique. [...] J'étais très fier. C'est vrai, quoi!
> C'est pas tous les jours que ceux-là voyaient des Nègres en colonie.
> (*MAM*, p. 65)

> [The following days we really enjoyed ourselves. [...] We visited the
> surrounding area. We carried our black mugs like flag bearers; we
> walked through the town. We looked like a tribe! People came out
> of their houses deliberately. They looked at us, they scrutinized our
> exotic soldier faces. [...] I felt very proud. Really, I did! It's not every
> day that those people got to see blacks on holiday.]

However, as with the performances in *Mirages de Paris*, the
tourist performances of *Maman a un amant* tell us as much, if not
more, about this tourist place (provincial France) as they do about
the Traorés' particular cultural background. For, as Mimi Sheller
and John Urry remind us, tourist destinations can be interpreted
as 'places to play and places in play' that involve performances by
both guests and hosts.[26] According to Sheller and Urry's paradigm,
then, it is not just the observers of the Traorés' exotic otherness who

are performing but all those whose activities, formal and informal, suggest a certain 'staging' of Pompidou. Thus Madame Trauchessec's cooking, cleaning and serving, her son Michel's informal guiding and perhaps even the ridiculously caricatured dialogue in the village café (an indiscreet discussion of a private affair of marital infidelity) all point to what Sheller and Urry identify as 'places [...] brought into being'. This allows the performances I have just described to be understood as a means of bringing into play notions of an unsophisticated, parochial, welcoming rural France. In addition, just as the staged authenticity of the cultures within the Exposition suggested alternative, complex realities within and outwith this bounded place, the intersecting performances of both the immigrant tourists and the rural hosts in *Maman a un amant* point to the need to de-centre discussion away from a homogeneous understanding of the immigrant family and instead focus on the complex interplay of mobilities that undermine fixed notions of place and identity. Consequently, just as the decision to go on holiday reveals an evolution in the Traorés' migrant identity, their very presence and their encounters with the Pompidou locals reveal a place and its population that are themselves constantly evolving through patterns of international migration, national relocation and rural exodus.

Despite clear overlaps with issues of performance in *Mirages de Paris*, it would be inaccurate to suggest that *Le petit prince de Belleville* and *Maman a un amant* bring African travellers in the West back to the heart of the alienating, labyrinthine space of *Mirages de Paris*. Certainly, there are shared elements in the experiences of the travelling African characters, most notably the persistence of the role of ethnicity in shaping perceptions of how they see and are seen. In a related manner, the questions of performance and the staging of identity continue to shape how these characters become at once observers of Western culture and spectacles for a Western audience. Nonetheless, the notions of performance and staging in African travel to the West do not have to be seen as inevitable nor, more importantly, do they have to lead to alienation. If the previous chapters prove anything, it is that African travel to the West is not a unitary phenomenon to be characterized in such a reductive way. To a certain extent, all cultures could be said to create traditions, and to engage in a continual process of performance and reinvention for complex sacred and secular purposes. And this is arguably even more true of the kinds of hyper-mobile societies that have been developing since the era of mass travel. The point in *Le petit prince de Belleville* and *Maman a un amant* is that such performances are not always seen as the detrimental force they come to represent in *Mirages de Paris*. Moreover, as was noted above, the roles of spectator and object of spectacle rotate so as to make their identification purely along ethnic lines redundant (although ethnic hierarchies and discrimination clearly do persist in other ways). Nobody, neither hosts nor tourists, is permanently detached from the performances that bring Pompidou into play, and all are subjects of discriminating gazes. In this way, Beyala's texts ultimately serve to underline the more positive aspects of staging and performance of identity by associating them with the more liberating and revitalizing forces of travel and cultural encounter.

Dressing for travel

In his excellent discussion of the vestimentary codes of Congolese *sapeurs*, Dominic Thomas illustrates how dress functions as a significant and intricate site for the articulation of identity in colonial and postcolonial contexts. For example, Thomas explains how, during the colonial era, clothing became a means to control the colonized body but also provided 'the occasion for the subversion of established modes and the rejection of the dictates of accepted norms. [...] The adoption of alternative aesthetic codes presents itself as a symbolic gesture aimed at reclaiming power.'[27] Although the above quotation addresses a different context, Thomas's assertion suggests how the issue of dress can be approached in the case of *Le petit prince de Belleville* and *Maman a un amant*. In effect, the sustained referencing of female dress and aesthetic norms throughout both texts suggests a specific semiotics of clothing that points at once to patriarchal views of female appearance and sexuality as well as to the main female character's own exploration and questioning of these issues. Indeed, over the course of both texts, attitudes to clothing emerge as the most effective means of tracing the complex renegotiation of M'am's identity provoked by travel and cultural encounter.

In order to progress in her personal journey, M'am begins to *make* and *sell* jewellery, a key product of the fashion industry. However, the way M'am and other female characters *wear* clothes is also of fundamental importance. For example, in the more sedentary context of *Le petit prince de Belleville*, female dress, not unsurprisingly, is largely seen to reflect a patriarchal and 'traditional' view of female identity and also to denote a clear distinction between African and French women. In M'am and Soumana's case, their manner of dressing and their relationship to clothes in general suggest a strong link between their culture of origin and the place allocated to them by patriarchal values. Indeed, unlike Abdou, who spends money the family can ill afford on new attire for the purposes of adulterous seduction, M'am and Soumana never dress to impress in this way. Instead, a routine part of their domestic activities is said to involve ironing and darning their husband's clothes. For the most part, description of the co-wives' clothes suggests that they act as they look. Succinct references to their traditional *boubous* evoke a garment less revealing of flesh and body contours than the type of 'inappropriate' clothing that elsewhere attracts the lascivious male gaze. On the contrary, the provocative dress sense of prostitutes and other more 'desirable' (according to the male perspective) females is recorded in detail in order to underline a fundamental distinction where attitudes to sexuality are concerned. Such expansiveness also extends to Loukoum's descriptions of the outward appearance of some of the young French females in Loukoum's class, and Goélène, Monsieur Tichit's daughter. Indeed, these girls' relationship to clothing appears to suggest a culturally rooted assertiveness and independence that also differs fundamentally from Abdou's submissive co-wives. (That is not to say that there is nothing troubling in the idea that these young French girls, through their appearance, seem to have internalized a complex set of expectations regarding female behaviour that are as phallocentric as those governing the behaviour of African female characters.) In addition, in a similar way to the darning mentioned above Lolita's casual offer to donate her shoes and socks to the poor of the Third World highlights the disposable nature of fashion and clothing in modern Western consumerist society as well as pointing to the stark material conditions separating her life from that of Loukoum and his family. In this regard, it is also notable that on the only occasion prior to her financially independent status that M'am does don Western-style dress the items of clothing are second-hand. The incident in question is the visit to the family home of Loukoum's biological mother, Aminata, whose revealing clothing immediately signals her out, in M'am's eyes, as 'une créature [...], une fille de-rien-du-tout' (*PPB*, p. 127) ['a tart, a girl worth nothing at all', p. 84]. Aminata's arrival is also notable because it illustrates the way in which clothes are used as a prop or disguise to 'perform' a particular identity. By changing into her second-hand Western attire in order to receive Aminata in her own home, M'am is seen to use clothes to play someone of higher social and moral standing and thereby deflect from her own failure to achieve status through reproduction.

It would be inaccurate, however, to suggest that over the course of *Le petit prince de Belleville* there is no evolution or ambiguity in M'am and Soumana's vestimentary norms and in the significance of their dress. As I noted earlier, there is a particular dynamism in the first part of the Loukoum diptych that is conveyed through mention of subtle changes in the co-wives' appearance. For example, railing against Abdou's infidelities (past and present) and her own impending death, Soumana makes a dramatic entrance to the family's New Year party and summons up her remaining dignity by dressing to kill her own despair. This is the only occasion where ethnic dress is described as elegant and imposing and it serves to underline the complexity of how any particular style of dress functions according to personal intention. However, here the impact of Soumana's ethnic dress is limited given that she is destined to fail to redress either the inevitable outcome of her illness or the gender inequalities she believes have destroyed her life. Nonetheless, in this instance Soumana's dress does succeed in becoming a highly symbolic assertion of her desire to confront oppression from within the home and to reject the conformity associated with her usual style of dress. And despite her failure, an earlier confession by Abdou suggests that changes in the appearance and behaviour of immigrant African women are indicative of a transition to a new situation that will prove disorienting for the previously all-dominant male:

> Les femmes se sont vidées, à mon insu. Elles ont ôté leurs pagnes et revêtu leurs corps de mousseline. Elles ont ôté les poils sous les aisselles et rasé l'angle du pubis. Plus rien n'est nommé. (*PPB*, p. 133)

> [The women have gutted themselves behind my back. They've taken off their pagnes and dressed themselves anew in muslin. They've removed the hair from under their armpits and shaved the pubic area. Nothing is called by its name any more.] (p. 91)

It is the holiday sequence of *Maman a un amant*, however, that once again provides the most fruitful context for examining the

interplay of physical mobility and vestimentary codes in the refash-
ioning of female migrant identities. In their discussion of tourism
mobilities, Mimi Sheller and John Urry note that 'places are not
simply encountered [...] but are performed through embodied play.
This playfulness', they argue, 'requires equipment for the body.'[28]
Needless to say, clothes form a fundamental part of such equipment
and are very much a reflection of the type of holiday in question
and the particular associations of the destination chosen. Earlier, the
Traoré family's understanding of tourist destination as status symbol
was underlined in their decision to lie to their neighbours and tell
them they were spending their holidays in sophisticated Cannes. An
extraordinary scene in *Le petit prince de Belleville* reveals that the
family is also aware that Cannes, as a luxury holiday resort and play-
ground of the wealthy, possesses its own vestimentary codes. Dressed
up in gloriously outlandish clothes and performing a wealthy, liberated woman, free to travel (expressed through the wearing of trousers), Soumana imagines she can escape the Belleville apartment and
leave for Cannes to become a 'real' actress:

> À Cannes, il y a les mers, les lords anglais qui se promènent sur la
> plage, il y a les bateaux, les oiseaux, les clowns dans les rues et des
> ballons qui tombent du ciel, des princesses de Monaco qui s'battent
> en caleçon sur les plages. J'aurai des belles robes, des manteaux de
> fourrure, des voitures, des bijoux. (*PPB*, p. 96)

> [In Cannes, there's the sea, there are English lords who take walks
> along the beach, there are boats, birds, clowns in the street, balloons
> falling from the sky, and princesses of Monaco who romp around
> on the beach in their swimsuits. I'll have gorgeous dresses, fur coats,
> cars, jewellery.] (p. 61)

Unlike Soumana, whose dress changes and performance are confined
to the home and a limited audience, M'am's holiday allows her to
continue an experimentation with Western modes that is primarily
conducted for her own benefit. This experimentation is earlier
launched by her transformation into business woman which she
marks sartorially by donning trousers in the home for the first time. In
Pompidou, however, M'am is shown to undergo an entire wardrobe
change. Sanctioned apparently by climate and season, M'am's shape-
less *boubous* are replaced by ever-tighter, more revealing garments.
As Ian Littlewood notes, this type of clothing can be seen as the
vestimentary norm of the sun holiday. However, they are more than

just practical and underline a certain exposure of the body that is intimately linked with contemporary Western holiday practices that '[thrust] on us an awareness of the physical in ourselves and other people, eroding the hierarchies asserted by conventional dress'.[29]

Littlewood may be correct in assuming that the hierarchies of class are temporarily erased by holiday fashion (although it is arguable that fashion is more complicated than he suggests and that issues of brand and style will still serve a discriminatory purpose). However, a close reading of M'am's holiday attire and the attention it draws to her physical appearance suggest initially a continued objectification of the female body by the male gaze. This thesis appears to be supported by descriptions of M'am's clothes and body that mirror those used to describe prostitutes in *Le petit prince de Belleville*. Indeed, M'am is explicitly referred to as a 'fille de-rien-du-tout' [a tart] by her husband, a term she herself has used earlier to describe Aminata. M'am's objectification is also suggested by the voyeuristic gaze to which she is constantly subjected each time her clothing is described. Reactions to her changing appearance are normally provided by Loukoum, who is clearly meant to illustrate the transfer from generation to generation of sexist, patriarchal views. However, Monsieur Tichit's reaction to her bikini, as well as the comments by local police in reaction to mere descriptions of her more revealing dress style, also show how the male characters, regardless of cultural origin, interact with women on the basis of clothing they clearly decode as sexually suggestive and inviting. Of course, it could also be argued that the explicitly sexual reactions of white French males to M'am's appearance indicate the recurrence of colonial stereotypes of the black female libido.

The bikini, the sartorial garment *par excellence* of female sexual liberation as well as female objectification, is highly emblematic of the frequently conflictual visual codes conveyed by dress.[30] Essentially, this garment 'même poids qu'un pop-corn' [weighing as much as a piece of popcorn] (*MAM*, p. 58) provides an opportunity for exploring another, more positive significance of the changes in M'am's style. Indeed, M'am's wearing of the bikini on a swimming excursion with Monsieur Tichit underscores, once again, how dress is imbued with meanings understood by wearer and observer. However, it is also clear that dress is manipulable and these meanings, therefore, do not always coincide. In this way, it is possible to argue that M'am's confident exposure of her body is not necessarily meant to convey the highly sexualized message Monsieur Tichit believes is being transmitted to him.

That the meanings of dress should conflict and contradict is precisely what Roland Barthes suggests in his discussion of the language of clothing. Barthes elucidates his ideas on clothing's meaning by linking them to Saussurian structural-linguistic analysis. Consequently, he is able to distinguish between *dress* (clothing's equivalent of Saussure's *langue*) as an 'institutional, fundamentally social reality' and *dressing* (Saussure's *parole*) as a 'second, individual reality [...] in which the individual actualizes on their body the general inscriptions of dress'.[31] *Clothing* is thus used in the way that Saussure uses *langage*; that is in order to refer to the generic whole formed by dress and dressing. Crucially, however, and despite the totalizing aspects of his methodology, Barthes also stresses that although dress and dressing can coincide, the meaning of dress can only be deduced by examining the way in which the wearer participates in clothing's semiological system: 'It is the degree of participation in the system (be it total submission, derivations, or aberrations) that is meaningful: the value of a system can only be understood via acceptances of, or challenges to it.'[32] In this way, Barthes seems to be saying, clothing's meanings can be renegotiated according to individual contexts. What is important, then, in M'am's case is not that men decode her dress as conveying an explicit sexual message destined exclusively for them but that she has learned to 'dress' herself in Barthes's sense of the term: it is she, and not others, who chooses how she will dress and what it is meant to reveal and convey of her inner self. Consequently, if M'am chooses the bikini to reveal herself, it should be seen neither as submissive to a masculine and highly sexualized vision of female beauty nor as a narcissistic preoccupation with self-image. Rather, M'am's dressing should be seen as self-definition that ultimately highlights *her* discovery of *her own* desires.

Increasing exposure of the body and the discovery of sexual pleasure in *Maman a un amant* seem initially designed to evoke both the sensual abandon and licentiousness associated with travel and holidays in the Western literary and cinematic imagination. (M'am's actions could also be construed as confirming a patriarchal view of female travellers as being either sexually vulnerable or sexually 'loose', and therefore requiring the presence of a protective male companion.[33]) But M'am has not recklessly submitted to sexual temptation. Instead, her affair bears certain resemblances to that depicted in *Shirley Valentine* as discussed by Ian Littlewood. For Littlewood, the holiday 'fling' that structures this 1986 Willy Russell play (and its highly popular 1989 film version) becomes a 'permanent revela-tion' and typifies 'a vital strand of tourism in which self-discovery and sexual discovery are twin sides of the same coin'.[34] In certain respects Littlewood's comments also echo a crucial aspect of Simone Fullager's discussion of desire within the context of female travel. As with M'am, whose discovery of her own desires includes, but is by no means limited to, sexual desire, Fullager identifies her own travel experiences as exemplifying the particular movement of desire as it functions in the liminal space of travel. This movement is character-ized as

> a movement of release, of letting go in order to be open to difference through an experience of desire that is an affective state. [...] The liminal space of travel offers a way of thinking through the tensions in-between, mind and body, mastery and abandon, movement and fixity. This liminality enables us to conceive of a positive desire to move towards the world, not in order to grasp, but rather in the wish to engage openly with the world in its difference. It is a desire for the journey, rather than a point of arrival, which requires a more fluid or mobile experience of subjectivity.[35]

With such a definition in mind it becomes possible to understand the wider significance of M'am's affair with Monsieur Tichit. What is especially significant is that her adultery does not become a two-week lapse from normal social and family structures but continues afterwards and offers her a more independent and viable way of life. However, this outcome should not be construed as granting the harmony of a happy conclusion. Rather, M'am's obvious desire for the journey means that the holiday instigates a process of constructing both her identity and her home. As such, she must face a number of important choices upon her return to Belleville. Many of these are painful (continued infidelity and the decision to leave her family), but many (such as learning to write) are transformative and confirm M'am as finally dwelling in travel.

Afterword

Postcolonial Eyes underlines in concrete terms the presence of a particular strand of francophone African literature that presents black Africans not as static objects of reflection for the West but as mobile, critically reflective subjects. I have illustrated how, in their own ways, each of the texts studied here contributes to the consolidation of 'inverted' patterns of travel and pre-eminently qualifies as travel literature projecting African views of other peoples and places. Throughout this study, the processes of comparison intrinsic to travel and its textualization have been consistently highlighted. The specific interpretative frameworks informing this comparative dimension have been unquestionably African, and the exploration of other cultures – their differences and their similarities – through travel has also served to highlight the complex nature of African societies themselves as they negotiate their place within the wider world. As the chapters of this study move from the 1931 Colonial Exposition in Paris to the more recent context of economic migration these interpretative frameworks shift and evolve according to the political, cultural and socio-historical contexts of individual texts.

If in *Mirages de Paris*, the earliest text studied, Africa very tentatively presents itself as a site from where comparisons may be made and theories may travel, this is done under crippling conditions of self-doubt and assumed cultural inferiority that appear to compromise the 'authority' of the traveller's observations and lead him, quite literally, into a dead end. Nonetheless, the notion of the 'West' as the seductive, powerful domain of truth and knowledge is subtly undermined by the African traveller's observations, a process that is developed in Aké Loba's *Kocoumbo, l'étudiant noir*. Here the 'risk' of observing and interpreting the 'West' according to an African frame of reference persists, but this time the traveller returns 'home' where, it is implied, the lessons of travel may be applied in practical ways that largely benefit the individual traveller. In the period from the late 1950s–60s, when decolonization and independence are either inevitable or newly achieved, an undeniable sense of hope and optimism pervades African textualizations of travel. This is translated into a growing sense of confidence that leads to a decided geographical diversification of African intercontinental travel and allows the authors of *Un Nègre à Paris*, *Patron de New York*, *L'Africain du Grœnland* and *Chalys d'Harlem* to engage in critical observations of 'Western' culture – in the majority of cases using the recognizably Western form of the travelogue – that are of more far-reaching value than the individual rewards of travel highlighted in Loba's text. For these journeys are as much epistemic as physical, and intended to show postcolonial Africa how it might begin to take its place in the world as an equal amongst others. In many respects, Calixthe's Beyala's fictionalized accounts of a Malian immigrant family appear to belie the hope and optimism of these earlier texts. Nonetheless, despite the 'abject' travel conditions that implicitly mark the original journey of these Africans to France, Beyala is more concerned with highlighting the ways in which immigrant travel can evolve into different practices of mobility that attempt to regain the confidence and optimism of newly independent African travellers. Her emphasis on women's experiences also points to important distinctions in travel's 'usefulness' and its role in enabling female travellers to discover and define identities.

This study has been motivated by diverse aims. One has simply been to draw attention to some of the voices and travels of Africans who have been silenced and immobilized by Western colonial discourses and literary traditions. By so doing, it is hoped that a distinctive body of African travel literature will be recognized as bearing witness both to the historical diversity of travel practices and the myriad of perspectives on other peoples and places. It has not been my intention, however, to argue that African writers can only record their experiences of mobility by means of European paradigms and discourses or that African textualizations of travel must invariably be read as the opposite number of Western travel literature. Throughout, it has been clear that African attitudes to and practices of travel remain relevant, contributing in particular to the value attributed to intercontinental travel. It is also important to stress that the incorporation of approaches to alterity in these texts should not be interpreted as an inevitable process of correcting or subverting the distorting perceptions of so many Western colonial/neo-colonial

accounts of journeys to Africa. What these texts collectively underline is that travel literature, regardless of the perspective from which
it is written, does not produce complete understandings or objective
truths about other cultures. Indeed, in *Patron de New York* we have
seen that an African traveller is capable of decontextualized generalizations and problematic assessments of cultural difference. I have
also alluded to the undeniably patriarchal view of women and moral-
izing tone that underpins some of Kpomassie's early observations on
Inuit lifestyle and which Debbie Lisle sees as evidence of 'behaviour
previously restricted to colonial powers'.[1] I believe, however, that the
history of colonization, the continued relevance of colonial ways of
visualizing Africans – be they on the move or not – and the undeniable importance of asymmetrical power relations between Africa and
much of the Western world means that, whatever negative cultural
prejudices these texts may reveal, they cannot easily be equated with
a regressive return to the practices of colonialist travel literature. First,
as travelling black subjects in overwhelmingly white cultures, these
authors are constantly faced with the objectification of their own
identity which means they are more aware of, and arguably more
critical of, the processes involved in such objectification. More significantly, in the cultural encounters described by Dadié, Kpomassie
and Diakhaté, and also in Beyala's texts, there is a distinct desire to
shift the focus away from difference – or devaluing interpretations
of difference – by insisting on a certain common humanity and by
proposing new ways of observing others that are both constructive
and enabling.

Another fundamental aim of this study has been to establish
the relevance of this study's corpus of works to the sophisticated
theoretical apparatus used for reading Western travel literature.
However, this is not to say that I have read African texts in order to
'prove' the claims of theory. The inevitable referencing of Western
forms and discourses of travel in *Postcolonial Eyes* should not simply
be seen as evidence of another example of analysing Africa according
to categories and conceptual tools that depend uncritically on a
Western epistemological order. Throughout, I have illustrated the
theoretical challenges raised by this African writing by underlining
the need to test, confirm, criticize and disprove certain theoretical
arguments where different contexts demand this approach. Most
specifically I have focused on the question of genre as a means, first,
to explore the exclusion of African authors from travel literature and,

secondly, to argue for their inclusion in this category. Indeed paying attention to form is fundamental to recognizing the existence of an African literature of travel and also to arguing for its relevance to the critical framework that has developed over recent years to analyse travel practices. This has meant acknowledging from the outset the influence of European travel literature and the ways in which it effectively transformed Africa into a textual subject to be discovered and analysed according to specific codes and myths. Identifying African travel literature then necessarily involves learning to read it alongside and against Western narratives of travel, examining where it adopts, rejects, develops and subverts generic conventions and also how it proposes not just an important perspective on Western cultures but also a new and more dynamic view of Africa and Africans. Attention to genre has also meant that the particular rhetorical and stylistic strategies and choices of the texts examined have also been highlighted and literariness has not been ignored at the expense of equally important historical and social contexts.

A consistent focus of this study has also been the connections between the economics and aesthetics of travel in the context of African writing. My highlighting of the material aspects of African travel practices points to a theoretical failure to account for the very real importance of material comfort, or lack thereof, to shaping motivations for and experiences of travel. At a time when migrants and nomads are frequently employed as metaphors for a deterritorialized existence, and travel and journeys construed as the leisure pursuits of time-rich, self-indulgent Western subjects, the texts studied here challenge any naive notion that African travellers might so easily be free of social and material constraints. Moreover, by highlighting the conflict between the practical concerns of embarking on a journey and the symbolic modes of describing the benefits of travel, these texts also expose the blind spots of travel criticism's metaphorical language. I have relied in particular on a loose interpretation of Cheryl Fish's conceptualization of travel 'as a field of usefulness' to describe what might be termed the 'heuristic impulse' evident in many of the texts studied, particularly 'conventional' travel narratives where the travelling authors appear anxious that their accounts be used for practical purposes: namely the transformation of independent African societies and the positive re-evaluation of African culture in a postcolonial global context. The emphasis on cultural similarity revealed in certain of these texts also exposes the ways in which critical discourse has come to highlight difference as the lifeblood of Western travel literature's observational practices and thereby elide the significance of cultural similarity or *wiedererkennen* and their significance to travel encounters.

This study has also tentatively raised the issue of language travel, particularly as it pertains to francophone African authors from the colonial era. Frequently, the exposure to language through travel that might be expected in texts such as those examined here is either absent or underplayed. However, as I have shown, this does not make the question of language in the context of African intercontinental travel insignificant. For the colonized francophone African traveller to France a language shared with the host culture never quite succeeds in erasing a fundamental and often alienating difference. Unlike white travellers with intimate and expert knowledge of French, the perfection of accent as the traveller's 'ultimate disguise' is never seen to function effectively for Africans.[2] For it would seem that s/he cannot travel unobserved, cannot conceal the traces of origin through language as her/his difference is seen before it is heard, interpreted before s/he can interpret. Conversely, inadequate knowledge of the other's language is never described as a hindrance in texts dealing with non-francophone destinations. This is not to say that colonial forms of visualizing and interpreting difference are irrelevant to such travel experiences. However, the degree of ease with which Kpomassie in particular, but also Diakhaté's protagonist and to a lesser extent Dadié in the United States, move through different linguistic realities suggests that language is not perceived as presenting quite the same obstacle to African travellers as it does to Western travellers. Indeed, the decidedly unimportant nature of 'language travels' suggests that many Africans, coming as they often do from more multilingual realities than Western travellers, may be better equipped to deal with the linguistic challenges of international travel.

Much remains to be said on African practices of travel and mobility. In particular, the various forms of travel in pre-colonial African culture need examination as does their representation in oral literature. Contemporary travel practices within the continent – both within and across Africa's national borders – have also been neglected and a more sustained analysis of their forms and significance would contribute greatly to the urgent task of particularizing the dominant forms of Western travel. The very distinctive tone, preoccupations and geographical diversification characterizing textualizations of intercontinental travel during the late 1950s–60s also deserves more sustained analysis. The francophone texts studied here would benefit from being read in relation to other African accounts of intercontinental travel during this era in order to gain a larger picture of how the hopes, anxieties and tensions of decolonization fit into specific global contexts such as the puppetry of the Cold War. The issue of geographical diversification could also be examined in relation to the 'migritude' authors mentioned in the introduction to determine the extent to which locations other than France and Africa figure in their work. In a related way, an axis of travel that warrants attention concerns that of French-born protagonists of African descent who return to explore and discover Africa, such as in Gaston-Paul Effa's *Voici le dernier jour du monde*.[3] Needless to say, such journeys frequently raise the age-old inequities between the global 'south' and 'north' yet also, as in the case of Abdourahman A. Waberi's *Aux États-Unis d'Afrique*, provide the basis upon which to invert these divisions by imagining Africa as the centripetal force pulling impoverished Western immigrants to its shores.[4] The issue of gender and travel, a particular focus of Chapter 6, is also a subject that has received insufficient critical attention. From a purely diachronic perspective there is an urgent need to determine when African women have embarked on intercontinental travel, where they have travelled and under what conditions. This would allow for a more sophisticated debate on the precise role of African women in travel literature and the extent to which their experiences could be said to converge or diverge from that of male travellers. By engaging directly with such questions critics could do much to challenge the tendency to fix Africa in the negative image of the 'Dark Continent'. Acknowledging the complex history, politics and aesthetics of travel and mobility in Africa would show how Africa is not unmoored from the rest of the world but intimately connected to it and contributing imaginatively to Michael Cronin's eloquent notion of 'the sustained enduring wonderwork of human geopoetics'.[5]

Notes

Introduction

1 Tim Youngs, 'Where are We Going? Cross-Border Approaches to Travel Writing', in *Perspectives on Travel Writing*, edited by Glen Hooper and Tim Youngs (Aldershot: Ashgate, 2004), pp. 167–80 (p. 169).

2 Patrick Holland and Graham Huggan, *Tourists with Typewriters: Critical Reflections on Contemporary Travel Writing* (Ann Arbor, MI: University of Michigan Press, 1998), p. 4.

3 James Clifford, *The Predicament of Culture: Twentieth-Century Ethnography, Literature and Art* (Cambridge, MA: Harvard University Press, 1988), p. 22.

4 Two notable exceptions are the anthologies *Always Elsewhere: Travels of the Black Atlantic*, edited by Alasdair Pettinger (London and New York: Cassell, 1998) and *Other Routes: 1500 Years of African and Asian Travel Writing*, edited by Tabish Khair and others (Bloomington, IN: Indiana University Press, 2005). Both include introductory essays (by Pettinger and Khair respectively) that offer helpful discussion of the issues determining the neglect of less well-known travel writing traditions.

5 Christopher Miller, *Nationalists and Nomads: Essays on Francophone Literature and Culture* (Chicago, IL: University of Chicago Press, 1998), p. 158.

6 Ibid., p. 167.

7 Mary Louise Pratt, *Imperial Eyes: Travel and Transculturation* (London and New York: Routledge, 1992), p. 31.

8 Ibid., pp. 74–75.

9 Ibid., p. 204. Emphasis in original.

10 Ibid., p. 84.

11 Sara Mills, *Discourses of Difference: An Analysis of Women's Travel Writing and Colonialism* (London and New York: Routledge, 1991), p. 174.

12 As Pratt and other influential critics of more contemporary travel writing have shown, the end of colonization does not signal the demise of colonial ways of perceiving and interpreting Africa. On this subject see, for example, Holland and Huggan, *Tourists with Typewriters*; Debbie Lisle, *The Global Politics of Contemporary Travel Writing* (Cambridge: Cambridge University Press, 2007); Kevin C. Dunn, 'Fear of a Black Planet: Anarchy Anxieties and Postcolonial Travel to Africa', *Third World Quarterly*, 25.3 (2004), pp. 483–99.

13 Syed Manzurul Islam, *The Ethics of Travel: From Marco Polo to Kafka* (Manchester: Manchester University Press, 1996), p. 45.

14 Martine Astier Loutfi, *Littérature et colonialisme: l'expansion coloniale vue dans la littérature romanesque française* (Paris: Mouton, 1971).

15 René Caillié, *Voyage à Tombouctou* (Paris: La Découverte, 1996 [1830]).

16 Tallandier publishers later reprinted many of these highly popular serialized accounts in single volumes as part of the series Bibliothèque des Grandes Aventures (1920–30). For an account of the *Journal des voyages* see Association des amis du roman populaire, *Le Rocambole: Bulletin des Amis du roman populaire. 6. Le Journal des voyages* (Maurepas: Association des amis du roman populaire, 1999).

17 Emmanuelle Sibeud, *Une Science impériale pour l'Afrique: la construction des savoirs africainistes en France, 1878–1930* (Paris: École des Hautes Études en Sciences Sociales 2002), p. 21.

18 Pierre-Philippe Fraiture, *La Mesure de l'autre: Afrique subsaharienne et roman ethnographique de Belgique et de France (1918–1940)* (Paris: Champion, 2007), p. 228.

19 Johannes Fabian, *Out of Our Minds: Reason and Madness in the Exploration of Central Africa* (Berkeley, CA: University of California Press, 2000), p. 227.

20 Ibid., p. 228.

21 Petrine Archer-Straw, *Negrophilia: Avant-Garde Paris and Black Culture in the 1920s* (London: Thames & Hudson, 2000), p. 38.

22 Laura E. Franey, *Victorian Travel Writing and Imperial Violence: British Writing on Africa, 1855–1902* (Basingstoke: Palgrave MacMillan, 2003), p. 15.

23 Pratt uses the term 'travelee' in her discussion of the relationship between colonizers/travellers and colonized/travelees. *Imperial Eyes*, p. 7.

24 Louis Sonolet and A. Pérès, *Moussa et Gigla: histoire de deux petits noirs* (Paris: Armand Colin, 1916). The book's preface outlines its 'pedagogical' aims which include encouraging the 'moral' and practical education of young colonized African students. This is to be achieved by helping them to 'discover' the resources of the country in which they live as well as showing them how France represents the pinnacle of civilization.

25 Roland Lebel, *Études de littérature coloniale* (Paris: J. Peyronnet, 1928), pp. 158–59. As a 'complete' corpus of travel writing by authors of mixed race, Lebel, one of the early critics of colonial literature, cites Léopold Panet's 'Relation d'un voyage du Sénégal à Mogador' (published in la *Revue coloniale*, 1850); the co-authored 1855 text *Sénégambie française* by Paul Holle and F. Carrère; abbé Boilat's *Esquisses sénégalaises* (1853); *Une excursion dans le Sine-Saloum* (1879) by Catholic priest Léopold Diouf; and also letters and proclamations by the Senegalese-born general Dodds who commanded the 1892–1894 Dahomey expedition.

26 Tim Fulford, Debbie Lee and Peter J. Kitson, *Literature, Science and Exploration in the Romantic Era: Bodies of Knowledge* (Cambridge: Cambridge University Press, 2004), p. 28.

27 Madeleine Borgomano, 'Le voyage "à l'africaine" et ses transformations selon *Amkoullel, l'enfant peul*', in *Les Discours de voyages: Afrique – Antilles*, edited by Romuald Fonkoua (Paris: Karthala, 1998), pp. 207–16 (p. 208).

28 Mildred Mortimer, *Journeys through the French African Novel* (Portsmouth, NH: Heinemann, 1990).

29 Ibid., p. 5.

30 Ursula Baumgardt, 'Voyages à travers la littérature peule', in *Les Discours de voyages: Afrique – Antilles*, edited by Romuald Fonkoua (Paris: Karthala, 1998), pp. 243–53.

31 Wilentz quotes Michelle Cliff's 1989 novel, *Abeng*, to explain the myth: 'The old men and women believed, before they had to eat salt during the sweated labor in the canefields, Africans could fly. They were the only people on this earth to whom God had given this power. Those who refused to be slaves and did not eat salt flew back to Africa.' Gay Wilentz, 'If you Surrender to the Air: Folk Legends of Flight and Resistance in African American Literature', *Melus*, 16.1 (1989–90), pp. 21–32 (p. 22).

32 Liz Gunner, 'Africa and Orality', in *The Cambridge History of African and Caribbean Literature*, edited by F. Abiole Irele and Simon Gikandi, 2 vols (Cambridge: Cambridge University Press, 2004), I, pp. 1–18 (p. 8).

33 Fabian, *Out of Our Minds*, p. 29.

34 The term 'voyage à l'envers' is used by Romuald Fonkoua to describe the journeys made by Africans to Europe in his essay 'Le "voyage à l'envers": Essai sur le discours des voyageurs nègres en France', in *Les Discours de voyages: Afrique – Antilles*, edited by Romuald Fonkua (Paris: Karthala, 1998), pp. 117–45.

35 Marc Michel, 'Les Troupes noires, la grande guerre et l'armée française', in *Tirailleurs sénégalais: zur bildlichen und literarischen Darstellung afrikanischer Soldaten im Dienste Franckreichs*, edited by János Riesz and Joachim Schultz (Frankfurt: Peter Lang, 1989), pp. 11–20.

36 Mortimer, *Journeys through the French African Novel*, p. 8. Bakary Diallo, *Force-bonté* (Paris: ACCT/ Nouvelles Éditions Africaines, 1926).

37 For an historical overview of the presence of African students in France see Fabienne Guimont, *Les Étudiants africains en France, 1950–1965* (Paris: L'Harmattan, 1997).

38 Cheikh Hamidou Kane, *L'Aventure ambiguë* (Paris: 10/18, 1979 [1961]). Pius Ngandu Nkashama, *Vie et mœurs d'un primitif en Essonne quatre-vingt-onze* (Paris: L'Harmattan, 1987).

39 Dominic Thomas, 'Francocentrism and the Acquisition of Cultural Capital', *Journal of Romance Studies*, 5.3 (2005), pp. 51–63 (p. 57).

40 Jacques Chevrier, 'Afrique(s)-sur-Seine: autour de la notion de "migritude"', *Notre Librairie: Revue des littératures du Sud*, 155–56 (2004), pp. 96–100.

41 Massaër Diallo's 'essay' is published in *Un Regard Noir: les Français vus par les Africains* (Paris: Autrement, 1984) together with Blaise N'Djehoya's surrealist short story of a Cameroonian student turned security guard in Paris, 'Bwanaland'. Véronique Tadjo, *L'Ombre d'Imana: Voyages jusqu'au bout du Rwanda* (Arles: Actes Sud, 2000).

42 Representations of intercontinental travel by Congolese writers include *Sans Rancune* (Paris, L'Harmattan, 2006 [1965]), a fictional account of an 'educational' journey to Brussels by Thomas Kanza, the first colonized Congolese lay student to study in Belgium. Maguy Kabamba's *La Dette coloniale* (Montreal: Humanitas, 1995) takes up this same theme in relation to a female student in a more recent context and Pie Tschibanda's *Un Fou noir au pays des blancs* (Paris: Broché, 2004) recounts the author's experience as a political refugee in Belgium. Zamenga Batukezanga is a member of the select group of francophone African authors to have penned non-fictional travelogues. In the early 1980s he published an account of a trip to the United States and later a collection of letters to his wife written when he attended a conference in Winnipeg, Canada. See *Lettres d'Amériques* (Kinshasa: Zabat, 1982) and *Chérie Basso* (Kinshasa: Éditions Saint Paul Afrique, 1989).

43 Loredana Polezzi's use of the term 'double absence' to describe similar issues in relation to the Italian tradition of travel writing is relevant here even if the reasons for this absence differ from those governing approaches to African texts. See *Translating Travel: Contemporary Italian Travel Writing in English Translation* (Aldershot: Ashgate, 2001), p. 1.

44 Valentin Y. Mudimbe has published two non-fictional journals that describe travels in the United States and Germany: *Carnets d'Amérique, septembre-novembre, 1974* (Paris: Éditions Saint-Germain-des-Près, 1976) and *Cheminements: Carnets de Berlin (avril-juin, 1999)* (Quebec: Humanitas, 2006). See also the two epistolary travel texts by Zamenga Batukezanga mentioned above.

45 John Frow, *Genre* (London and New York, 2006), p. 2.

46 Ibid., p. 73.

47 Alistair Fowler, *Kinds of Literature: An Introduction to the Theory of Genres and Modes* (Oxford: Clarendon Press, 1982).

48 Jacques Derrida, 'The Law of Genre', in *Acts of Literature*, edited by Derek Attridge (London and New York: Routledge, 1991), pp. 221–352 (p. 224).

49 Derrida, 'The Law of Genre', p. 228.

50 Stephen Heath, 'The Politics of Genre', in *Debating World Literature*, edited by Christopher Prendergast (London: Verso, 2004), pp. 163–74 (p. 170).

51 Jan Borm, 'Defining Travel: On the Travel Book, Travel Writing and Terminology', in *Perspectives on Travel Writing*, edited by Glen Hooper and Tim Youngs (Aldershot: Ashgate, 2004), pp. 13–26 (p. 19).

52 Kimberley J. Healy, *The Modernist Traveler, French Detours, 1900–1930* (Lincoln, NE, and London: University of Nebraska Press, 2003), p. 17.

53 Polezzi, *Translating Travel*, p. 1.

54 Mark Simpson, *Trafficking Subjects: The Politics of Mobility in Nineteenth-Century America* (Minneapolis, MN: University of Minnesota Press, 2005), p. xvi.

55 Ibid.

56 Both Tim Cresswell and John Urry refer respectively to the development of a 'mobility turn' and 'mobilities paradigm' in critical theory. See Tim Cresswell, *On the Move: Mobility in the Modern Western World* (London and New York: Routledge, 2006) and John Urry, *Mobilities* (Cambridge: Polity Press, 2007).

57 Cresswell, *On the Move*, p. 2.

58 Ibid., p. 220.

59 Charles Forsdick, *Travel in Twentieth-Century French and Francophone Cultures: The Persistence of Diversity* (Oxford: Oxford University Press, 2005), p. xii.

60 Frow, *Genre*, p. 27.

61 Ibid., p. 25. Emphasis in original.

62 See Peter Hulme amd Tim Youngs, *Talking about Travel Writing: A Conversation between Peter Hulme and Tim Youngs* (Leicester: English Association. Issues in English 8, 2007), p. 3.

63 Simon Gikandi, *Reading the African Novel* (London: James Currey, 1987). Gikandi here proposes four different categories for the texts he discusses: the parabolical novel, biographical narratives, subjective narratives and the political novel. See also Stephanie Newell, *Popular Fiction: 'Thrilling Discoveries in Conjugal Life' and Other Tales* (Oxford: James Currey, 2000); Forsdick, *Travel in Twentieth-Century French and Francophone Cultures*; Debra Kelly, *Autobiography and Independence:*

Selfhood and Creativity in North African Postcolonial Writing in French (Liverpool: Liverpool University Press, 2005); Maeve McCusker, *Patrick Chamoiseau: Recovering Memory* (Liverpool: Liverpool University Press, 2007).

64 Holland and Huggan, *Tourists with Typewriters*, p. 5. My emphasis.

65 Ibid.

66 Michel de Certeau, *Heterologies: Discourse on the Other*, trans. Brian Massumi (Manchester: Manchester University Press, 1986), p. 69. De Certeau is here commenting on Montaigne's 'Les Cannibales' which he sees as subverting, in a subtle manner, the authority of travel writing's meta-discourse by having the 'savage' himself return.

67 Jószef Böröcz, 'Travel Capitalism: The Structure of Europe and the Advent of the Tourist', *Comparative Studies in Society and History*, 33.4 (1992), pp. 708–41 (p. 711).

68 Cheryl J. Fish, *Black and White Women's Travel Narratives: Antebellum Explorations* (Gainesville, FL: University of Florida Press, 2001), p. 3.

69 Holland and Huggan, *Tourists with Typewriters*, p. 109.

70 John Urry, *Consuming Places* (London and New York: Routledge, 1994).

71 There is of course a Western trend of turning penniless travelling into an adventurous experiment. Paul Morand wittily examines such materially challenged travel practices in his *Conseils pour voyager sans argent* (Paris: Émile Hazan et Cie, 1930).

72 Michael Cronin, *Across the Lines: Travel, Language, Translation* (Cork: Cork University Press, 2000), p. 19.

73 Simon Gikandi, 'Theory, Literature, and Moral Considerations', *Research in African Literatures*, 32.4 (2001), pp. 1–18 (p. 1).

74 Dennis Porter, '*Orientalism* and its Problems', in *Colonial Discourse and Post-Colonial Theory: A Reader*, edited by Patrick Williams and Laura Chrisman (Hemel Hempstead: Harvester Wheatsheaf, 1993), pp. 150–61 (p. 153).

Chapter One

1 Socé is also the author of *Karim* (1935), a novel that describes the fate of its eponymous protagonist when he travels from rural Senegal to live in Dakar. A less frequently mentioned fact is that Socé was a co-founder, with fellow Negritude writers Senghor, Damas and Aimé Césaire, of the journal *L'Étudiant noir*.

2 Raoul Girardet, *L'idée coloniale en France de 1871 à 1962* (Paris: Hachette/Pluriel, 1972). As Christopher Miller notes, 'a curious silence governs key issues' concerning Fara's trip to Paris. He is not a live exhibit at the Exposition, and the novel gives no specific description as to what exactly he does there in a professional capacity. Moreover, although his arrival and original intended date of departure coincide with the dates of the Exposition, it is never explicitly stated that he has been chosen to travel to the Exposition. Miller, *Nationalists and Nomads*, p. 64. Much of Chapter 2 of Miller's study, 'Hallucinations of France and Africa', is devoted to Socé's novel.

3 Interestingly, Socé's is not the first novel to use an exhibition of this kind as the context for an inter-racial love story. Louise Faure-Favier's treats the same theme in her novel *Blanche et Noir* (1928), which takes place against the background of the 1889

Universal Exhibition. See Roger Little, 'Blanche et Noir: Louise Faure-Favier and the Liberated Woman', *Australian Journal of French Studies*, 36.2 (1999), pp. 214–28.

4 The significance of Socé's treatment of miscegenation in *Mirages de Paris* is dealt with in depth by Edwin Hill, 'Imagining *Métissage*: The Politics and Practice of *Métissage* in the French Colonial Exposition and Ousmane Socé's *Mirages de Paris*', *Social Identities*, 8.4 (2002), pp. 619–45.

5 Miller, *Nationalists and Nomads*, p. 65.

6 *Mirages de Paris* has attracted a significant amount of critical interest in recent years. As well as Miller's examination of the text in *Nationalists and Nomads* and Edwin Hill's article, see also the brief but cogent analyses by Roger Little, *Between Totem and Taboo: Black Man, White Woman in Francographic Literature* (Exeter: University of Exeter Press, 2001) and Forsdick, *Travel in Twentieth-Century French and Francophone Cultures*. Socé's novel is also the subject of more sustained analysis by Dominic Thomas in *Black France: Colonialism, Immigration, and Transnationalism* (Bloomington, IN: Indiana University Press, 2007).

7 Bernard Mouralis, *L'Europe, l'Afrique et la folie* (Paris: L'Harmattan, 1993), p. 101.

8 Paulin Hountondji, 'Charabia et mauvaise conscience: psychologie du langage chez les intellectuels colonisés, *Présence Africaine*, 61 (1961), pp. 11–31 (p. 30). Emphasis in original.

9 For a general view of this subject within an Anglophone context see of course Bill Ashcroft, Gareth Griffiths and Helen Tiffin, *The Empire Writes Back: Theory and Practice in Post-Colonial Literatures* (London and New York: Routledge, 1989). For a study of this issue within a francophone African context see, for example, Jean-Claude Blachère, *Négritures: les écrivains d'Afrique noire et la langue française* (Paris: L'Harmattan, 1993).

10 Mary Besemeres, 'Anglos Abroad: Memoirs of Immersion in a Foreign Language', *Biography*, 28.1 (2005), pp. 27–42 (p. 28). None of the texts examined by Besemeres are by colonial or postcolonial authors and all are by native, originally monolingual, English speakers who learn, or attempt to learn, a foreign language when adults.

11 Ibid. Besemeres is careful to point out that not all translingual travel narratives are inherently dialogic.

12 The relevance of Fanon's theories on language and the colonized in *Black Skin, White Masks* is all too obvious here. For a helpful analysis of this aspect of Fanon's thinking as reflected in the work of Edouard Glissant see Celia M. Britton *Edouard Glissant and Postcolonial Theory: Strategies of Language and Resistance* (Charlottesville, VA: University of Virginia Press, 1999), pp. 84–93.

13 Dominic Thomas notes how one of these French passengers switches from the familiar *tu* to the more formal *vous* once Fara has demonstrated linguistic proficiency and has therefore distanced himself 'from the African component of his identity, which is only perceived in negative terms'. Thomas, *Black France*, p. 69.

14 Hountondji, 'Charabia et mauvaise conscience', p. 13.

15 Interestingly, Birago Diop claims that Socé originally intended to entitle his novel 'Panamite', a term explained in a footnote of the novel itself (p. 171) as 'mal de Paris', in other words a type of inverted 'homesickness'. Paname is also the popular name for Paris. See Birago Diop: '"J'avais appris à lire pour pouvoir écrire"', *Notre Librairie*, 81 (1989), pp. 62–69.

16 Miller, *Nationalists and Nomads*, p. 56. Emphasis in original.

17 Ibid., p. 62.

18 See 'Introduction', in George Revill and Richard Wrigley (eds), *Pathologies of Travel* (Amsterdam: Rodopi, 2000), pp. 1–20 (p. 3).

19 Ibid.

20 See Fabian, *Out of Our Minds*. Although Fabian understands 'Madness' in a loose sense intended to convey the notion of the 'ecstatic', i.e. instances where Western travellers exist 'outside the rationalized frames of exploration' (p. 7), he nonetheless illustrates how such prosaic events as attacks by insects and vermin as well as tropical illnesses and experiments with drugs and sexual behaviour quite literally drove many European travellers in Africa out of their minds.

21 Jonathan Andrews, 'Letting Madness Range: Travel and Mental Disorder, c1700–1900', in Revill and Wrigley (eds), *Pathologies of Travel*, pp. 25–88 (p. 28).

22 W.E.B. Du Bois, *The Souls of Black Folk* (Harmondsworth: Penguin, 1996 [1903]), p. 5.

23 With regard to the number of visitors, critical works provide very divergent figures with some quoting in the region of 3 million visitors (Carole Sweeney, '"Le Tour du Monde en Quatre Jours": Empire, Exhibition and the Surrealist Order of Things', *Textual Practice*, 19.1 [2005], pp. 131–47); others such as Christopher Miller suggest circa 8 million (*Nationalists and Nomads*, p. 68); and yet more critics suggest 34 million (Raoul Girardet in *L'Idée coloniale en France de 1871 à 1962*, p. 175).

24 See, for example, *Documents: Exposition coloniale Paris, 1931*, edited by Sylvie Palà (Paris: Bibliothèques de la Ville de Paris, 1981); Paul Greenhalgh, *Ephemeral Vistas: The Expositions Universelles, Great Exhibitions and World's Fairs, 1851–1939* (Manchester: Manchester University Press, 1988); Catherine Hodeir and Michel Pierre, *L'Exposition Coloniale* (Brussels: Éditions Complexe, 1991); Herman Lebovics, *True France: The Wars over Cultural Identity, 1900–1945* (Ithaca, NY: Cornell University Press, 1992); Panivong Norindr, *Phantasmatic Indochina: French Colonial Ideology in Architecture, Film and Literature* (Durham, NC: Duke University Press, 1996).

25 In *True France*, Lebovics reminds us that six European colonial powers, and the United States, were represented. Only Great Britain declined the invitation to participate.

26 Lebovics, *True France*, pp. 55–56.

27 Miller, *Nationalists and Nomads*, p. 69.

28 Charles Forsdick, 'Revisiting Exoticism: From Colonialism to Postcolonialism', in *Francophone Postcolonial Studies: A Critical Introduction*, edited by Charles Forsdick and David Murphy (London: Arnold, 2003), pp. 46–55 (p. 49).

29 For a cogent analysis of the question of live exhibits in world fairs, see Raymond Corbey, 'Ethnographic Showcases, 1870–1930', *Cultural Anthropology*, 8.3 (1993), pp. 338–69. The French historians Nicolas Bancel, Pascal Blanchard, Gilles Bœtsch, Eric Deroo and Sandrine Lemaire have also published a very thorough account of 'human zoos' in *Human Zoos: Science and Spectacle in the Age of Empire* (Liverpool: Liverpool University Press, 2008 [2002]).

30 It is worth mentioning here the condemnatory view of colonialism presented in the counter exhibition, *La Vérité sur les colonies*. This unofficial exhibition ran

concurrently with the main Exposition and was organized by a group of surrealist artists and writers including Louis Aragon, Paul Eluard, André Breton and Tristan Tzara. For a more detailed account of this event see Sweeney, 'Le Tour du Monde en Quatre Jours' and Lebovics, *True France*, pp. 105–10. For more general discussion of ideological opposition to the Exposition, see Elizabeth Ezra, *The Colonial Unconscious: Race and Culture in Inter-war France* (Ithaca, NY: Cornell University Press, 2000), pp. 26–30.

31 For Pratt, 'autoethnographic' texts reveal a practice whereby colonized subjects represent themselves in the colonizer's own terms. Such texts, she argues, '[involve] partial collaboration with and appropriation of the idioms of the conqueror'. *Imperial Eyes*, p. 7.

32 Robert Pageard argues that Socé is the first black francophone author to have written a truly 'African' portrait of Europe. See Robert Pageard, 'L'image de l'Europe dans la littérature ouest-africaine d'expression française', in *Connaissance de l'étranger: mélanges offerts à la mémoire de Jean-Marie Carré* (Paris: Didier, 1964), pp. 323–46.

33 Homi K. Bhabha, 'The Other Question: Stereotype, Discrimination and the Discourse of Colonialism', in *The Location of Culture* (London: Routledge, 1994), pp. 66–84 (p. 66). I am also using here Bhabha's related influential essay on stereotypes and difference, 'Of Mimicry and Man: The Ambivalence of Colonial Discourse', in *The Location of Culture*, pp. 85–92.

34 Bhabha, 'The Other Question', p. 76.

35 Dean MacCannell, *The Tourist: A New Theory of the Leisure Class* (Basingstoke: MacMillan, 1976).

36 MacCannell, here, is referring to Daniel Boorstin's derogatory use of the term 'pseudo-event' to denote the intellectually dissatisfying nature of tourist attractions and sight-seeing. *The Tourist*, p. 103.

37 Ibid., p. 93

38 Bhabha, 'The Other Question', p. 66.

39 MacCannell, *The Tourist*, p. 93. Emphasis in original.

40 Bhabha, 'The Other Question', p. 76. My emphasis.

41 Thomas, *Black France*, pp. 66–72.

42 Timothy Mitchell, 'Orientalism and the Exhibitionary Order', in *Colonialism and Culture*, edited by Nicholas B. Dirks (Michigan: University of Michigan Press, 1992), pp. 289–317.

43 Mitchell, 'Orientalism and the Exhibitionary Order', p. 295.

44 Ibid., p. 299.

45 Ibid., p. 299.

46 Ibid., p. 300.

47 Neil Lazarus, 'The Fetish of "the West" in Postcolonial Theory', in *Marxism, Modernity and Postcolonial Studies*, edited by Crystal Bartolovich and Neil Lazarus (Cambridge: Cambridge University Press, 2002), pp. 43–64 (p. 44), my emphasis. Here Lazarus is discussing the implications for postcolonial theory of a dematerialized interpretation of 'the West'.

48 Mitchell, 'Orientalism and the Exhibitionary Order', p. 301.

Chapter Two

1 Gérard Aké Loba was born in Abidjan in 1929. Apart from his well-known first novel, *Kocoumbo l'étudiant noir*, he is the author of two other novels, *Les Dépossédés* (1973) and *Le Sas des parvenus* (1990). Kane's masterpiece is contemporaneous with Loba's.

2 Pius Adesanmi, 'Redefining Paris: Trans-Modernity and Francophone African Migritude Fiction', *Modern Fiction Studies*, 51.4 (2005), pp. 958–75 (pp. 962–63). For an accessible study of Kane's novel see J. P. Little, *Cheikh Hamidou Kane: L'Aventure ambiguë* (London: Grant & Cutler, Critical Guides to French Texts, 2000).

3 Adesanmi, 'Redefining Paris', p. 964.

4 Interestingly, in order to further stress the independence of this individual, he is said to be the owner of the village's only bicycle. However, the text also illustrates that access to forms of mechanized transport and increased distances mean that the bicycle's association with status will soon become redundant. Indeed, as Xavier Godard points out, today in Africa the bicycle is more likely to be associated with poverty and 'backward', rural populations. See 'V comme Vélo, ou le grand absent des capitales africaines', in Xavier Godard (ed.), *Les Transports et la ville en Afrique au sud du Sahara* (Paris: Karthala, 2002), pp. 343–56.

5 Loba provides no exact dates in the novel. However, in a rare article (online) devoted to the text, Katharina Städtler claims that Kocoumbo finishes his African education in 1942. See 'Regards africains sur la ville de Paris', *France-Mail-Forum*, 23 (August 2001), www.france-mail-forum.de/fmf23/neu/23sstaed.html (accessed 15 June 2008). This would place events in Paris in the late 1940s to mid-1950s. This tallies with certain clues provided in the text such as the rise of air travel and the mention of a brother who has died in the Second World War.

6 See Forsdick, *Travel in Twentieth-Century French and Francophone Cultures*, p. 113.

7 See Marian Aguiar, 'Smoke of the Savannah: Traveling Modernity in Sembène Ousmane's *God's Bits of Wood*', *Modern Fiction Studies*, 49.2 (2003), pp. 284–305 (p. 296). This fascinating analysis centres on the conflicting views of the railway in this classic Senegalese novel about the 1947 West African railway strike. Aguiar notes how, for the novel's older generation in particular, rail transport is an alienating technology and is seen as being heavily enmeshed in the violent history of colonization. For them, the railway's legacy cannot, therefore, be viewed as positive. For the younger generation, clearly more imbued by a political atmosphere moving towards decolonization, the railway, and the technology it represents, is seen as more culturally and historically neutral and thus to be appropriated for their own aspirations, regardless of where it originates. This view of a 'technology of agency' is clearly that which Kocoumbo's father comes to espouse. It is also evident in Kocoumbo's own reaction to the Paris metro (pp. 85–86) and his later rejection of Marxist theories concerning modern Western technology's alienating tendencies (p. 249). However, as Aguiar carefully elucidates, such a view can also be seen as an indication of the continuing influence of colonialist and Eurocentric views of 'universalism' that present progress as following a single (Western) path.

8 Ships, of course, represent an important chronotope in Paul Gilroy's seminal

study, *The Black Atlantic: Modernity and Double Consciousness* (London and New York: Verso, 1993). According to Gilroy, 'ships immediately focus attention on the middle passage, on the various projects for redemptive return to an African homeland, on the circulation of ideas and activists as well as the movement of key cultural and political artefacts: tracts, books, gramophone records, and choirs' (p. 4). Whether Loba intends it or not, the travelling conditions of the majority of the African passengers do evoke the 'racialized' travel practices of the middle passage.

9 Brenda Chalfin, 'Cars, the Customs Service, and Sumptuary Rule in Neoliberal Ghana', *Comparative Studies in Society and History*, 50.2 (2008), pp. 424–53 (p. 427).

10 For a brief history of the motor car and Africa see, 'The Story of Africa between World Wars: Air and Road', www.bbc.co.uk/worldservice/africa/features/storyofafrica/13chapter9.shtml (accessed 17 June 2008).

11 Chalfin, 'Cars, the Customs Service, and Sumptuary Rule in Neoliberal Ghana', p. 430.

12 Kristin Ross notes that although the car was no longer considered a luxury item at the time Loba is writing, only one in eight French citizens owned a car in 1961. See *Fast Cars, Clean Bodies: Decolonization and the Reordering of French Culture* (Cambridge, MA: MIT Press, 1996), p. 27.

13 Forsdick, *Travel in Twentieth-Century French and Francophone Cultures*, p. 129.

14 Ibid., p. 112.

15 See Bhabha, 'Of Mimicry and Man', in *The Location of Culture*, pp. 85–92.

16 Interestingly, it is not just car ownership that highlights Durandeau's obsession with belonging to a white social elite characterized by access to more luxurious travel practices. In Marseilles, his disgust with the growing democratization of international travel amongst fellow Africans is reminiscent of the inter-war elitism of many Western anti-tourist commentators. See *Kocoumbo*, p. 75.

17 Edward Said, 'Travelling Theory', in *The World, the Text and the Critic* (London: Vintage, 1991 [1983]), pp. 226–47 (p. 226). Said's primary concern in this essay is to illustrate the ways in which 'revolutionary' or 'progressive' theories can become 'tamed' in the process of travelling and lose their radical potential when applied in different contexts. Later, in the companion essay 'Travelling Theory Reconsidered', in *Reflections on Exile and other Literary and Cultural Essays* (London: Granta Books, 2001 [2000]), pp. 436–52, Said considers the reverse outcome and examines how travel can prompt theory to develop a more transgressive dimension.

18 Said, 'Travelling Theory', p. 226.

19 Of course elitism also existed in its metropolitan counterpart, but to a lesser – and undoubtedly less intentional – extent. On this question of elitism in French education, and its survival until at least the middle of the twentieth century, see Joseph N. Moody, *French Education Since Napoleon* (New York: Syracuse University Press, 1978).

20 Said, 'Travelling Theory Reconsidered', pp. 436–52 (p. 436).

21 On this question of the paradox of colonial educational policy see, for example, Alice Conklin, *A Mission to Civilize: The Republican Idea of Empire in France and West Africa, 1885–1930* (Stanford, CA: Stanford University Press, 1997); J. P. Little's 'Introduction' to the re-edition of Georges Hardy's 1917 text, *Une*

Conquête morale (Paris: L'Harmattan, Collection 'Autrement Mêmes', 2005) and Chapter 2 of Dominic Thomas's *Black France*.

22 Jean Suret-Canale, *French Colonialism in Tropical Africa, 1900–1945*, trans. Till Gottheiner (New York: Pica Press, 1971 [1964]), p. 380. My emphasis.

23 Tony Chafer, 'France's *Mission Civilisatrice* in Africa: French Culture not for Export', in *Popular Culture and Mass Communication in Twentieth-Century France*, edited by Rosemary Chapman and Nicolas Hewitt (Lampeter: Edwin Mellen Press, 1992), pp. 142–64 (p. 149).

24 It is not clear whether Kocoumbo has a 'certificat d'études primaires indigènes' or the more advanced 'certificat d'études primaires supérieures', although his age would suggest the latter. However, ultimately whichever qualification he has is immaterial given that, as Tony Chafer insists, neither would have been recognized in France. See Chafer, 'France's *Mission Civilisatrice*'.

25 Adesanmi, 'Redefining Paris', p. 961.

26 Ibid.

27 David Scott, *Semiologies of Travel: From Gautier to Baudrillard* (Cambridge: Cambridge University Press, 2004), p. 62.

28 Brent Hayes Edwards, *The Practice of Diaspora: Literature, Translation, and the Rise of Black Internationalism* (Cambridge, MA: Harvard University Press, 2003), p. 240.

29 Several critics, including those working in a francophone context, have dealt with the question of Marxism's failure to address effectively the question of 'race' and the colonies. For example, in the *Practice of Diaspora*, Brent Hayes Edwards speaks of the 'lumbering, veiled racism' of the French Communist Party (Parti Communiste Français) in the 1920s and '30s (p. 262) and examines in depth how the efforts of African intellectuals such as Tiemoko Garan Kouyaté to establish a race-based labour movement were perceived as a threat to working-class unity. Christopher Miller also notes that despite the attraction of Communism's (and the PCF's) anti-colonial credentials and financial support for many African intellectuals, 'communist thinking [...] seemed to be as trapped in cultural stereotyping as colonialist ideology was'. See *Nationalists and Nomads*, p. 19. Miller also explains how, from the 1930s, the PCF became less resolute in its support of independence for the colonies, a policy it had openly espoused in the 1920s. On this subject see also Girardet, *L'Idée coloniale en France*, p. 204.

Chapter Three

1 Regarding the date of the trip on which *Un Nègre à Paris* is based, it is Dadié himself, in an interview with Bennetta Jules-Rosette, who provides this information. See Bennetta Jules-Rosette, *Black Paris: The African Writers' Landscape* (Urbana, IL: University of Illinois Press, 1998), pp. 140–46. As well as *Patron de New York* and *La Ville où nul ne meurt* (Paris: Présence Africaine, 1969) Dadié also published a short newspaper article in his native Ivory Coast on a trip to Japan, 'Le Japon, pays découvert qui reste à découvrir', *Fraternité-Matin*, 11 October 1968, p. 9.

2 The brief nature of Bertin's stay also helps to support the thesis that he is a tourist or holidaymaker. For Fred Inglis, it is precisely this notion of brief and

'bracketed time' that contributes to defining the 'form' of the holiday as we have come to recognize it. See *The Delicious History of the Holiday* (London and New York: Routledge, 2000), p. 9.

3 Jean-Didier Urbain, *L'Idiot du voyage: histoires de touristes* (Paris: Payot, 1993), p. 16. For more on anti-tourist discourse in the Western history of travel, see James Buzard, *The Beaten Track: European Tourism, Literature and the Ways to Culture* (Oxford: Clarendon, 1993).

4 Urbain is not alone in attempting to defend and rehabilitate the tourist. Both Dean MacCannell and Jonathan Culler have argued convincingly for tourists' sophisticated semiological understanding of their particular travel experiences. See MacCannell, *The Tourist*, and Jonathan Culler, 'Semiotics of Tourism', *American Journal of Semiotics*, 1.1–2 (1981), pp. 127–40.

5 Urbain, *L'Idiot du voyage*, p. 19. I have been unable to discover any statistics related to the recreational travel practices of black Africans. There are, however, studies available of the holiday/tourist practices of white South Africans on the continent. See, for example, Jonathan Crush and Paul Wellings, 'The Southern African Pleasure Periphery, 1966–83', *The Journal of Modern African Studies*, 21.4 (1983), pp. 673–98.

6 Elisabeth Mudimbe-Boyi, 'Travel, Representation, and Difference, Or How Can One Be a Parisian?', *Research in African Literatures*, 23.3 (1992), pp. 25–39 (p. 28).

7 Of course, the reference to air travel also points to the enhanced mobility provided by modern technology which also underpins the rise of mass tourism.

8 Malcolm Crick, 'Representations of International Tourism in the Social Sciences; Sun, Sex, Sights, Savings and Servility', *Annual Review of Anthropology*, 18 (1989), pp. 307–44. According to Crick, Western cultural critics in particular often relate to tourists as though the latter were distant, embarrassing relatives whose existence signifies undesired but unavoidable interaction, and whose travel practices highlight uncomfortable overlaps with supposedly more authentic travel.

9 Quoted in Claude Dunot, 'Bernard Binlin Dadié', *L'Afrique littéraire et artistique*, 5 (1969), pp. 16–21 (p. 20).

10 See Fernando Lambert, 'Bernard Dadié: l'écriture et le voyage', *L'Afrique littéraire et artistique*, 85 (1989), pp. 35–41.

11 See Nicole Vincileoni, *L'Œuvre de Bernard B. Dadié* (Issy-les-Moulineaux: Les Classiques africains, 1986); Pierre Daninos, *Les Carnets du Major W. Marmaduke Thompson: découverte de la France et des Français* (Paris: P. de Tartas, 1954).

12 Both Vincileoni and Karen C. Hatch, in the introduction to her translation of *Un Nègre à Paris*, argue that Tanhoe Bertin is in fact a persona of the author. Both cite the significance of the travelling narrator's name to support their claim: Tanhoe is the name of a river in the Ivory Coast. Vincileoni also suggests that Bertin is a composite of Bernard and Dadié's middle name, Binlin.

13 The term interlingual translation comes from Roman Jakobson and is defined by Michael Cronin in his study of language in travel as 'the interpretation of verbal signs by means of verbal signs from another language'. See *Across the Lines*, p. 2.

14 Ibid. Given the travelling context of *Un Nègre à Paris*, this 'monolingual' perspective could also be said to correspond to Jakobson's notion of '*intralingual translation*' as defined by Cronin: 'the interpretation of verbal signs by means of other signs belonging to the same language'.

15 I am not suggesting here, however, that the relationship of Dadié's travelling narrator with the French language is one of complete familiarity. Instead, his constant references to the oddities of French suggest a connection based at once on intimate knowledge and distance. Indeed, despite their very different linguistic contexts, aspects of Dadié's relationship to French remind us of the seminal moment in James Joyce's *A Portrait of the Artist as a Young Man* (Harmondsworth: Penguin, 1992 [1916]) when Dubliner Stephen Daedalus reflects on a conversation he has with the English dean of studies at his university: 'The language in which we are speaking is his before it is mine. [...] His language, *so familiar and so foreign*, will always be for me an acquired speech. I have not made or accepted its words' (p. 205, my emphasis).

16 Montesquieu, *Les Lettres persanes* (Paris: Livres de poche, 2003 [1721]).

17 Dustin Griffin, *Satire: A Critical Reintroduction* (Lexington, KY: University Press of Kentucky, 1994), p. 70.

18 Ibid. It should be stressed that Griffin does not entirely reject the idea of the satirist as moralist but argues persuasively that moral concerns are not at the centre of satirical writing. Instead, he sees satire as being open-ended, a 'rhetoric of inquiry, of provocation, of display, of play' (p. 38).

19 Linda Hutcheon, *Irony's Edge: The Theory and Politics of Irony* (London and New York: Routledge, 1994), p. 48. Hutcheon provides a very cogent and useful analysis of irony's different functions and their associated affective charges, which range from the relatively benign to the offensive. Hutcheon uses university literature departments as an example of a 'discursive community' that would view irony's reinforcement as necessary for greater 'precision of communication' (p. 48). One could also imagine literary communities playing such a role. Irony in Dadié's writing would thus become a means for acceptance into a community that would arguably accept Montesquieu and Daninos more readily. However, as Hutcheon explains, each function of irony has a negative and a positive articulation, and it would, therefore, also be possible to see such ironic reinforcement as merely 'decorative' and 'subsidiary' (a tendency which is not entirely absent from Dadié's sometimes laboured attempts at constantly 'performing' the witty narrator). For Hutcheon, a related function of reinforcement would be irony's ludic role that is also very much in evidence in Dadié's writing. When seen favourably, Hutcheon points to this function's quality of 'benevolent teasing' can be viewed as relatively benign (p. 49). When viewed negatively, irony's ludic function can, Hutcheon asserts, be interpreted as irresponsible, and as 'trivializing the essential seriousness of art' (p. 49).

20 This aspect of Glissant's thinking is discussed by Celia Britton in *Edouard Glissant and Postcolonial Theory*, p. 83.

21 Quoted in Dunot, 'Bernard Binlin Dadié', p. 17.

22 Michael Syrotinski, *Singular Performances: Reinscribing the Subject in Francophone African Writing* (Charlottesville, VA: University of Virginia Press, 2002), p. 70.

23 Ibid., p. 82. Nicole Vincileoni also identifies Dadié's subversive intentions in the three texts she classifies as his 'carnets de voyage' [travelogues]. See *L'Œuvre de Bernard B. Dadié*.

24 Ibid., pp. 72, 82.

25 Ibid., p. 69.

26 Charles A. Knight, *The Literature of Satire* (Cambridge: Cambridge University Press, 2004), p. 4.

27 Hutcheon, *Irony's Edge*, p. 17.

28 Johannes Fabian, *Time and the Other: How Anthropology makes its Object* (New York: Columbia University Press, 1983), p. 17.

29 Ibid., p. 31. Emphasis in original.

30 Lisle, *The Global Politics of Contemporary Travel Writing*, pp. 218, 229–30.

31 Ibid., p. 240.

32 Fabian, *Time and the Other*, p. 17.

Chapter Four

1 See, for example, Philippe Dewitte, *Les Mouvements nègres en France, 1919–1959* (Paris: L'Harmattan, 1985); Michel Fabre, *From Harlem to Paris: Black American Writers in France, 1840–1980* (Urbana, IL: University of Illinois Press, 1991); Tyler Stovall, *Paris Noir: African Americans in the City of Light* (Boston, MA: Houghton Mifflin, 1996); Miller, *Nationalists and Nomads*; Archer-Straw, *Negrophilia*; Ezra, *The Colonial Unconscious*; Edwards, *The Practice of Diaspora*; *Journal of Romance Studies*, 5.3 (2005), special issue on 'Black Paris' edited by Sam Haigh and Nicki Hitchcott; *Modern Fiction Studies*, 51.4 (2005), special issue on 'Paris, Modern Fiction and the Black Atlantic'; Thomas, *Black France*.

2 Edwards, *The Practice of Diaspora*, p. 3

3 Ibid.

4 Maran, winner of the 1921 Goncourt prize, was born in Martinique to Guyanese parents and worked as a colonial administrator in Chad before returning to Paris where he played a vital role in 1920s transatlantic cultural and intellectual exchange between Harlem and the French capital. On this subject see Michel Fabre, 'René Maran, the New Negro and Negritude', *Phylon*, 36.3 (1974), pp. 340–51. Tovalou-Houenou, one-time soldier, lawyer and socialite, was born in Dahomey (now Benin) and was founder of *Les Continents*, the first black newspaper in France (on which Maran also collaborated), and also of the Ligue Universelle pour la Défense de la Race Noire. In his role as head of this organization he travelled to the United States in 1924. For more on this personality, see Iheanachor Egonu, '*Les Continents* and the Francophone Pan-Negro Movement', *Phylon*, 41.1 (1980), pp. 12–24 and Edwards, *The Practice of Diaspora*. Finally, Fanon's transatlantic journeys saw him travel from the Caribbean to France to North Africa and finally to the United States where he died in 1961.

5 These are not the only Francophone African texts that highlight west-bound transatlantic travel. *Carnets d'Amérique, septembre–novembre, 1974* by V.-Y. Mudimbe and *Lettres d'Amérique* by his Congolese compatriot Zamenga Batukezanga, as the titles suggest, are accounts of travel to America. However, both journeys took place later than the texts studied here. Both Bernard Dadié and Léopold S. Senghor have published poems about New York which are examined by Janis L. Pallister in 'Outside the Monastery Walls: American Culture in Black African and Caribbean Poetry', *The Journal of Popular Culture*, 17.1 (1983), pp. 74–82. In addition, Mariama Bâ's highly influential text *Une si longue lettre* (Dakar:

Les Nouvelles Éditions Africaines, 1979) presents the main protagonist, Ramatou-laye, writing from Senegal to her friend Aïssatou who has left the country to go to the United States. American-based African writers Emmanuel Dongala and Alain Mabanckou have also published texts that explore the complex network of black cultural influences that move back and forth across the Atlantic between Africa and America. See for example Dongala's *Jazz et vin de palme* (Paris: Le Serpent à plumes, 1982) and Mabanckou's *Lettre à Jimmy* (Paris: Fayard, 2007). In anglophone African literature, an account of a studentship in Princeton, *America, Their America* (London: Heinemann, 1964) by Nigerian author John P. Clark shows him to be an eloquent and insightful commentator on American society of the time.

   6 Agustin Lao-Montes, 'Decolonial Moves: Trans-locating African Diaspora Spaces', *Cultural Studies*, 21.2–3 (2007), pp. 309–38 (p. 311).

   7 Certainly, there is growing acknowledgement that Harlem's distinct identity developed as much on the basis of ethnic dynamics as 'racial' ones. For obvious reasons of numerical importance, however, studies of this question focus almost exclusively on anglophone Caribbean immigration. See, for example, Irma Watkins-Owens, *Blood Relations: Caribbean Immigrants and the Harlem Community, 1900–1930* (Bloomington and Indianapolis: Indiana University Press, 1996) and Michelle A. Stephens, 'Black Transnationalism and the Politics of National Identity: West Indian Intellectuals in Harlem in the Age of War and Revolution', *American Quarterly*, 50.3 (1998), pp. 592–608. For an example of critical discussion of franco-phone Caribbean migration to the United States see J. Michael Dash, *Haiti and the United States: National Stereotypes and the Literary Imagination* (New York: Saint Martin's Press, 1997).

   8 There is a growing body of critical work devoted to accounts of 'homeland' journeys by African Americans. See, for example, John Cullen Gruesser, *Black on Black: Twentieth-Century African American Writing about Africa* (Lexington, KY: University Press of Kentucky, 2000). A related trajectory that figures in this Atlantic criss-crossing is the issue of the 'return' of members of the African diaspora in the context of contemporary tourism. This journey, analysed for example in Edward M. Bruner's article on slavery tourism to Ghana, is a complex admixture of the almost 'sacred' elements of a return to slavery's roots, and what might be termed the more 'profane' elements of certain tourist practices. See Edward M. Bruner, 'Tourism in Ghana: The Representation of Slavery and the Return of the Black Diaspora', *American Anthropologist*, 98.2 (1996), pp. 290–304 and Paulla A. Ebron's study of a similar phenomenon in Senegal, 'Tourists as Pilgrims: Commercial Fashioning of Transatlantic Politics', *American Ethnologist*, 26.4 (1999), pp. 910–32.

   9 The political context of *Chalys d'Harlem* is complex and the precise political affiliations of the eponymous protagonist difficult to ascertain. In the course of his narrative, Chalys does mention, during a conversation with an acknowledged DuBois supporter (p. 116), the acrimonious dispute between this middle-class black intel-lectual, who was closely associated with the moderate and integrationist National Association for the Advancement of Colored People (NAACP), and Marcus Garvey, the Jamaican-born founder of the separatist Universal Negro Improvement Associa-tion (UNIA). Another explicit mention of Garvey (p. 64) would seem to suggest that Chalys, and those in his 'organization', are not active members of the UNIA. The central role in *Chalys d'Harlem* of the fourth Pan-African Conference organized by

DuBois in Harlem in 1927 and actively supported by Chalys and his companions also seems to offer some basis for suggesting that they are closer to the beliefs and methodologies of the NAACP. (Interestingly, Garvey was in jail in 1927 and decreed there would be no annual UNIA convention that year.) Nonetheless, Chalys is not averse to more radical political approaches, and his respect for the passion, but not the intolerance, of the 'Black-Muslim' (p. 52) movement would suggest that Garvey, for all his 'demagoguery' (p. 116), would not be dismissed. Equally, Garvey's thesis that an economic project should form a fundamental element of a transnational politics of black affirmation and liberation would suggest that the ideological influence of the UNIA leader is not irrelevant or indeed antithetical to Chalys's own political sympathies (no more than DuBois's can be said to be naturally compatible with them). As Barbara Blair explains, Garvey was not just a theorist of black internationalism, he also put his economic theories into practice by founding a commercial wing of the UNIA that established and supported small businesses in Harlem (the question of black business ventures is central to Diakhaté's representation of Harlem). See Barbara Blair, 'Pan-Africanism as Process: Adelaide Casley Hayford, Garveyism, and the Cultural Roots of Nationalism', in *Imagining Home: Class, Culture and Nationalism in the African Diaspora*, edited by Sidney J. Lemelle and Robin D.G. Kelley (London: Verso, 1994), pp. 121–44. Another key element suggesting the relevance of Garvey's ideas to the text concerns Chalys's preference for 'traditional African' dress at political demonstrations and his particular interest in the nationalist symbolism of newly independent Senegal. According to Michelle A. Stephens, Garvey saw his annual UNIA convention as a counter to the 'white' League of Nations and encouraged delegates to wear 'national', or nationally imagined costumes to these lively affairs. Specific mention of the impact of these events is made in *Chalys d'Harlem* (p. 64). See Stephens, 'Black Transnationalism and the Politics of National Identity'. For a detailed discussion of the ideological differences between Garvey and DuBois see Tony Martin, *Race First: The Ideological and Organizational Struggles of Marcus Garvey and the Universal Negro Improvement Association* (Westport, CT: Greenwood Press, 1976). Ultimately, the only thing that can be said with certainty about the politics of *Chalys d'Harlem* is that it espouses the transnational dimension of a specifically Black Atlantic identity that Garvey and DuBois ultimately shared, whatever the complex nature of the differences that divided them.

10 Senegal became a UN member state in 1960. The date of Fall's New York trip, as well as several mentions of the UN headquarters is no doubt intended to underline Senegal's imminent entry on to the world stage.

11 Michael Syrotinski interprets the text slightly differently and attributes the difference in composition of *Patron de New York* to the length of Dadié's stay that results, in his view in a more 'settled and reflective account'. *Singular Performances*, p. 82.

12 This emphasis on economics is not so surprising when one considers, as Irma Watkins-Owens does, how enterprise and racial politics were intimately linked in Harlem of this era: 'Between 1900 and 1930 almost any individual of African descent engaged in business, however small, could expect to be lauded in the black press as a racial hero.' See Watkins-Owens, *Blood Relations*, p. 126.

13 The 1927 Pan-African Congress in New York was organized by DuBois and took place while Marcus Garvey was in prison. Agustin Lao-Montes describes these

pan-African conferences, and the 1950s–60s movements for decolonization in Africa, as the climax of transnational black politics. See 'Decolonial Moves: Trans-locating African Diaspora Spaces'.

14 Even if it is based on myth, Chalys's family history is also a reminder of the importance of thinking about African travel practices historically and of recognizing a tradition of travel that developed prior to European colonization. On this subject see the chapter entitled 'African Roots of Black Seafaring' in W. Jeffrey Bolster, *Black Jacks: African American Seamen in the Age of Sail* (Cambridge, MA: Harvard University Press, 1997). Bolster describes how the expertise and skill of West African canoeists was vital for the smooth running of the slave trade and later contributed to the development of seafaring knowledge in Europe and America.

15 Gilroy, *The Black Atlantic*, p. 133.

16 Tom Nissley, *Intimate and Authentic Economies: The American Self-Made Man from Douglass to Chaplin* (London and New York: Routledge, 2003).

17 Ibid., p. 6.

18 Ibid., pp. 26–27.

19 Ibid., p. 27.

20 This disappointment must be understood against the specific context of the African-American job market of the time. In her study of Harlem between 1900 and 1930, Irma Watkins-Owens explains the limited job opportunities that existed for the black population, the impact of low pay and the absence of any effective collective bargaining power. In such a climate it is obvious how social networks and word of mouth played a vital role. See Watkins-Owens, *Blood Relations*.

21 William Boelhower, '"I'll teach you how to flow": On Figuring Out Atlantic Studies', *Atlantic Studies*, 1.1 (2004), pp. 28–48.

22 Nissley, *Intimate and Authentic Economies*, p. 5.

23 Boelhower, '"I'll teach you how to flow"', p. 30.

24 Whether Diakhaté intended it or not, it is possible to discern in the importance attributed to the shipping trade the influence of Marcus Garvey's economic theories. Garvey was convinced of the role steamships could play in establishing effective communication across the Black Atlantic world. As part of a strategy that would allow Black Atlantic populations, including Africans, to counter European monopolies on shipping he therefore established the Black Star Line, a black-owned international shipping company. Ultimately this commercial venture proved to be a financial disaster of monumental proportions. However, the ideological function of the Black Star Line as a transnational network geared towards greater African control of the international distribution of resources is clearly evident in the importance Chalys's attributes to shipping in independent Senegal. In addition, Chalys's emphasis on the Senegalese flag in the context of shipping is a reminder of a more explicit attempt to link shipping, political and economic identity and national identity: after independence Ghana superimposed a black star on its new national flag in a direct reference to Garvey's company. For more on the Black Star Line see Martin, *Race First*.

25 Indeed the text's one-sided exploration of economic advancement means that the question of an alternative view to labour and American capitalist modernity is ignored. For example, Elisa L. Glick identifies Harlem's speakeasy culture and also the figure of the African-American dandy in the 1920s–30s as important reminders of the rejection of values associated with market imperatives and commodity culture.

For the dandy, in particular, the dogma of work, production and progress harked back to the alienating practices of slavery and therefore compromised individual and collective freedom. See 'Harlem's Queer Dandy: African-American Modernism and the Artifice of Blackness', *Modern Fiction Studies*, 49.3 (2003), pp. 414–42. Similarly, the fleeting but positive comments concerning Roosevelt and the New Deal in *Chalys d'Harlem* do not reflect what Steve Valocchi has identified as the racially based nature of certain New Deal policies that discriminated against African Americans. See 'The Racial Basis of Capitalism and the State, and the Impact of the New Deal on African Americans', *Social Problems*, 41.3 (1994), pp. 347–62.

26 The purpose of Dadié's American trip is briefly mentioned by David Allen Case in his largely negative review of the American travel book, 'Bernard Binlin Dadié's Observations', *The Journal of African Travel-Writing*, 1 (1996), pp. 90–92. At no time in *Patron de New York* does Dadié himself refer to his particular political status or to the precise nature of his American journey.

27 Syrotinski, *Singular Performances*, p. 85.

28 Here, I am paraphrasing James Clifford's opening remarks in his well-known essay 'Traveling Cultures' where he describes some of the places and spaces of transit (including hotels and airports) which he sees as symbolizing late twentieth-century travel practices and relations. See 'Traveling Cultures', in *Cultural Studies*, edited by Laurence Grossberg, Cary Nelson and Paula Treichler (New York and London: Routledge, 1992), pp. 96–116.

29 In *Seducing the French: The Dilemma of Americanization* (Berkeley, CA: University of California Press, 1993), Richard Kuisel identifies the question of conformity as central to French perceptions of America. Despite impressively high standards of living, American consumer society was seen by such intellectuals as Jean Baudrillard, Michel Crozier and George Duhamel to quell radicalism and to produce a uniform culture and environment. Dadié's familiarity with French intellectual life would suggest that he was not ignorant of such thinking. For more on post-1945 French travellers to America, in particular Baudrillard, see Scott, *Semiologies of Travel*, and Forsdick, *Travel in Twentieth-Century French and Francophone Cultures*.

30 Dadié's subtle linking of transit time and space (the one-way systems of airport corridors) to the complex nature of American consumer society is another example of his prescient thinking on air travel practices. In her study of recent airport architecture, Justine Lloyd examines how airport planners have devised means of strengthening the links between travel and consumerism by creating more economically useful spaces within the circulating spaces of airports. See 'Airport Technology, Travel, and Consumption', *Space and Culture*, 6.2 (2003), pp. 93–109.

31 The Portuguese repression of post-1945 nationalist movements in Angola was noted for its violence. Following a rebellion in 1961, for example, between 30,000 and 50,000 Angolans were killed and many were exiled. Portugal itself became involved in an economically disastrous guerrilla war in its African colonies on which it spent at least half its national budget. Inevitably this destabilized the European country and led to a *coup d'état* in 1974. Significantly NATO, of which the United States was of course the most powerful member, supported Portugal in this colonial war. Angola was granted independence in 1975. For more on this subject see Elikia M'Bokolo, 'Equatorial West Africa', in *General History of Africa*, edited by Ali A. Mazrui, 8 vols (Oxford: James Currey, 1993), VIII, pp. 192–220.

32 This perception of America as a 'new' country and wayward child was common in post-war Europe and is mentioned several times by Kuisel in *Seducing France*.

33 Alvin Z. Rubenstein and Donald E. Smith, 'Anti-Americanism in the Third World', *Annals of the American Academy of Political Science*, 497 (1988), pp. 35–45 (p. 40). Unfortunately, the authors deal only very briefly with the subject of a specifically African anti-Americanism. They mention the dissatisfaction of African leaders with America's lack of resolve in ending South Africa's apartheid regime and also their discontent at being pawns in the Soviet–American relations of the Cold War.

34 Kuisel, *Seducing the French*, p. 4.

35 In her introduction to the American translation, Jo Patterson establishes Dadié's itinerary: Ann Arbor, MI, New York, Atlanta, Chicago, Nashville, Indianapolis, New Orleans and Washington, DC.

36 Case, 'Bernard Binlin Dadié's Observations', p. 92.

37 Thomas, *Black France*, p. 77.

Chapter Five

1 See Frances Bartkowski, *Travelers, Immigrants, Inmates: Essays in Estrangement* (Minneapolis/London: University of Minnesota Press, 1995). Bartkowski's chapter, 'From Snakes to Ice: Tété-Michel Kpomassie's *An African in Greenland*', pp. 72–81, is one of the few critical analyses of this text.

2 For a more detailed analysis of this relationship see Mike Robinson, 'Between and Beyond the Pages: Literature–Tourism Relationships', in Mike Robinson and Hans-Christian Andersen, *Literature and Tourism: Essays in the Reading and Writing of Tourism* (London: Thompson Learning, 2002), pp. 39–79.

3 Robert Gessain, *Les Esquimaux du Grœnland à l'Alaska* (Paris: Éditions Bourrelier & Cie, 1947). Gessain's text is part of the ethnographic-inspired collection 'La joie de connaître' which features such titles as *La Vie des noirs d'Afrique* and *Au Village de France: la vie traditionnelle des paysans*. The approach of this illustrated book (photographs and sketches) is largely simplistic and romanticized, claiming to introduce the reader – specifically identified as French – to the traditional life of Eskimos whilst deliberately avoiding engagement with what it terms 'les modifications apportées par les contacts avec les diverses *nations civilisées*' [the changes brought about by contact with different *civilized nations*] (p. 12, my emphasis). Where there is discussion of the role of Denmark in Greenland, it is characterized by unambiguous praise for that country's supposedly progressive and enlightened colonial policy.

4 Scott, *Semiologies of Travel*, p. 170. There are, however, important differences between Kpomassie's desire to read in order to escape his cultural origins and Leiris's use of his boxes of books (largely European classics), to create, according to Scott, 'a safety barrier between him and the different symbolic systems of the native societies' (p. 168).

5 Holland and Huggan, *Tourists with Typewriters*, p. 67. The authors identify the 'exotic' Arctic as one of these 'zones'.

6 Of course the translation of these texts into Danish rather than the local language is emblematic of the use of literature by European colonial powers to promote their culture as a sacred monument that silences inferior local culture. See, for example,

the much-quoted 1835 'Minute on Indian Education' by Thomas Macaulay where he suggests that a single shelf of a good European library is worth the whole native literature of India. In *Selections from Educational Records (1781–1839)*, edited by H. Sharp (Delhi: National Archives of India, 1965 [1920]), pp. 107–17.

7 Lisle, *The Global Politics of Contemporary Travel Writing*, p. 89. Emphasis in original.

8 See Talal Asad, 'Introduction', in *Anthropology and the Colonial Encounter*, edited by Talal Asad (Atlantic Highlands, NJ: Humanities Press, 1973), pp. 9–19 (pp. 14–15). French contemporaries of Asad also highlighted the links between anthropology and colonial history. See, for example, Gérard Leclerc, *Anthropologie et colonialisme: essai sur l'histoire de l'africanisme* (Paris: Fayard, 1972) and Jean Copans, *Anthropologie et impérialisme* (Paris: François Maspéro, 1975).

9 Nicholas Thomas, 'Against Ethnography', *Cultural Anthropology*, 6.3 (1991), pp. 306–22 (p. 309).

10 Tim Ingold, 'Introduction' to account of 1992 debate,'The past is a foreign country', in *Key Debates in Anthropology*, edited by Tim Ingold (London and New York: Routledge, 1996), pp. 199–248 (p. 201). Ingold's notion of the 'ethnographic present' is of course reminiscent of Johannes Fabian's argument regarding anthropology's 'denial of coevalness' in its representation of non-Western cultures.

11 Clifford, *Predicament of Culture*, p. 47.

12 According to Mark Nuttall, judgements on the 'promiscuous' sexual habits of the Inuit are commonplace amongst foreign researchers who fail to take account of indigenous cultural norms. See *Arctic Homeland: Kinship, Community and Development in Northwest Greenland* (London: Belhaven Press, 1992). Where Kpomassie is concerned, it is interesting that the polygamous relationship of his own father is never judged in the way that Inuit relationships are.

13 Scott, *Semiologies of Travel*, p. 75. Holland and Huggan also discuss the difference between ethnography and travel writing, which they see primarily as one of 'emphasis'. Like Scott, they see ethnography as primarily scientific and travel writing as being 'self-consciously autobiographical, intentionally anecdotal, and (in some cases) deliberately ethnocentric'. However, they are careful to acknowledge travel writing's debt to ethnography and ultimately conclude that distinctions between them are at best problematic. *Tourists with Typewriters*, p. 11.

14 See James Clifford, 'Introduction: Partial Truths', in, *Writing Culture: The Poetics and Politics of Ethnography*, edited by James Clifford and George E. Marcus (Berkeley, CA: University of California Press, 1986), pp. 1–26.

15 Holland and Huggan, *Tourists with Typewriters*, p. 68.

16 Clifford, 'Partial Truths', p. 6.

17 Clifford, 'Partial Truths', p. 9. Another well-known subversion of Western ethnographic discourse is Yambo Ouologuem's portrait of the anthropologist Shrobenius (a thinly disguised reference to the German Africanist Frobenius) in his novel *Le Devoir de violence* (Paris: Seuil, 1968), translated by Ralph Manheim as *Bound to Violence* (London: Heinemann, 1968). 'Ethnologie inversée' also informs Massaër Diallo's study of the persistence of irrational belief systems in French society as evidenced in the practice of French clients consulting Paris-based African marabouts. See 'Les marabouts de Paris' in the volume he co-authored with Blaise N'Djehoya, *Un Regard noir: les Français vus pas les Africains*.

18 Thomas, 'Against Ethnography', p. 309.

19 Thomas, 'Against Ethnography', p. 317.

20 de Certeau, *Heterologies*, p. 70.

21 For more on the influence of pan-African ideology on African anti-colonial movements of this time see S.K.B. Asante, 'Pan-Africanism and Regional Integration', in *General History of Africa*, edited by Ali A. Mazrui, 8 vols (Oxford: James Currey, 1993), VIII, pp. 724–43.

22 Kpomassie's 'language travels' are suggested but never explored in the text. As with the colonized African travellers discussed in earlier chapters, Kpomassie gives little or no sense of the process of foreign language acquisition. Nor does he explain the level of linguistic attainment achieved in the various languages he speaks, and learns to speak (as well as Mina, his own mother tongue, and knowledge of French and English he clearly learns sufficient Danish to enable him to read texts in that language. He also appears to gain a good grasp of the local Greenland language during his sixteen-month stay.) His linguistic competence appears simply as a given and his own cultural experiences appear to have normalized translation to such a degree that it appears largely unworthy of comment. This is yet another reminder of the often multilingual abilities of colonized travelling Africans.

23 It is no surprise that Kpomassie should find work in the Guinean embassy in Accra. As he himself states, the Ghanaian capital became a hub of pan-African activity in the 1950s–60s, mirroring the philosophy of the most pan-African of all political leaders of the time, Ghanaian president Kwame Nkrumah. Amongst his most supportive allies was the Guinean president Ahmed Sekou Touré. However, Kpomassie's experiences seem to confirm S.K.B. Asante's claim that the pan-Africanist ideology of the 1960s rarely went beyond the stage of theoretical discussion. See 'Pan-Africansm and Regional Integration'. Asante's chapter explores in detail the differences and divisions that led to the overwhelming refusal of African countries to sacrifice perceived national interests in the name of continental political and economic unity.

24 Greenland has been subject to some form of European colonization since the Norwegian Erik the Red's first exploration of the island in AD 981. Although the colony he established declined in the fourteenth and fifteenth centuries, the island's rich seas continued to attract the attention of Scottish and Scandinavian whalers until, eventually, the Danish Lutheran missionary Hans Egede established a trade and mission post in Nuuk in 1721. Denmark continued to administer the island from the early eighteenth century but it was 1921 before the European colonial power claimed sovereignty over the entire island. In 1953 Greenland became the Danish equivalent of the French overseas departments and in 1979 was granted home rule. In 1985 Greenland became the first country to leave the European Union. For more on Greenland's history, see David Sugden, *Arctic and Antarctic: A Modern Geographical Synthesis* (Oxford: Basil Blackwell, 1982).

25 Mark Nuttall argues that, before this, the largely isolationist and paternal attitude of the Danes meant that the Inuit were not exploited and 'this certainly was a significantly different attitude from other imperial powers'. However, Nutall's study also makes clear that from the eighteenth century the hierarchal attitudes so familiar amongst other colonizing powers did govern interactions with the Inuit population. See 'Greenland: Emergence of an Inuit Homeland', in *Polar Peoples:*

Self-Determination and Development, edited by Minority Rights Group (London: Minority Rights Publications, 1994), pp. 1–28 (p. 6).

26 Sugden, *Arctic and Antarctic*, pp. 263–68.

27 Holland and Huggan, *Tourists with Typewriters*, p. 100.

28 Forsdick, *Travel in Twentieth-Century French and Francophone Cultures*, pp. 3, 69.

29 This nostalgic and elitist travel discourse is usually associated with Western inter-war travel writing when the growing democratization of travel led to a backlash against emerging, usually mass travel practices. For Charles Forsdick, criticism of travel's increasing acceleration by 1930s French travel writers is part of a wider generic preoccupation with entropic decline and implies 'a paradoxical aristocracy of the gaze associated with the means of transport selected'. *Travel in Twentieth-Century French and Francophone Cultures*, p. 94. Here, however, as with Kpomassie's earlier experience of the aurora borealis, the emphasis is on the subjective feelings and emotional reactions of one seduced by landscape rather than a colonialist visual engagement that seeks to interpret and control it.

30 Holland and Huggan, *Tourists with Typewrites*, p. 100.

31 Patrick Holland and Graham Huggan, 'Varieties of Nostalgia in Contemporary Travel Writing', in *Perspectives on Travel Writing*, edited by Glenn Hooper and Tim Youngs (Aldershot: Ashgate, 2004), pp. 139–51 (p. 140). Rosaldo's highly influential concept of 'imperialist nostalgia', the mourning for what one has destroyed oneself, occurs alongside 'a peculiar sense of mission, "the white man's burden", where civilized nations stand duty-bound to uplift so-called savage ones. In this ideologically constructed world of ongoing progressive change, putatively static savage societies become a stable reference point for defining (the felicitous progress of) civilized identity. "We" (who believe in progress) valorize innovation, and then yearn for more stable worlds, whether these reside in our past, in other cultures, or in the conflation of the two.' See the chapter on 'Imperialist Nostalgia' in his study *Culture and Truth: The Remaking of Social Analysis* (Boston, MA: Beacon Press, 1993), pp. 68–87 (p. 70).

32 Bartkowski, *Travelers, Immigrants, Inmates*, pp. 79, 81.

Chapter Six

1 Caren Kaplan, *Questions of Travel: Postmodern Discourses of Displacement* (Durham, NC: Duke University Press, 1996), p. 2.

2 Janet Wolff, 'On the Road Again: Metaphors of Travel in Cultural Criticism', *Cultural Studies*, 7.2 (1993), pp. 224–39 (p. 224). Emphasis in original.

3 Tim Cresswell, 'Imagining the Nomad: Mobility and the Postmodern Primitive', in *Space and Social Theory: Interpreting Modernity and Postmodernity*, edited by Georges Benko and Ulf Strohmayer (Oxford: Blackwell, 1997), pp. 360–79 (p. 377).

4 Sara Mills, *Discourses of Difference: An Analysis of Women's Travel Writing and Colonialism* (London and New York: Routledge, 1991), p. 196.

5 Holland and Huggan, *Tourists with Typewriters*, p. 112.

6 Susan Bassnett, 'Travel Writing and Gender', in *The Cambridge Companion to Travel Writing*, edited by Peter Hulme and Tim Youngs (Cambridge: Cambridge University Press, 2002), pp. 225–41.

7 For an overview of scholarship in the area of Western women's travel writing see Bassnett, 'Travel Writing and Gender'.

8 Cresswell, *On the Move*, p. 178.

9 Paul White, 'Geography, Literature and Migration', in *Writing Across Worlds: Literature and Migration*, edited by Russell King, John Connell and Paul White (London and New York: Routledge, 1995), pp. 1–19 (p. 1).

10 Beyala is the author of two texts that conform in many respects to essays: *Lettre d'une Africaine à ses sœurs occidentales* (Paris: Spengler, 1995) and *Lettre d'une Afro-française à ses compatriotes* (Paris: Mango, 2000). More recently, she has published erotic fiction. For more detailed discussion of her work, including the controversy surrounding accusations of plagiarism levelled against her, see Nicki Hitchcott, *Calixthe Beyala: Performances of Migration* (Liverpool: Liverpool University Press, 2007).

11 Creswell, *On the Move*, p. 3. Cresswell here is opposing mobility to 'movement', which he sees as 'mobility abstracted from contexts of power'.

12 I am thinking here of texts such as Jean Roger Essomba's novel *Le Paradis du Nord* (Paris: Présence Africaine, 1996) where the detailed description of the immigrant journey (from motivation, departure, journey through Africa and Europe) presents this form of travel as a particular type of risk-laden, tragic but also arguably heroic adventure. A more explicit example is the photographic essay by Sarah Caron and Isabelle Fougère, *Odyssée moderne: voyage avec les migrants clandestins du Sahara à la grande bleue* (Marseille: Images en manœuvre, 2004).

13 In the anthology of African and Asian travel writing, *Other Routes*, the editors include an extract from the German-language memoirs of Emily Said-Ruete, a Zanzibar-born 'African-Arab Princess' and convert to Christianity who travelled throughout Europe in the late nineteenth century. One could also mention non-African portrayals of African women in Europe such as *Ourika* by Claire de Duras (Exeter: University of Exeter Press, 1993 [1823]) or similar African male-authored portrayals such as Ousmane Sembene's fictional account of a modern-day slave, 'La Noire de...' which features in the collection of short stories *Voltaïque* (Paris: Présence Africaine, 1962). The extremely rare textualizations of intercontinental female travel by African women writers include Mariama Bâ's reference to the American-based Senegalese correspondent of *Une si Longue Lettre*, Ken Bugul's representation of the failed 'educational' journey of a young Senegalese student in Brussels, *Le Baobab fou* (Dakar: Les Nouvelles Éditions Africaines, 1984) and Véronique Tadjo's account of two trips to Rwanda in *L'Ombre d'Imana*. For more on the broader history of African women's writing see, Juliana Makuchi Nfah-Abbenyi, *Gender in African Women's Writing: Identity, Sexuality and Difference* (Bloomington, IN: Indiana University Press, 1998) and Nicki Hitchcott, *Women Writers in Francophone Africa* (Oxford: Berg, 2000).

14 Wolff, 'On the Road Again', p. 232. Emphasis in original.

15 Although M'am has official status and is in possession of the necessary legal papers, Nicki Hitchcott correctly points out that it is Soumana, as mother of Abdou's children, who would be entitled to stay under French immigration law. *Calixthe Beyala: Performances of Migration*, p. 70.

16 For example, Meaghan Morris examines how the 'stifling home' becomes the place from which male journeys of discovery and adventure begin, and to which,

in the end, they return. 'At Henry Parkes Motel', *Cultural Studies*, 2.1 (1988), pp. 1–47.

17 White, 'Geography, Literature and Migration', p. 4.

18 Ellen Furlong, 'Making Mass Vacations: Tourism and Consumer Culture in France, 1930s to 1970s', *Comparative Studies in Society and History*, 40.2 (1998), pp. 247–86 (p. 249). In France, paid holiday time was approved by law in 1936. For an excellent critical overview of the history of *congés payés* in France, see Jean Viard, *La Révélation vacancière* (La-Tour-d'Aigues: Groupe d'études des mutations régionales, 1981).

19 Jean-Didier Urbain, *Paradis verts: désirs de campagne et passions résidentielles* (Paris: Payot, 2002), p. 13.

20 Jean Viard, *Penser les vacances* (Arles: Actes Sud, 1984), pp. 132–40. Viard's methodology pre-empts aspects of Kristin Ross's notion of 'interior colonialism' and the reordering of the 'everyday' life of French citizens following decolonization. See *Fast Cars, Clean Bodies*. A similar approach is used by Herman Lebovics in his assessment of how the former colonies shaped the French state's attempts to impose a unified vision of a national cultural heritage following the loss of its colonies. See *Bringing the Empire Back Home: France in the Global Era* (Durham, NC: Duke University Press, 2004).

21 Rosaldo, *Culture and Truth*, p. 68.

22 Ibid., p. 70.

23 Urbain discusses in detail the complex issue of rurophobia in Chapter 2 of *Paradis verts*.

24 Furlong, 'Making Mass Vacations', p. 248.

25 Hitchcott, *Calixthe Beyala: Performances of Migration*, p. 72.

26 Mimi Sheller and John Urry, 'Introduction: Places to Play, Places in Play', in *Tourism Mobilities: Places to Play, Places in Play*, edited by Mimi Sheller and John Urry (London and New York: Routledge, 2004), pp. 1–10.

27 Thomas, *Black France*, p. 161. For a discussion of the symbolism of dress in the exercise of British colonial domination see Helen Callaway, 'Dressing for Dinner in the Bush: Rituals of Self-Definition and British Imperial Authority', in *Dress and Gender: Making and Meaning*, edited by Ruth Barnes and Joanne B. Eicher (Oxford: Berg, 1992), pp. 232–47. Callaway devotes a section of this article to the codes and trends of dress amongst nineteenth-century female travellers.

28 Sheller and Urry, 'Places to Play, Places in Play', p. 5.

29 Ian Littlewood, *Sultry Climates: Travel and Sex* (Cambridge, MA: Da Capo Press, 2001), p. 213.

30 Jacques Heim designed the bikini in France in 1946, ten years after the Front populaire introduced paid holidays. The two-piece swimsuit was unquestionably influential in promoting the Western image of the female body beautiful as tanned, slim and toned. In her rich and nuanced discussion of the bikini's symbolism, Teresia K. Teaiwa notes how the bikini 'politically negates the female body by exposing it'. However, Teaiwa is ultimately more concerned with what she identifies as the bikini's two colonized referents: the 'generic South Sea noble savage' and 'dispossessed Bikinians'. See, 'Bikinis and other S/pacific N/oceans', in *Voyaging through the Contemporary Pacific*, edited by David Hanlon and Geoffrey M. White (Oxford: Rowman & Littlefield, 2000), pp. 91–112. (pp. 96, 99). For a more general design

history of the bikini, see Anne-Laure Quilleret's article, 'L'épopée du bikini', *Le Monde*, 3 August 2002, p. 18.

31 Roland Barthes, 'History and Sociology of Clothing: Some Methodological Observations', in *The Language of Fashion*, edited by Andy Stafford and Michael Carter, trans. Andy Stafford (Oxford: Berg, 2006), pp. 3–20 (pp. 8–9).

32 Ibid., p. 13.

33 For example, in a *hadith* from *The Translation of the Meanings of Sahih Al-Bukhari* by Sunni Islamic scholar al-Bukhari, women are explicitly prohibited from travelling alone overnight without a respectable, preferably male, chaperone who must be related by blood or marriage. See Volume II, p. 109 of the nine-volume edition translated by Muhammad Muhsin Khan (New Delhi: Kitab Bhavan, 1987). In her discussion of seventeenth-century travel narratives by Catholic Spanish nuns in the Americas, Elisa Sampson Vera Tudela discusses the slippage between moral vulnerability and sexual deviance in popular perceptions of these women. She quotes Alonso de Andrade's 1642 text, *Tratodo de la Virgen* where he claims 'from pilgrim woman to prostitute there is but little difference'. See *Colonial Angels: Narratives of Gender and Spirituality in Mexico, 1580–1750* (Austin, TX: University of Texas Press, 2000), p. 1.

34 Littlewood, *Sultry Climates*, p. 100.

35 Fullager sees travel as transforming the essentially phallocentric and sexual economy of desire and allowing women to explore alternative meanings of the term. Simone Fullager, 'Narratives of Travel: Desire and the Movement of Feminine Subjectivity', *Leisure Studies*, 21.1 (2002), pp. 57–74 (p. 65).

Afterword

1 Lisle, *The Global Politics of Contemporary Travel Writing*, p. 89.

2 Cronin, *Across the Lines*, p. 46.

3 Gaston-Paul Effa, *Voici le dernier jour du monde* (Monaco: Éditions du Rocher, 2005).

4 Abdourahman A. Waberi, *Aux États-Unis d'Afrique* (Paris: J.-C Lattès, 2006).

5 Cronin, *Across the Lines*, p. 157.

Bibliography of Works Cited

Primary Sources

Beyala, Calixthe, *Le petit prince de Belleville* (Paris: Albin Michel, 1992); *Loukoum: The 'Little Prince' of Belleville*, trans. Marjoljin de Jager (Oxford: Heinemann, 1995).
——, *Maman a un amant* (Paris: J'ai lu, 1993).
Dadié, Bernard, *Un Nègre à Paris* (Paris: Présence Africaine, 1959); *An African in Paris*, trans. Karen C. Hatch (Urbana, IL: University of Illinois Press, 1994).
——, *Patron de New York* (Paris: Présence Africaine, 1964); *One Way: Bernard Dadié Observes America*, trans. Jo Patterson (Urbana, IL: University of Illinois Press, 1994).
Diakhaté, Lamine, *Chalys d'Harlem* (Dakar: Les Nouvelles Éditions Africaines, 1978).
Kpomassie, Tété-Michel, *L'Africain du Grœnland* (Paris: Flammarion, 1981); *An African in Greenland*, trans. James Kirkup (New York: The New York Review of Books, 2001 [1983]).
Loba, Aké, *Kocoumbo, l'étudiant noir* (Paris: Flammarion, 1960).
Socé Diop, Ousmane, *Mirages de Paris* (Paris: Nouvelles Éditions Latines, 1964 [1937]).

Secondary Works

Adesanmi, Pius, 'Redefining Paris: Trans-Modernity and Francophone African Migritude Fiction', *Modern Fiction Studies*, 51.4 (2005), pp. 958–75.
Aguiar, Marian, 'Smoke of the Savannah: Travelling Modernity in Sembène Ousmane's *God's Bits of Wood*', *Modern Fiction Studies*, 49.2 (2003), pp. 284–305.
Al-Bukhari, Sahih, *The Translation of the Meanings of Sahih Al-Bukhari*, trans. Muhammad Muhsin Khan (New Delhi: Kitab Bhavan, 1987).
Anderson, Hans Christian and Mike Robinson (eds), *Literature and Tourism* (London: Continuum, 2002).
Andrews, Jonathan, 'Letting Madness Range: Travel and Mental Disorder, c1700–1900', in *Pathologies of Travel*, ed. George Revill and Richard Wrigley (Amsterdam: Rodopi, 2000), pp. 25–88.
Archer-Straw, Petrine, *Negrophilia: Avant-Garde Paris and Black Culture in the 1920s* (London: Thames & Hudson, 2000).

Asad, Talal (ed.), *Anthropology and the Colonial Encounter* (London: Ithaca Press, 1973).

Asante, S.K.B., 'Pan-Africanism and Regional Integration', in *General History of Africa*, ed. Ali A. Mazrui, 8 vols (Oxford: James Currey, 1993), VIII, pp. 724–43.

Ashcroft, Bill, Gareth Griffiths and Helen Tiffin, *The Empire Writes Back: Theory and Practice in Post-Colonial Literatures* (London and New York: Routledge, 1989).

Association des amis du roman populaire, *Le Rocambole: Bulletin des Amis du roman populaire. 6. Le Journal des voyages* (Maurepas: Association des amis du roman populaire, 1999).

Bâ, Mariama, *Une si longue lettre* (Dakar: Les Nouvelles Éditions Africaines, 1979).

Bancel, Nicolas, Pascal Blanchard, Gilles Boëtsch, Éric Deroo, Sandrine Lemaire and Charles Forsdick (eds), *Human Zoos: Science and Spectacle in the Age of Empire* (Liverpool: Liverpool University Press, 2008 [2002]).

Barthes, Roland, 'History and Sociology of Clothing: Some Methodological Observations', in *The Language of Fashion*, ed. Andy Stafford and Michael Carter, trans. Andy Stafford (Oxford: Berg, 2006), pp. 3–20.

Bartkowski, Frances, *Travelers, Immigrants, Inmates: Essays in Estrangement* (Minneapolis, MN: University of Minnesota Press, 1995).

Bassnett, Susan, 'Travel Writing and Gender', in *The Cambridge Companion to Travel Writing*, ed. Peter Hulme and Tim Youngs (Cambridge: Cambridge University Press, 2002), pp. 225–41.

Batukezanga, Zamenga, *Lettres d'Amérique* (Kinshasa: Zahat, 1982).

——, *Chérie Basso* (Kinshasa: Éditions Saint Paul Afrique, 1989).

Baumgardt, Ursula, 'Voyages à travers la littérature peule', in *Les Discours de voyages: Afrique – Antilles*, ed. Romuald Fonkoua (Paris: Karthala, 1998), pp. 243–53.

Besemeres, Mary, 'Anglos Abroad: Memoirs of Immersion in a Foreign Language', *Biography*, 28.1 (2005), pp. 27–42.

Beyala, Calixthe, *Lettre d'une Africaine à ses sœurs occidentales* (Paris: Spengler, 1995).

——, *Lettre d'une Afro-française à ses compatriotes* (Paris: Mango, 2000).

Bhabha, Homi K., *The Location of Culture* (London and New York: Routledge, 1994).

Blachère, Jean-Claude, *Négritures: les écrivains d'Afrique noire et la langue française* (Paris: L'Harmattan, 1993).

Blair, Barbara, 'Pan-Africainism as Process: Adelaide Casley Hayford, Garveyism, and the Cultural Roots of Nationalism', in *Imagining Home: Class, Culture and Nationalism in the African Diaspora*, ed. Sidney J. Lemelle and Robin D.G. Kelley (London: Verso, 1994), pp. 121–44.

Boelhower, William '"I'll teach you how to flow": On Figuring Out Atlantic Studies', *Atlantic Studies*, 1.1 (2004), pp. 28–48.

Bolster, W. Jeffrey, *Black Jacks: African American Seamen in the Age of Sail* (Cambridge, MA: Harvard University Press, 1997).

Borgomano, Madeleine, 'Le voyage "à l'africaine" et ses transformations selon

Amkoullel, l'enfant peul', in *Les Discours de voyages: Afrique – Antilles*, ed. Romuald Fonkoua (Paris: Karthala, 1998), pp. 207–16.

Borm, Jan, 'Defining Travel: On the Travel Book, Travel Writing and Terminology', in *Perspectives on Travel Writing*, ed. Glen Hooper and Tim Youngs (Aldershot: Ashgate, 2004), pp. 13–26.

Böröcz, Jószef, 'Travel Capitalism: The Structure of Europe and the Advent of the Tourist', *Comparative Studies in Society and History*, 33.4 (1992), pp. 708–41.

Boyce Davies, Carole, *Black Women, Writing and Identity: Migrations of the Subject* (London and New York: Routledge, 1994).

Britton, Celia M., *Edouard Glissant and Postcolonial Theory: Strategies of Language and Resistance* (Charlottesville, VA: University of Virginia Press, 1999).

Bruner, Edward M., 'Tourism in Ghana: The Representation of Slavery and the Return of the Black Diaspora', *American Anthropologist*, 98.2 (1996), pp. 290–304.

Bugul, Ken, *Le Baobab fou* (Dakar: Les Nouvelles Éditions Africaines, 1984).

Buzard, James, *The Beaten Track: European Tourism, Literature and the Ways to Culture* (Oxford: Clarendon, 1993).

Caillié, René, *Voyage à Tombouctou* (Paris: La Découverte, 1996 [1830]).

Callaway, Helen, 'Dressing for Dinner in the Bush: Rituals of Self-Definition and British Imperial Authority', in *Dress and Gender: Making and Meaning*, ed. Ruth Barnes and Joanne B. Eicher (Oxford: Berg, 1992), pp. 232–47.

Caron, Sarah and Isabelle Fougère, *Odyssée moderne: voyage avec les clandestins du Sahara à la grande bleue* (Marseille: Images en manœuvre, 2004).

Case, David Allen, 'Bernard Binlin Dadié's Observations', *The Journal of African Travel-Writing*, 1 (1996), pp. 90–92.

Certeau, Michel de, *Heterologies: Discourse on the Other* (Minneapolis, MN: University of Minnesota Press, 1986).

Chafer, Tony, 'France's *Mission Civilisatrice* in Africa: French Culture not for Export', in *Popular Culture and Mass Communication in Twentieth-Century France*, ed. Rosemary Chapman and Nicolas Hewitt (Lampeter: Edwin Mellen Press, 1992), pp. 142–64.

Chalfin, Brenda, 'Cars, the Customs Service, and Sumptuary Rule in Neoliberal Ghana', *Comparative Studies in Society and History*, 50.2 (2008), pp. 424–53.

Chevrier, Jacques, 'Afrique(s)-sur-Seine: autour de la notion de "migritude"', *Notre Librairie: Revue des littératures du Sud*, 155–156 (2004), pp. 96–100.

Clark, John P., *America, their America* (London: Heinemann, 1964).

Clifford, James, *The Predicament of Culture: Twentieth Century-Ethnography, Literature and Art* (Cambridge, MA: Harvard University Press, 1988).

——, 'Notes on Travel and Theory', *Inscriptions*, 5 (1989), pp. 177–88.

——, 'Traveling Cultures', in *Cultural Studies*, ed. Lawrence Grossberg, Cary Nelson and Paula Treichler (New York and London: Routledge, 1992), pp. 19–116.

——, *Routes: Travel and Translation in the Late Twentieth Century* (Cambridge, MA: Harvard University Press, 1997).

Clifford, James and George Marcus (eds), *Writing Culture* (Berkeley, CA: University of California Press, 1986).

Conklin, Alice, *A Mission to Civilize: The Republican Idea of Empire in France and West Africa, 1885–1930* (Stanford, CA: Stanford University Press, 1997).

Copans, Jean, *Anthropologie et impérialisme* (Paris: François Maspéro, 1975).

Corbey, Raymond, 'Ethnographic Showcases, 1870–1930', *Cultural Anthropology*, 8.3 (1993), pp. 338–69.

Cresswell, Tim, 'Imagining the Nomad: Mobility and the Postmodern Primitive', in *Space and Social Theory: Interpreting Modernity and Postmodernity*, ed. Georges Benko and Ulf Strohmayer (Oxford: Blackwell, 1997), pp. 360–79.

——, *On the Move: Mobility in the Modern Western World* (London and New York: Routledge, 2006).

Crick, Malcolm, 'Representations of International Tourism in the Social Sciences; Sun, Sex, Sights, Savings and Servility', *Annual Review of Anthropology*, 18 (1989), pp. 307–44.

Cronin, Michael, *Across the Lines: Travel, Language, Translation* (Cork: Cork University Press, 2000).

Crush, Jonathan and Paul Wellings, 'The Southern African Pleasure Periphery, 1966–83', *The Journal of Modern African Studies*, 21.4 (1983), pp. 673–98.

Culler, Jonathan, 'Semiotics of Tourism', *American Journal of Semiotics*, 1.1–2 (1981), pp. 127–40.

Dadié, Bernard, 'Le Japon, pays découvert qui reste à découvrir', *Fraternité-Matin*, 11 October 1968, p. 9.

Daninos, Pierre, *Les Carnets du Major W. Marmaduke Thompson: découverte de la France et des Français* (Paris: P. de Tartas, 1954).

Dash, J. Michael, *Haiti and the United States: National Stereotypes and the Literary Imagination* (New York: Saint Martin's Press, 1997).

Derrida, Jacques, 'The Law of Genre', in *Acts of Literature*, ed. Derek Attridge (London and New York: Routledge, 1991), pp. 221–352.

Dewitte, Philippe, *Les Mouvements nègres en France, 1919–1959* (Paris: L'Harmattan, 1985).

Diallo, Bakary, *Force-bonté* (Paris: ACCT/Les Nouvelles Éditions Africaines, 1926).

Diallo, Massaër and Blaise N'Djehoya, *Un Regard noir: les Français vus pas les Africains* (Paris: Autrement, 1984).

Diop, Birago, '"J'avais appris à lire pour pouvoir écrire"', *Notre Librairie*, 81 (1989), pp. 62–69.

Dongala, Emmanuel, *Jazz et vin de palme* (Paris: Le Serpent à plumes, 1982).

DuBois, W.E.B., *The Souls of Black Folk* (Harmondsworth: Penguin, 1996 [1903]).

Dunot, Claude, 'Bernard Binlin Dadié', *L'Afrique littéraire et artistique*, 5 (1969), pp. 16–21.

Dunn, Kevin C., 'Fear of a Black Planet: Anarchy Anxieties and Postcolonial Travel to Africa', *Third World Quarterly*, 25.3 (2004), pp. 483–99.

Duras, Claire de, *Ourika* (Exeter: University of Exeter Press, 1993 [1823]).

Ebron, Paulla A., 'Tourists as Pilgrims: Commercial Fashioning of Transatlantic Politics', *American Ethnologist*, 26.4 (1999), pp. 910–32.

Edwards, Brent Hayes, *The Practice of Diaspora: Literature, Translation and the Rise of Black Internationalism* (Cambridge, MA: Harvard University Press, 2003).

Effa, Gaston-Paul, *Voici le dernier jour du monde* (Monaco: Éditions du Rocher, 2005).

Egonu, Iheanachor, '*Les Continents* and the Francophone Pan-Negro Movement', *Phylon*, 41.1 (1980), pp. 12–24.

Essomba, Jean Roger, *Le Paradis du Nord* (Paris: Présence Africaine, 1996).

Ezra, Elizabeth, *The Colonial Unconscious: Race and Culture in Interwar France* (Ithaca, NY: Cornell University Press, 2000).

Fabian, Johannes, *Time and the Other: How Anthropology Makes its Object* (New York: Columbia University Press, 1983).

——, *Out of Our Minds: Reason and Madness in the Exploration of Central Africa* (Berkeley, CA: University of California Pres, 2000).

Fabre, Michel, Fabre, 'René Maran, the New Negro and Negritude', *Phylon*, 36.3 (1974), pp. 340–51.

——, *From Harlem to Paris: Black American Writers in France, 1840–1980* (Urbana, IL: University of Illinois Press, 1991).

Fonkoua, Romuald (ed.), *Les Discours de voyages: Afrique – Antilles* (Paris: Karthala, 1998).

Forsdick, Charles, 'Revisiting Exoticism: From Colonialism to Postcolonialism', in *Francophone Postcolonial Studies: A Critical Introduction*, ed. Charles Forsdick and David Murphy (London: Arnold, 2003), pp. 46–55.

——, *Travel in Twentieth-Century French and Francophone Cultures: The Persistence of Diversity* (Oxford: Oxford University Press, 2005).

Fowler, Alistair, *Kinds of Literature: An Introduction to the Theory of Genres and Modes* (Oxford: Clarendon Press, 1982).

Fish, Cheryl J., *Black and White Women's Travel Narratives: Antebellum Explorations* (Gainesville, FL: University Press of Florida, 2004).

Fraiture, Pierre-Philippe, *La Mesure de l'autre: Afrique subsaharienne et roman ethnographique de Belgique et de France (1918–1940)* (Paris: Champion, 2007).

Franey, Laura E., *Victorian Travel Writing and Imperial Violence: British Writing on Africa, 1855–1902* (London: Palgrave, 2003).

Frow, John, *Genre* (London and New York: Routledge, 2006).

Fulford, Tim, Debbie Lee and Peter J. Kitson, *Literature, Science and Exploration in the Romantic Era: Bodies of Knowledge* (Cambridge: Cambridge University Press, 2004).

Fullager, Simone, 'Narratives of Travel: Desire and the Movement of Feminine Subjectivity', *Leisure Studies*, 21.1 (2002), pp. 57–74.

Furlong, Ellen, 'Making Mass Vacations: Tourism and Consumer Culture in France, 1930s to 1970s', *Comparative Studies in Society and History*, 40.2 (1998), pp. 247–86.

Gessain, Robert, *Les Esquimaux du Grœnland à l'Alaska* (Paris: Éditions Bourrelier & Cie, 1947).

Gide, André, *Voyage au Congo suivi du Retour du Tchad. Carnets de route* (Paris: Gallimard, 1927–28).

Gikandi, Simon, *Reading the African Novel* (London: James Currey, 1987).

——, 'Theory, Literature, and Moral Considerations', *Research in African Literatures*, 32.4 (2001), pp. 1–18.

Gilroy, Paul, *The Black Atlantic: Modernity and Double Consciousness* (London and New York: Verso, 1993).

Girardet, Raoul, *L'Idée coloniale en France de 1971 à 1962* (Paris: Hachette/Pluriel, 1972).

Glick, Elisa L., 'Harlem's Queer Dandy: African-American Modernism and the Artifice of Blackness', *Modern Fiction Studies*, 49.3 (2003), pp. 414–42.

Gobineau, Joseph-Arthur, comte de, *Essai sur l'inégalité des races humaines* (Paris: Firmin-Didot & Cie, 1854).

Godard, Xavier (ed.), *Les Transports et la ville en Afrique au sud du Sahara* (Paris: Karthala, 2002).

Greenhalgh, Paul, *Ephemeral Vistas: The Expositions Universelles, Great Exhibitions and World's Fairs, 1851–1939* (Manchester: Manchester University Press, 1988).

Griffin, Dustin, *Satire: A Critical Reintroduction* (Lexington, KY: University Press of Kentucky, 1994).

Gruesser, John Cullen, *Black on Black: Twentieth-Century African American Writing about Africa* (Lexington, KY: University Press of Kentucky, 2000).

Guimont, Fabienne, *Les Étudiants africains en France, 1950–1965* (Paris: L'Harmattan, 1997).

Gunner, Liz, 'Africa and Orality', in *The Cambridge History of African and Caribbean Literature*, ed. F. Abiole Irele and Simon Gikandi, 2 vols (Cambridge: Cambridge University Press, 2004), I, pp. 1–18.

Hardy, George, *Une Conquête morale* (Paris: L'Harmattan, Collection 'Autrement Mêmes', 2005 [1917]).

Healy, Kimberley J., *The Modernist Traveler: French Detours, 1900–1930* (Lincoln, NE: University of Nebraska Press, 2003).

Heath, Stephen, 'The Politics of Genre', in *Debating World Literature*, ed. Christopher Prendergast (London: Verso, 2004), pp. 163–74.

Hill, Edwin, 'Imagining *Métissage*: The Politics and Practice of *Métissage* in the French Colonial Exposition and Ousmane Socé's *Mirages de Paris*', *Social Identities*, 8.4 (2002), pp. 619–45.

Hitchcott, Nicki, *Women Writers in Francophone Africa* (Oxford: Berg, 2000).

——, *Calixthe Beyala: Performances of Migration* (Liverpool: Liverpool University Press, 2007).

Hodeir, Catherine and Michel Pierre, *L'Exposition Coloniale* (Brussels: Éditions Complexe, 1991).

Holland, Patrick and Graham Huggan, *Tourists with Typewriters: Critical Reflections on Contemporary Travel Writing* (Ann Arbor, MI: The University of Michigan Press, 1998).

——, 'Varieties of Nostalgia in Contemporary Travel Writing', in *Perspectives on Travel Writing*, ed. Glenn Hooper and Tim Youngs (Aldershot: Ashgate, 2004), pp. 139–51.

Hountondji, Paulin 'Charabia et mauvaise conscience: psychologie du langage chez les intellectuels colonisés', *Présence Africaine*, 61 (1961), pp. 11–31.

Hulme, Peter and Tim Youngs, *Talking about Travel Writing: A Conversation between Peter Hulme and Tim Youngs* (Leicester: English Association. Issues in English 8, 2007).

Hutcheon, Linda, *Irony's Edge: The Theory and Politics of Irony* (London and New York: Routledge, 1994).

Inglis, Fred, *The Delicious History of the Holiday* (London and New York: Routledge, 2000).

Ingold, Tim (ed.), *Key Debates in Anthropology* (London and New York: Routledge, 1996).

Islam, Syed Manzurul, *The Ethics of Travel: From Marco Polo to Kafka* (Manchester: Manchester University Press, 1996).

Journal of Romance Studies, 5.3 (2005), special issue on 'Black Paris' edited by Sam Haigh and Nicki Hitchcott.

Joyce, James, *A Portrait of the Artist as a Young Man* (Harmondsworth: Penguin, 1992 [1916]).

Jules-Rosette, Bennetta, *Black Paris: The African Writers' Landscape* (Urbana, IL: University of Illinois Press, 1998).

Kane, Cheikh Hamidou, *L'Aventure ambiguë* (Paris: 10/18, 1979 [1961]).

Kanza, Thomas, *Sans Rancune* (Paris: L'Harmattan, 2006 [1965]).

Kaplan, Caren, *Questions of Travel: Postmodern Discourses of Displacement* (Durham, NC: Duke University Press, 1996).

Kelly, Debra, *Autobiography and Independence: Selfhood and Creativity in North African Postcolonial Writing in French* (Liverpool: Liverpool University Press, 2005).

Khair, Tabish et al. (eds), *Other Routes: 1500 Years of African and Asian Travel Writing* (Bloomington, IN: Indiana University Press, 2005).

Knight, Charles A., *The Literature of Satire* (Cambridge: Cambridge University Press, 2004).

Kuisel, Richard, *Seducing the French: The Dilemma of Americanization* (Berkeley, CA: University of California Press, 1993).

Lambert, Fernando, 'Bernard Dadié: l'écriture et le voyage', *L'Afrique littéraire et artistique*, 85 (1989), pp. 35–41.

Lao-Montes, Agustin, 'Decolonial Moves: Trans-locating African Diaspora Spaces', *Cultural Studies*, 21.2–3 (2007), pp. 309–38.

Lazarus, Neil, 'The Fetish of "the West" in Postcolonial Theory', in *Marxism, Modernity and Postcolonial Studies*, ed. Crystal Bartolovich and Neil Lazarus (Cambridge: Cambridge University Press, 2002), pp. 43–64.

Lebel, Roland, *Études de littérature coloniale* (Paris: J. Peyronnet, 1928).

Lebovics, *True France: The Wars over Cultural Identity, 1900–1945* (Ithaca, NY: Cornell University Press, 1992).

——, *Bringing the Empire Back Home: France in the Global Era* (Durham, NC: Duke University Press, 2004).

Leclerc, Gérard, *Anthropologie et colonialisme: essai sur l'histoire de l'africanisme* (Paris: Fayard, 1972).

Little, Pat, *Cheikh Hamidou Kane: L'Aventure ambiguë* (London: Grant & Cutler, Critical Guides to French Texts, 2000).

Little, Roger, 'Blanche et Noir: Louise Faure-Favier and the Liberated Woman', *Australian Journal of French Studies*, 36. 2 (1999), pp. 214–28.

——, *Between Totem and Taboo: Black Man, White Woman in Francographic Literature* (Exeter: University of Exeter Press, 2001).

Littlewood, Ian, *Sultry Climates: Travel and Sex* (Cambridge, MA: Da Capo Press, 2001).

Lisle, Debbie, *The Global Politics of Contemporary Travel Writing* (Cambridge: Cambridge University Press, 2007).

Lloyd, Justine, 'Airport Technology, Travel, and Consumption', *Space and Culture*, 6.2 (2003), pp. 93–109.

Loti, Pierre, *Roman d'un Spahi* (Paris: Flammarion, Folio, 1992).

Loutfi, Martine Astier, *Littérature et colonialisme: l'expansion coloniale vue dans la littérature romanesque française* (Paris: Mouton, 1971).

Mabanckou, Alain, *Lettre à Jimmy* (Paris: Fayard, 2007).

Macauley, Thomas, 'Minute on Indian Education', in *Selections from Educational Records (1781–1839)*, ed. H. Sharp (Delhi: National Archives of India, 1965 [1920]), pp. 107–17.

MacCannell, Dean, *The Tourist: A New Theory of the Leisure Class* (Basingstoke: MacMillan, 1976).

McCusker, Maeve, *Patrick Chamoiseau: Recovering Memory* (Liverpool: Liverpool University Press, 2007).

Martin, Tony, *Race First: The Ideological and Organizational Struggles of Marcus Garvey and the Universal Negro Improvement Association* (Westport, CT: Greenwood Press, 1976).

M'Bokolo, Elikia, 'Equatorial West Africa', in *General History of Africa*, ed. Ali A. Mazrui, 8 vols (Oxford: James Currey, 1993), VIII, pp. 192–220.

Michel, Marc, 'Les Troupes noires, la grande guerre et l'armée française', in *Tirailleurs sénégalais: zur bildlichen und literarischen Darstellung afrikanischer Soldaten im Dienste Franckreichs*, ed. János Riesz and Joachim Schultz (Frankfurt: Peter Lang, 1989).

Miller, Christopher, *Nationalists and Nomads: Essays on Francophone African Literature and Culture* (Chicago: University of Chicago Press, 1998).

Mills, Sara, *Discourses of Difference: An Analysis of Women's Travel Writing and Colonialism* (London and New York: Routledge, 1991).

Mitchell, Timothy, 'Orientalism and the Exhibitionary Order', in *Colonialism and Culture*, ed. Nicholas B. Dirks (Ann Arbor, MI: University of Michigan Press, 1992), pp. 289–317.

Modern Fiction Studies, 51.4 (2005), special issue on 'Paris, Modern Fiction and the Black Atlantic'.

Montesquieu, *Les Lettres persanes* (Paris: Livres de poche, 2003 [1721]).

Moody, Joseph N., *French Education since Napoleon* (New York: Syracuse University Press, 1978).

Morand, Paul, *Conseils pour voyager sans argent* (Paris: Émile Hazan & Cie, 1930).

Mortimer, Mildred, *Journeys through the French African Novel* (Portsmouth, NH: Heinemann, 1990).

Morris, Meaghan, 'At Henry Parkes Motel', *Cultural Studies*, 2.1 (1988), pp. 1–47.

Mouralis, Bernard, *L'Europe, l'Afrique et la folie* (Paris: L'Harmattan, 1993).

Mudimbe, Valentin Y., *Carnets d'Amérique, septembre-novembre, 1974* (Paris: Saint Germain des Près, 1974).

——, *Cheminements: Carnets de Berlin (avril-juin, 1999)* (Quebec: Humanitas, 2006).

Mudimbe-Boyi, Elisabeth, 'Travel, Representation and Difference, or how can one be a Parisian', *Research in African Literatures*, 23.3 (1992), pp. 25–39.

Newell, Stephanie, *Popular Fiction: 'Thrilling Discoveries in Conjugal Life' and Other Tales* (Oxford: James Currey, 2000).

Nfah-Abbenyi, Juliana Makuchi, *Gender in African Women's Writing: Identity, Sexuality and Difference* (Bloomington, IN: Indiana University Press, 1998).

Ngandu Nkashama, Pius, *Vie et mœurs d'un primitif en Essonne quatre-vingt-onze* (Paris: L'Harmattan, 1987).

Nissley, Tom, *Intimate and Authentic Economies: The American Self-Made Man from Douglass to Chaplin* (London and New York: Routledge, 2003).

Norindr, Panivong, *Phantasmatic Indochina: French Colonial Ideology in Architecture, Film and Literature* (Durham, NC: Duke University Press, 1996).

Nuttall, Marc, *Arctic Homeland: Kinship, Community and Development in Northwest Greenland* (London: Belhaven Press, 1992).

——, 'Greenland: Emergence of an Inuit Homeland', in *Polar Peoples: Self-Determination and Development*, ed. Minority Rights Group (London: Minority Rights Publications, 1994), pp. 1–28.

Ouologuem, Yambo, *Le Devoir de violence* (Paris: Seuil, 1968), *Bound to Violence*, trans. Ralph Manheim (London: Heinemann, 1968).

Pageard, Robert, 'L'image de l'Europe dans la littérature ouest-africaine d'expression française', in *Connaissance de l'étranger: mélanges offerts à la mémoire de Jean-Marie Carré* (Paris: Didier, 1964), pp. 323–46.

Palà, Sylvie (ed.), *Documents: Exposition coloniale Paris, 1931* (Paris: Bibliothèques de la Ville de Paris, 1981).

Pallister, Janis L., 'Outside the Monastery Walls: American Culture in Black African and Caribbean Poetry', *The Journal of Popular Culture*, 17.1 (1983), pp. 74–82.

Pettinger, Alasdair (ed.), *Always Elsewhere: Travels of the Black Atlantic* (London and New York: Cassell, 1998).

Polezzi, Loredana, *Translating Travel: Contemporary Italian Travel Writing in English Translation* (Aldershot: Ashgate, 2001).

Porter, Dennis, '*Orientalism* and its Problems', in *Colonial Discourse and Post-Colonial Theory: A Reader*, ed. Patrick Williams and Laura Chrisman (Hemel Hempstead: Harvester Wheatsheaf, 1993), pp. 150–61.

Pratt, Mary Louise, *Imperial Eyes: Travel Writing and Transculturation* (London and New York: Routledge, 1992).

Quilleret, Anne-Laure, 'L'épopée du bikini', *Le Monde*, 3 August 2002, p. 8.

Revill, George and Richard Wrigley (eds), *Pathologies of Travel* (Amsterdam: Rodopi, 2000).

Rosaldo, Renato, *Culture and Truth: The Remaking of Social Analysis* (Boston, MA: Beacon Press, 1993).

Ross, Kristin, *Fast Cars, Clean Bodies: Decolonization and the Reordering of French Culture* (Cambridge, MA: MIT Press, 1996).

Rubenstein, Alvin Z. and Donald E. Smith, 'Anti-Americanism in the Third World', *Annals of the American Academy of Political Science*, 497 (1988), pp. 35–45.

Sabatier, Peggy R., '"Elite" Education in French West Africa: The Era of Limits, 1903–1945', *The International Journal of African Historical Studies*, 11.2 (1978), pp. 247–66.

Said, Edward, *Orientalism* (New York: Vintage, 1978).

——, 'Travelling Theory', in *The World, the Text and the Critic* (London: Vintage, 1991 [1983]), pp. 226–47.

——, 'Travelling Theory Reconsidered', in *Reflections on Exile and Other Literary and Cultural Essays* (London: Granta Books, 2000), pp. 436–52.

Scott, David, *Semiologies of Travel: From Gautier to Baudrillard* (Cambridge: Cambridge University Press, 2004).

Sembene, Ousmane, *Le Docker noir* (Paris: Présence Africaine, 1973 [1956]).

——, *Voltaïque* (Paris: Présence Africaine, 1962).

Sheller, Mimi and John Urry (eds), *Tourism Mobilities: Places to Play, Places in Play* (London and New York: Routledge, 2004).

Sibeud, Emmanuelle, *Une Science impériale pour l'Afrique: la construction des savoirs africanistes en France, 1878–1930* (Paris: École des Hautes Études en Sciences Sociales, 2002).

Simpson, Mark, *Trafficking Subjects: The Politics of Mobility in Nineteenth-Century America* (Minneapolis, MN: University of Minnesota Press, 2005).

Sonolet, Louis and A. Pérès, *Moussa et Gigla: histoire de deux petits noirs* (Paris: Armand Colin, 1916).

Städtler, Katharina, 'Regards africains sur la ville de Paris', *France-Mail-Forum*, 23 (August 2001), www.france-mail-forum.de/fmf23/neu/23sstaed.html (accessed 15 June 2008).

Stephens, Michelle, 'Disarticulating Black Internationalism: West Indian Radicals and *The Practice of Diaspora*', *Small Axe*, 17 (2005), pp. 100–11.

'The Story of Africa between World Wars: Air and Road', www.bbc.co.uk/worldservice/africa/features/storyofafrica/13chapter9.shtml (accessed 17 June 2008).

Stovall, Tyler, *Paris Noir: African Americans in the City of Light* (Boston, MA: Houghton Mifflin, 1996).

Sugden, David, *Arctic and Antarctic: A Modern Geographical Synthesis* (Oxford: Basil Blackwell, 1982).

Suret-Canale, Jean, *French Colonialism in Tropical Africa, 1900–1945*, trans. Till Gottheiner (New York: Pica Press, 1971 [1964]).

Sweeney, Carole, '"Le Tour du Monde en Quatre Jours": Empire, Exhibition and the Surrealist Order of Things', *Textual Practice*, 19.1 (2005), pp. 131–47.

Syrotinski, Michael, '"When in Rome…": Irony and Subversion in Bernard Dadié's Travel-Writing', *The Journal of African Travel-Writing*, 7 (1999), pp. 66–79.

——, *Singular Performances: Reinscribing the Subject in Francophone African Writing* (Charlottesville, VA: University of Virginia Press, 2002).

Tadjo, Véronique, *L'Ombre d'Imana: Voyages jusqu'au bout du Rwanda* (Arles: Actes Sud, 2000).

Teaiwa, Teresia, K., 'Bikinis and other S/pacific N/oceans', in *Voyaging through the Contemporary Pacific*, ed. David Hanlon and Geoffrey M. White (Oxford: Rowman & Littlefield, 2000), pp. 91–112.

Thomas, Dominic, 'Francocentrism and the Acquisition of Cultural Capital', *Journal of Romance Studies*, 5.3 (2005), pp. 51–63.

——, *Black France: Colonialism, Immigration and Transnationalism* (Bloomington, IN: Indiana University Press, 2007).

Thomas, Nicholas, 'Against Ethnography', *Cultural Anthropology*, 6.3 (1991), pp. 306–22.

Tschibanda, Pie, *Un Fou noir au pays des blancs* (Paris: Broché, 2004).

Tudela, Elisa Sampson Vera, *Colonial Angels: Narratives of Gender and Spirituality in Mexico, 1580–1750* (Austin, TX: University of Texas Press, 2000).

Urbain, Jean-Didier, *L'Idiot du voyage: histoires de touristes* (Paris: Payot, 1993).

——, *Paradis verts: désirs de campagne et passions résidentielles* (Paris: Payot, 2002).

Urry, John, *Consuming Places* (London and New York: Routledge, 1994).

——, *Mobilities* (Cambridge: Polity Press, 2007).

Valocchi, Steve, 'The Racial Basis of Capitalism and the State, and the Impact of the New Deal on African Americans', *Social Problems*, 41.3 (1994), pp. 347–62.

Viard, Jean, *La Révélation vacancière* (La-Tour-d'Aigues: Groupe d'études des mutations régionales, 1981).

——, *Penser les vacances* (Arles: Actes Sud, 1984).

Vincileoni, Nicole, *L'Œuvre de Bernard B. Dadié* (Issy-les-Moulineaux: Les Classiques africains, 1986).

Waberi, Abdourahman A., *Aux États-Unis d'Afrique* (Paris: J.-C Lattès, 2006).

Watkins-Owens, Irma, *Blood Relations: Caribbean Immigrants and the Harlem Community, 1900–1930* (Bloomington, IN: Indiana University Press, 1996).

White, Paul, 'Geography, Literature and Migration', in *Writing Across Worlds: Literature and Migration*, ed. Russell King, John Connell and Paul White (London and New York: Routledge, 1995), pp. 1–19.

Wilentz, Gay, 'If You Surrender to the Air: Folk Legends of Flight and Resistance in African American Literature', *Melus*, 16.1 (1989–90), pp. 21–32.

Wolff, Janet, 'On the Road Again: Metaphors of Travel in Cultural Criticism', *Cultural Studies*, 7.2 (1993), pp. 224–39.

Youngs, Tim, 'Where Are We Going? Cross-Border Approaches to Travel Writing', in *Perspectives on Travel Writing*, ed. Glen Hooper and Tim Youngs (Aldershot: Ashgate, 2004), pp. 167–80.

Index